FLY FISHING
& CONSERVATION
IN VERMONT

FLY FISHING & CONSERVATION IN VERMONT

STORIES OF THE
BATTENKILL AND BEYOND

TIM TRAVER

Published by The History Press
Charleston, SC
www.historypress.com

Copyright © 2020 by Tim Traver
All rights reserved

First published 2020

Manufactured in the United States

ISBN 9781467141321

Library of Congress Control Number: 2019954280

Notice: The information in this book is true and complete to the best of our knowledge. It is offered without guarantee on the part of the author or The History Press. The author and The History Press disclaim all liability in connection with the use of this book.

All rights reserved. No part of this book may be reproduced or transmitted in any form whatsoever without prior written permission from the publisher except in the case of brief quotations embodied in critical articles and reviews.

CONTENTS

Acknowledgements 7
Introduction 11

1. The Ottauquechee River, Part I 13
2. Lake Runnemede 21
3. The Black River 24
4. Lewis Creek 30
5. Caspian Lake 38
6. The Battenkill 43
7. Lake Mitchell Trout Club 54
8. The Lower Connecticut River 57
9. The Family Fishing Festival 63
10. The White River 67
11. The Winooski River 73
12. Lake Champlain 81
13. The Ottauquechee River, Part II 91
14. The Rod Makers 101
15. The Walloomsac River 107
16. The Connecticut River 112
17. Stratton Pond 119
18. The Mettawee River 123
19. Miller Pond 130
20. Mill River 136

Contents

21. Little River, Mad River, Dog River	139
22. The White River, Third Branch	147
23. Jon Conner	155
24. The Lamoille River and Sterling Pond	162
25. Lamoille River Headwaters	168
26. Growing Fish	173
27. The White River, West Branch	176
28. Lake Willoughby	183
29. The Leicester River	190
30. The Upper Connecticut River	194
31. Little Averill Lake	201
32. Jobs Pond	210
33. Saving the Missisquoi	212
Appendix A. Recipes	225
Appendix B. The Upright Caddis Emerger, by Thomas Ames	231
Selected Bibliography	233
About the Author	237

ACKNOWLEDGEMENTS

I could never have completed this book without the help of a whole lot of people who took the time to show me their water, explain their work and connect me to their colleagues working in the field, some of whom I'm sure I've neglected to list here. Thanks to the Abenaki voices who gently reminded me that when you fish in Vermont, you are on the ancestral lands of the People of the Dawn Lands. Special thanks to Ron Rhodes, Connecticut River steward and dam remover extraordinaire who opened up his address book and introduced me to his wide network of river restorers, including various staff and volunteers of Trout Unlimited. I couldn't have gotten far without the excellent support of the fisheries biologists at the Vermont Fish and Wildlife Department who, without exception, helped me get to the information I needed. And here's a special shout-out to the department's director of the Let's Go Fishing program, Cory Hart, and his team of volunteers for introducing children and families across Vermont to the joys and responsibilities of fishing. You are all an inspiration.

When I needed a boat, I turned to the Martin brothers at Adirondack Guide Boat in Ferrisburg, who set me up with a perfect lightweight rowing canoe I could afford and lift above my head. Thanks to those who endured days on the stream with me, either as guides or fishing companions, including old friend and fishing partner Jon Vara, who hauled a canoe with me a mile and a half into Cow Mountain Pond; Caitlin Fox, who braved the beaver dams on the wild Leister; Wayne Ellis, who hiked into the upper watershed of the Lamoille River for wild brook trout; Battenkill

Acknowledgements

master angler Doug Lyons; Clark Amadon, chair of the Mad River–Dog River TU chapter in central Vermont; fishing pal Steve Hoffman for outings during the Hex hatch; tree planter, fly fishing teacher and retired Ottauquechee River guide Marty Banak and the folks at Greater Upper Valley TU Chapter; bamboo rod maker and dedicated fly angler Brian Ganley for some productive trips up to the NEK, including a most interesting anthropological foray at Paul Stream; and retired state biologist Len Girardi for a great day at Willoughby Lake. Thanks, too, to Jon Vincent for a lovely morning at Lake Mitchell Trout Club.

Thanks to friend and colleague Joan Allen, whose work with the Vermont Land Trust and the Nature Conservancy has left miles of river frontage better off. Also, thanks to writer/photographer Tom Ames, whose knowledge of hatches and whose books have long been an inspiration. Hats off to Greg Russ and Mary Russ at the White River Partnership, which has an amazing set of projects going with federal, state and local partners. Also, kudos to the highly effective folks at Friends of the Winooski, who just keep plugging along doing good by the river with the largest watershed in Vermont, and to Steve Libby and the remarkable Vermont River Conservancy, with projects across the state of Vermont.

The hidden value of writing a fishing guide is what you learn and who you meet along the way. Thanks to Bob Shannon with the Fly Rod Shop; Ken Sprankle, U.S. Fish and Wildlife Service's Connecticut River fisheries program coordinator; Jennie Shurtleff, program coordinator for the Woodstock History Center; and Don Tobi with Champlain International. Special thanks to the Town of Swanton for its help in understanding the issues and opportunities of the Missisquoi River: Reg Belliveau, village manager; David Jescavage, town administer; Ron Kilburn, president of the Swanton Historical Society; Elizabeth Nance, Swanton economic development coordinator; Bill Scully, hydroelectric developer; and Chris Smith, state coordinator for the Partners for Fish and Wildlife Program, Lake Champlain Fish and Wildlife Conservation Office. Thanks to Steve Boyajian for his photos and thoughts on fishing the famed steelhead runs on Lake Memphremagog (another book is in order). Thanks to Tom Chairvolloti, Lake Champlain fish culture specialist with the Vermont Fish and Wildlife Department, and to ace fly caster and tyer Jon Conner of Sharon, who shared stories of his grandfather, a famed nineteenth-century commissioner of fish and wildlife in Vermont. Thanks to chef and friend Sylvia Davatz; Jon Demasi, Orvis Guide and fishing writer; James Ehlers, executive director of Lake Champlain International; and

Acknowledgements

VNRC's Brian Fitzgerald. Kudos to Sally and David Laughlin, two of Vermont's most distinguished environmental heroes. Thanks Tom Rosenbauer at Orvis for hooking me up to good photos and to Paul Schullery. Thanks, always, to the good folks at the American Museum of Fly Fishing in Manchester, Vermont.

I never would have completed this work without the support of Mollie Traver, Kalmia Traver and Toben Traver, writers and editors exemplar! And thanks to my wife, Delia Clark, for her unerring support.

A portion of the proceeds from the sale of this book support the work of the White River Partnership and Vermont River Conservancy.

INTRODUCTION

It's a perfect early May morning in Vermont. Shadbush is close to blooming, and the thermometer has hit the low sixties. Water temps are running mid-fifties—just how we anglers like it. The air is fresh, swept clean of the funk of mud season and old wood-frame homes. The unfurling leaves are in hues of pink to rust to pale green. The world invites exploration. Rumor has it there's a hatch coming off the White River. Time to rig the fly rod!

This work is aimed at anyone, new or old to the sport of fly fishing, who's looking to fish interesting places in interesting times. While this is an angler's guide, it's a selective one. My hope is that by traveling to a handful of rivers, ponds and lakes, and exploring their stories, readers will get an angler's view of the whole varied world of fly fishing in Vermont.

Vermont, as state fisheries biologist Tom Jones put it, is an angler's paradise. This has as much to do with Vermonters as it has to do with Vermont. The real fishing experts out there are the ones who are dialed in to their home waters and who work not only to fish that water but to restore and protect it as well. My success here rests in hooking you up to these people. They are an inspiring and, I'll warn you, provincial lot. On provinciality and fishing, Jon Conner, a seventy-year-old lifer fly angler/fly tyer who fishes only a few rivers close to Sharon, Vermont, put it this way: "I'd rather drive fifteen minutes and fish for two hours than drive two hours and fish for fifteen minutes." Perhaps no one quite knows the Ottauquechee River, lower sections of the White River and the middle and upper sections of the Connecticut River better than Jon. And yet many of us prefer long-

Introduction

distance travel with a fly rod. Look no further than Jon's grandfather John Wheelock Titcomb. Titcomb was chairman of the Vermont Fish and Game Commission, serving from 1891 to 1902. An early fish culturalist, Titcomb didn't stay local at all. He's credited with bringing the first salmonids, and the first trout hatchery, to Argentina (plus brook trout to Bariloche and later brown trout to the Río Gallegos). Vermont is exceedingly amenable to travelers from afar with fly rods.

On provinciality and conservation action, a wise old conservationist named Lilla McLane-Bradley, one of the founders of the Upper Valley Land Trust, liked to say, "People love the places they get to know best—what's close at hand—and they work to protect what they love." She was an incredibly can-do leader, and her optimism was our mantra at the Upper Valley Land Trust, a group that today, thirty years after its founding, has protected more than fifty thousand acres of land, much of it along rivers and streams in Vermont. Many of the land trust's projects in the Connecticut River Valley—a favorite trail, a hilltop, a swimming hole, a river frontage, a wild pond, a farm—took years for local people, working with land trust professionals, to accomplish. These citizen conservationists prevailed because of their deep caring for the place, and no one was working for pay. Anglers give time and money because they want to leave the place better than how they found it. When you set foot in Vermont waters with a fishing rod in hand, you become part of a long-running stewardship and restoration story with a history of success and a challenging future.

Chapter 1

THE OTTAUQUECHEE RIVER, PART I

Saturday, May 10, 2018

My home river, the Ottauquechee ("*ah*-tah-kwee-chee"), is a good place to start my peregrinations this fishing season. It's about a five-minute walk from the house. The Ottauquechee Valley is picture-book Vermont. The dam at the bottom of the street and the red covered bridge just below it, often photographed during leaf-peeping season, date back to the early nineteenth century. The river runs through a landscape of small hills, orchards, pastures, eighteenth- and nineteenth-century homes and well-built stone walls, together with the amenities of Woodstock village and its Green. It can be a surprisingly fun place to fish through June. The sections through Woodstock below the iron bridge and the covered bridge off the Village Green are iconic Vermont. I float the reach above the dam in Taftsville. Until Tropical Storm Irene in August 2011, the Taftsville Dam generated electricity. Much farther back, in the early 1800s, the original dams powered sawmills and a tool-making foundry. After the river gets stocked in late May, for six weeks or so the trout rise to a variety of hatches in the evening, and trying to catch them becomes a minor obsession in June. Relatively speaking, there is little fishing pressure on much of the Ottauquechee, particularly upstream of Bridgewater, which includes the lovely North Branch, a wild brook trout reach that extends into the remote and undeveloped lands of the Chateauguay area. Rarely do I see another boat on the river in the ponded waters above Taftsville, and fishing pressure from shore is light.

Taftsville, Vermont, early nineteenth century, from a postcard, 1909. *Courtesy of the Woodstock History Center.*

The real sport on the Ottauquechee, though, is arguably going after large holdover rainbow trout in the early spring and fall. A handful of locals in-the-know chase these big fish from Woodstock down to the Quechee Gorge. The expert on these is a guy named Marty Banak.

Marty, in my book, is Mr. Ottauquechee. He guided and taught out of a barn at Marshland Farm on the river for thirty years until handing over the business to Pete Meyer, an excellent regional guide. Marty is an active Trout Unlimited (TU) member who organizes tree planting on the banks up and down the river. While his bread and butter during his guiding years was arguably stocked yearling rainbow trout in the Ottauquechee and White, as well as his fly fishing school for new anglers, it was those larger holdover fish that perked him up in May. These early fish are wild, strong and tough to find. When I have the chance to go after them with Marty, I take it.

We met up at the Taftsville Country Store, parked beside a pile of marshmallow hay bales in a farmer's field, and headed downhill to the first big bend in the river below the Taftsville Covered Bridge. Marty ran through the drill at the top of the big dogleg pool downstream. The cast was upstream and across a fast current to the deep water on the far shore. I tied on a streamer; I was using a sinking line. Marty had a Hornberg on a sinking leader. He began casting and wading down, and I cycled in behind him, casting and moving down the pool.

We didn't catch a damn thing.

Half an hour later, we were back in the car for a ride downstream. Here, the discerning eye can find a very fishing guide–like aid: a rope for arthritic knees, in place to help you down a steep bank. The pool below, invisible from River Road, is invitingly green, the water funneled into the center of the river over an abruptly dropping ledge. This is the kind of place fish really ought to be. So…why aren't they? We fished in water about one hundred yards apart, anticipating the jolting hits that never came, and enjoyed the very best that a May day in Vermont can give, if it can't give a fish. There were a dozen pools that have produced large fish scattered between us and Quechee, including the golf course section and pools you can scout from the edge of the road. Access is good throughout, and with a little sleuthing, you can find these fish.

Walking back downriver to the hidden path up through the woods to the steep section and its climbing aid, Marty posed out loud a question he's been pondering over for many years, convinced that it hasn't been realized: "What is the potential of this river? What could the Ottauquechee become?" It's a question that gets asked by anglers about the rivers they care about nationwide. He thinks that erratic water flows are currently the deal breaker on the Ottauquechee. The river begins some years with plenty of water, and then drought reduces the channel to a trickle. Could flows be addressed? Trout seem to survive here in spite of erratic flows, warm temperatures and the next flood.

The bucolic Ottauquechee has been highly "modified by human action," to borrow an expression from the river's best-known native son, George Perkins Marsh, a nineteenth-century statesman/writer, considered to be the founder of the American conservation movement. There are no fewer than five dams and a major gorge between the Taftsville Covered Bridge and the river's confluence at the Connecticut River nine miles away. Three of these hold back millponds dating to the mid-eighteenth century, and there were many more dams and waterwheels back then on the main stem and tributaries. The millwheels ran coffin shops, bobbin mills, leather tanneries and sawmills and produced everything needed, from linseed oil to scythes, axe handles, leather boots and shoes. Upstream and down from Taftsville were large woolen mills. These were rivers and landscapes shaped by the early years of the Industrial Revolution and the conversion of wild lands to settled towns and farmlands.

Marty Banak. *Photo by author.*

Marty's question about restoring the river to its full potential is a George Perkins Marsh question. Born on the banks of the Ottauquechee in Woodstock at the beginning of the nineteenth century, Marsh grew up during the heyday of dam building, mill development, the construction of roads and bridges, trains and the transformation of the valley by the clearing of its forests. He spent his youth walking around these hills and this river, then shorn of trees, and witnessed the Merino sheep boom—and its bust. He saw the coming of the railroad up this valley. Even though he suffered from poor eyesight, he read widely on geography, history and biology and began in Woodstock to put together in his mind this grand narrative of the relationship between human actions, human industry and the various thousands of endeavors that degraded nature. It was a grim picture.

Marsh's seminal book, *Man and Nature: Or, Physical Geography as Modified by Human Action*, didn't get published until 1864. By then, Marsh had long since left Woodstock to live and travel widely in Europe. He was appointed by President Zachary Taylor as minister resident in the Ottoman empire and then, by President Abraham Lincoln, as the first United States minister to Italy. *Man and Nature* combined Marsh's boyhood experience in Woodstock with years of study, travel and observation abroad. He was the longest-serving ambassador in United States history. His fundamental insight was that humans and their actions were the major shaping influence of the face of the earth—not volcanoes, earthquakes and tropical storms, but human industry. And it wasn't all negative in his mind. He had an abiding faith in human craft and the human urge to improve, to civilize itself. He saw relationships in the broadest contexts. He looked at the treeless expanses and ruined soils of the Mediterranean basin, for instance, and saw the impact that warfare, Roman tyranny, the overtaxation of peasants and poor husbandry practices had had on those devastated landscapes. He was teasing out relationships between the social and the ecological before the term *ecology* was even invented, trying to understand how the world works—the way a modern-day climate scientist or an ecosystem scientist would today, only without their tools.

In one specific way, George Perkins Marsh was in broad agreement with Marty Banak. In *Man and Nature*, Marsh linked the cutting off of hillside forests and the overgrazing of Merino sheep flocks to the torrential runoffs in spring, as well as to the floods, erosion and droughts that the Ottauquechee Valley experienced in the 1850s. These are Marty's "erratic flows." At the heart of Marsh's book is the relationship between woods and waters. Marsh would likely have answered Marty's question with an idea that modern angling environmentalists would instantly understand today: If you want to improve the fishing, plant trees. (And do a lot of other things, too, like create fish-passage technologies at dams that block fish migrations, protect the connection rivers have to their floodplains and build sewage treatment plants.) Forests and riparian buffers shade and cool water, filter out sediments and recharge groundwater, all of which helps to even out flows. The benefits of wide forested buffers along river valleys are profound.

There were other ideas from Marsh that Marty would applaud. Marsh called for fishing regulations and for a federal, multistate approach to migratory fish management. In the 1850s, Marsh published a report for the Vermont legislature on the decline of Vermont fishes. His report was one of the earliest calls for governmental management of fish and wildlife resources. He identified some of the causes of fish declines, including overfishing, fishing at and during spawning runs, pollution, dam building and what he suspected to be other causes related to "minute" life forms invisible to the naked eye. Today's problems with nutrient loading and blue-green algae blooms come to mind. One of his recommendations was a program of fish culture—restoring fish populations through the growing and stocking of native and nonnative fish. Not long after Marsh's report and his publication of *Man and Nature*, Vermont and the other New England states became early adopters of fish culture–based restoration. Marsh's ideas resonated

George Perkins Marsh, Woodstock, Vermont's native son. *Photo by Mathew Brady, courtesy of the Library of Congress.*

with his good friend Spencer Baird, who was appointed commissioner of the first U.S. Commission of Fish and Fisheries (less formally, the U.S. Fish Commission) in 1871. Spencer Baird initiated an enthusiastic program of fish culture nationwide. Incidentally, while in Turkey, Marsh collected fish for Baird, whose primary job was serving as second in command at the Smithsonian Institution. Some of Marsh's Turkish fish are stored down in the bowels of the Smithsonian to this day.

I'm not sure how Marty feels about stocking. The reality of trout fishing in Vermont is that we heavily rely on stocked trout for the enjoyment of our sport—and for the occasional meal, though not only on stocked trout. There are wild populations of brown trout and rainbow trout. Native wild brook trout populations, recent studies show, are holding up well and thriving in all corners of the state, despite climate change—so far. But the threat of climate change to fisheries is very real and present. Vermont's mountain chains provide the cold water that trout need, but temperatures are on the rise and so are the frequency and intensity of storms.

Over the past twenty or so years, Vermont Fish and Wildlife has made significant changes to its stocking policies and program. Much attention today is going toward promoting and protecting wild trout populations and dealing with ecosystem fundamentals. Stocking today is more focused than it has ever been and generally occurs only in waters that don't have the potential to support natural reproduction. There is less stocking of fry and more stocking of trophy-sized fish today in select locations for early season fisheries attractive to locals and tourist anglers alike. All brook trout stocked today are triploid trout (meaning they cannot successfully produce offspring). This has worked very well for all who like to fly fish with the hopes of catching an eighteen-inch-plus brook trout.

What would it take to restore the Ottauquechee River to its fullest potential? Actions we are probably not willing or able to take yet. But given an extravagantly generous allowance of time, it's possible to imagine an Ottauquechee shaded by enormous old-growth silver maples and other floodplain species; a river valley where the humans get their energy from the sun; a river carrying loads of drowned wood measured in tonnage; a river that can flow into its floodplains; a river whose parallel roads are repaired with natural processes in mind, including flood protection; a river where old railroad dikes are removed and redundant dams are ancient history. In this imagined world, environmentally sensitive hydro projects that don't contribute to worsening climate change could play a role, assuming they take into account fish passage and optimal flows.

To riff on Aldo Leopold, it's going to take thinking like a forest, thinking like a river, changing radically how we build, the energy we use, the transportation systems that move us and the democracy we practice to give a river back its fullest potential. It will take advanced reengineering and the widespread deployment of green design—small actions that have large consequences—and repurposed will. And it may take some expertly placed dynamite to reach back to a river's potential, to do well by rivers and land. George Perkins Marsh was the first of a long line of conservationists coming from this valley. We'll explore some of his contemporary protégés further in.

Chapter 2

LAKE RUNNEMEDE

Friday, May 11, 2018

Even though fishing with a bow and arrow is legal in Vermont, you don't see it practiced much anymore, at least not on the eastern side of the state. Nor do many of the fly fishers I know dabble in that kind of fishing approach. I think of spring bow hunting as a remnant practice from an older time—a subsistence practice. I'm glad some still partake. Seeing a bow hunter reminds me of images I've seen of Abenaki fishers hunting with three-pronged spears for giant muskellunge and spawning lake sturgeon along the banks of the Missisquoi River.

But it did surprise me to find a bow hunter at Lake Runnemede. Lake Runnemede is a conserved property today, popular with dog walkers and birdwatchers and now part of the town of Windsor's Paradise Park, protected with help from the Upper Valley Land Trust. The bow hunter was standing like a statue on a wooden box he'd placed on the edge of the dike that contains the pond at its shallower north end. A woman with two poodles had just edged her way nervously around him when we came up. Below the dike are thriving beaver meadows, cattails and phragmites. Sometimes all of that can be alive with birds in early May. That morning we saw small flocks of redstarts and yellow warblers.

His name was John, and he told me he'd been bow hunting here for years—initially for carp. Carp, he said, were once as thick as a shag carpet in Runnemede, but not any longer. He liked carp as fertilizer for his garden.

Today, though, carp are all but gone, and he was looking for large pike—not for compost, but for food. "This is a decent pike pond, isn't it?" I asked. John said that some years it can be. I'd also heard that bowfin had been caught here, and he corroborated that, adding that bowfin must have been illegally introduced, since they're only native in Lake Champlain. Anyway, he was headed back to the Connecticut River—to the Hartland side of Sumner Falls, just a few miles away—because the bass fishing there yesterday had been stupendous. "A fish every cast."

Why include a warm-water pond in a book about fly fishing? Because it's an excellent spot to fly fish for warm-water species. No boats allowed, but from the vantage point of a slightly elevated dike, you've got several hundred yards of unobstructed back and forward casting room. Perch, pike, pickerel, bass and, who knows, maybe even bowfin. A great place to practice casting, to bring beginners and to encounter families and other fishers using lures and bait. Ask them what they're catching and see if you can coax up the same.

I first laid eyes on Runnemede in the late 1980s, when I worked for the Upper Valley Land Trust. The landowner, Alex, a crusty Yankee gentleman, contacted us and asked how he might go about conserving the property. But he couldn't give much value away, he warned. He needed money for his retirement. We drove out to his fields—some thirty acres leased to a local farmer—and the lake, not far from the center of old Windsor, the birthplace of Vermont and home to the state's longest covered bridge. The aesthetics were spectacular. From the edge of the pond, the view to the west is of commanding Mount Ascutney, a volcanic peak that sits unmistakably alone in this middle valley of the Connecticut River. On the far side of the pond, up a terrace of gravels and sands left by the glaciers, perches a row of wood-frame houses—the northern reach of the neighborhoods of Windsor. Surrounding were all the elements: the forests of Paradise Park, the extensive wetlands of a marsh, the beginnings of Mill Brook, the lake and the edge of the village. This place was a linchpin to the nature, culture and history of Windsor.

Back in the late 1980s, things were changing in the land and water conservation fields in Vermont. Private, nonprofit land trusts were on the rise. One of the earliest, the Ottauquechee Land Trust, changed its name to the Vermont Land Trust in 1987. The State of Vermont had established the Vermont Housing and Conservation Board (VHCB) that same year. There was dedicated funding for projects like Lake Runnemede that conserved farm and forestland and benefited local communities. What was unique about

Boys fishing in Woodstock, Vermont, late nineteenth century. *Courtesy of the Woodstock History Center.*

VHCB was that it supported often competing goals so that affordable housing and open space needs could be considered together.

This particular property got very high marks. It included prime farmland, wetlands and water bodies adjacent to town-owned conserved land. There was the added benefit of public trails through an exceptional natural area, within walking distance to the center of town. The wetlands to the north were added later through a gift to the town by the landowner. To all these benefits was added the fishing: the disparaged carp, the lurking pike, the sweet and edible perch, the bowfin (an ancient fish that occupies its own taxonomic family) and the bass, introduced willy-nilly across Vermont and New Hampshire in the 1860s. What makes fishing important, in a place a kid can ride a bike to? That wiggling, slimy, slippery, sharp, living thing may offer children the most visceral, dramatic and ultimately unforgettable connection they make to the land at an early age. A fish can be a potent link to home.

Chapter 3

THE BLACK RIVER

Friday, May 11, 2018

In the afternoon, the sun finally showing, I drove about a half hour south of Taftsville, hopping on I-91 at Hartland (Exit 9) and then off again at Ascutney (Exit 8), west onto Route 131 to the trophy section of the Black River. It was cool and windy, with water temps still in the low fifties, but the sky was blue and there was no more rain in the forecast.

The Black's trophy water, stocked with two-year-old rainbow and brown trout, begins downstream at Downers Covered Bridge just off Route 131 and runs upstream four miles to the Iron Bridge at Howard Hill Road. (Note: The well-known ice cream place at Downers Four Corners, at the intersection of Route 106 just up the road, sells fried catfish too and soft ice cream made with real maple syrup.) Most of the trophy section is visible from Route 131 and is easily accessible. There are steep riprapped banks along parts of the river where sections of roadway were washed out by Tropical Storm Irene. Be careful on those.

Before going into the fly fishing on the Black, a word about Tropical Storm Irene. When we talk about Vermont rivers and trout fishing these days, talk invariably turns to Irene. A slow-moving hurricane downgraded to a tropical storm somewhere over the mid-Atlantic states, Irene crept up the spine of Vermont on August 27–28, 2011, dumping more than six inches of rain. Central and south-central Vermont, where the USGS recorded record discharges from eight stream gauges, were hit hardest.

Irene caught Vermonters by surprise. The long Labor Day weekend was filled with images of covered bridges floating away, roads washed out and towns isolated. Cavendish, on the Black, was hit hard, flooding part of the old town and washing away large sections of Route 131. In my hometown of Taftsville, flooding overwhelmed a mobile home park and houses downstream. Culverts and drainage swales overflowed on the hilly roads, too, not where you'd expect flood damage to occur. Happy Valley Road, which runs along Happy Valley Brook, became a river, gullied and cratered with six-foot-deep potholes by the end of the day. This was a common story throughout dirt-road Vermont, which is most of it. Our covered bridge was knocked off its supporting ledges. Propane cylinders, liberated from the gas company in Woodstock, came down like a flotilla of mini-submarines. One made it to the Atlantic at Long Island Sound.

In the aftermath, crews of volunteers dug silt out of homes. In town, we got out our chainsaws and trucks and cut our way through massive logjams pushed against the shade trees near shore. There were odd and poignant items mixed in with the tons of tree trunks—a kerosene lantern, patio furniture, clothing, bicycles and children's toys—reminding everyone of the human scale of a flood's devastation. This was our reckoning with a five-hundred-year storm. We can expect more of them in this era of climate change.

As dramatic as the floodwaters were, the damage to rivers like the Black was mostly due to the road rebuilding that went on in the storm's long aftermath. The builders went about rapidly reconnecting the state's road system—a matter of public health, safety and welfare. But while we need the connectivity of our road systems, the hydrodynamics and natural histories of our rivers, in the rush to rebuild, were overlooked. Rivers are living systems, more complex than cut-and-fill road systems, which are often built snug to riverbanks and cutting through floodplains.

Vermont Fish and Wildlife's partial assessment in 2012 estimated a total of "77 miles of stream with major degradation to aquatic habitat resulting from post-flood stream channel alteration activities." Based on its long-term monitoring studies, it estimated that "where aquatic habitat has been severely altered through streambed and natural wood mining, channel widening and straightening, complex habitat features will need to reestablish before improvements in fish and aquatic populations can be expected....The recovery of longer reaches may take decades and will depend upon the availability and mobility of upstream sources of coarse streambed material and natural wood, as well as the magnitude and

Flooding from Tropical Storm Irene, Woodstock Village.
Photo taken by Alison Clarkson, courtesy of the Woodstock History Center.

frequency of future flood events." And the frequency of flood events is expected to sharply rise as global temperatures warm.

In the recent paper "Mechanisms of Abrupt Extreme Precipitation Change Over the Northeastern United States," data show a 53 percent increase in precipitation after 1996 over 1901–95. The months of September and October contributed most of the increase due to more hurricanes and tropical storms, but major contributions also came in the form of greater precipitation from fronts and extratropical cyclones during June, July and March. The increase in precipitation from extreme events is associated with warmer Atlantic sea surfaces and more water vapor in the atmosphere. There will be more Irenes.

The good news, post-Irene, was the wakeup call the storm provided. Lessons were learned. New outreach and training programs were instituted for state agencies and communities, particularly for transportation workers. New "Flood Ready" data were collected for towns, and educators developed new school curricula using tools like stream tables. The legislature responded to the need for improved emergency response with Act 138. The new legislation gave the state's River Management Program new enforcement authorities and guidelines for river and stream alteration, and towns have new tools for river corridor protection. The overall result, in the wake of Irene, is that Vermont is well on the road toward improved community resiliency and river health. This is all good news for anglers.

Vermont's trophy trout program began in 1994, when Vermont Fish and Wildlife stocked four rivers with sixteen- to eighteen-inch two-year-old rainbow and brown trout. The idea was to create "an enhanced and exciting opportunity for anglers to chase bigger fish through May and June." The feel of a two-pound rainbow on the line is pretty persuasively exciting, and the program caught hold.

Vermont's trophy trout river reaches, eight in all today, have good public access, as well as the structure and habitat needed to support fish populations through June and often well into July. These reaches are not capable, at least for now, of supporting reproducing stocks of native fish (although they may contain feeder streams that are). They heat up in July and don't have the cold-water inputs needed to support wild populations through an entire season. These fisheries are located throughout the state and provide a kind of roadmap for exciting fishing travel across Vermont in the early season.

Anywhere from eighteen thousand to twenty thousand two-year-old fish are released into the eight trophy sections annually across the state now. In the Black, the total is about two thousand fish, three quarters of which are rainbows and one quarter browns, stocked across four miles in two batches two weeks apart in May. The Black's deep pools and boulder-strewn habitat make for excellent fish cover.

Special regulations apply to all eight quality trout reaches like this stretch of the Black. Anglers can keep two fish per day—although a very high number are caught and released—and there are no tackle restrictions. A worm or a lure is perfectly legal. These aren't fly fishing-only waters, although fly anglers do make up the majority. The idea is to spread around the catch.

In 2013 and 2014, Vermont Fish and Wildlife conducted creel studies on the Black to determine fishing pressure and fishing success. Average fishing hours per mile across the two years were around 6,700. That's high. About 70 percent of the fish stocked were caught; the average catch per angler hour was 0.7/hour. That's also high. Expert anglers are likely to do better than the average, and plenty of anglers will come up with zeroes on a single trip. Keep that in mind. Like investing in the stock market, there are no guaranteed gains. Fish were caught on the Black an average of three times.

How to fish the Black? Don Cutter is a consummate Upper Valley region angler, a member of the Lake Mitchell Trout Club and a true believer in the Woolly Bugger, especially early and late in the season. The gist of Don's advice on the Black: 1) Get your fly down deep—Don uses a full sinking line; 2) Keep your line in the water—"You're not going to catch anything with a fly in the air"; 3) Change flies. If a black Woolly Bugger is bombing, try orange or green. Or go with a streamer and fish it like a minnow. If fishing any stocked trophy water, Don's advice is to move. "Stocked fish," he added, "hang around the stocking point only for a few days. The fish get hungry and acclimated to natural food, then begin to move and redistribute. So you have to move to find them." While that sounds like folksy anecdote, it's consistent with the research on stocked-fish movements. Stocked trout in Pennsylvania studies stayed put for a few days and then moved mostly downstream. On average, rainbows began moving in three days, brook trout in ten and browns in seven. I asked hatchery staff how they stock Black River fish and was told, "By the five-gallon pail, a few at a time." Volunteers show up to help. These are high-class trout (silk-lined buckets and opera-goers) after all. No unceremonious dumping of the trout horde in one place. Don's advice to move worked for me.

Local Orvis-endorsed guide John DeMasi, who has spent a lot of time with clients chasing large trout on the Black, told me that even though he sees a range of hatches, some quite impressive, he finds the two-year-old stocked fish on the Black not always that receptive to them. One exception has been the sulfur hatch. John told me that sulfurs produce good activity and can be fished through all the stages, from nymph to dun. Something to try.

I went searching for about two hours and didn't raise a fish between the Downers Covered Bridge to a point two miles upstream, a section that was low gradient, wide and without much promise. But walking downstream from there to a corner far from the road, I found a lovely pool up against a ledge on the far bank holding fish. I was playing with sinking line too, although a sink-tip line or a weighted leader probably would have been fine.

The Black attracts a lot of anglers by late May and early June. I've seen New Hampshire, Connecticut and New York plates and anglers using everything from heavily dressed, brightly colored size-8 streamers to size-16 Pheasant Tail nymphs. These are strong fish, from sixteen to eighteen inches and up to two pounds. Have fun.

Interesting Cavendish trivia: When the Russian dissident writer Aleksandr Solzhenitsyn—author of *One Day in the Life of Ivan Denisovich, Cancer Ward* and *The Gulag Archipelago*—was exiled from the Soviet Union in 1974, along with his books, he chose the little town of Cavendish, Vermont, on the Black River for his home in exile. He lived with his wife, Natalia, and their children in privacy and seclusion there to continue his work writing the history of the Russian Revolution and the rise of the Soviet Union—particularly of the Stalin years. His multivolume masterpiece on the Russian Revolution, *The Red Wheel*, was released in early 2018. When the Solzhenitsyns came to Cavendish, Aleksandr asked that the town's people honor his need for privacy. They more than complied, refusing to give out his whereabouts to throngs of curious tourists hoping for a glimpse of a Russian dissident and journalists hoping for an interview. His children grew up not in seclusion, but rather as public members proper of the town of Cavendish. They went to public schools, they played soccer and took music lessons, and Natalia was (and is) well known around town as a good-humored and active community member. During his seventeen years in Cavendish, Solzhenitsyn wrote more than 400,000 words, rarely leaving the sanctuary of his home, except for trips to the Dartmouth Library. He left Cavendish and returned to Moscow in 1994 and died there in 2008. He probably never fished the Black.

Chapter 4

LEWIS CREEK

Governor McCullough, of Vermont, when seen by a representative of Forest and Stream *at his office in New York city, declared that it was his firm intention to do all in his power to stop the further pollution of the waters of* [Lake Champlain] *by the offending mills, and also to put an end to illegal seining.*
—Forest and Stream *61 (1903)*

Sunday, May 13, 2018

It's Mother's Day, and my wife and I were celebrating in the car on the road to the Burlington airport, whereupon I put her on a plane to Alaska (this was not some form of Russian exile; she actually had work-for-pay in Alaska). I headed for the first time this season down the eastern shore of Lake Champlain to my job, which is, strangely, *fishing around*. Honestly, I was getting accustomed to a fishing work life. My fish-wife, Delia, approved and was adjusting to my river road trips abroad. She had her own summer plans to hike the Long Trail and was counting on me to shuttle, resupply and generally support her exhausting effort, which I would gladly do. That was a fair quid pro quo. If fishing forced me also into the mode of chauffeur with fishing rod, driving up and down the Green Mountain chain for pickups and deliveries, then that could work well for both of us. Maybe I would become an Uber angler?

Known by local anglers as a steelhead fishery in the early season, followed by spawning smallmouth bass (catch and release before June 1), Lewis Creek isn't far from "metropolitan" Burlington to the north, although it's a haul from Taftsville—as is much of western Vermont, thanks to the mountain chain that divides us. The upper parts of the Lewis Creek watershed are found in the towns of Starksboro, Monkton and Bristol, encompassing the woodlands and farms up in the shadowlands of the Green Mountains. There are, as an angling friend once described them, "lipstick case–sized" wild brook trout in those upper parts of Lewis Creek. But fly anglers are drawn more to the floodplains at the mouth in early April into early May. Access to this lower stretch is at the Route 7 bridge in Ferrisburgh. Park on the right side of Lewis Creek Drive just north of the bridge crossing and head either up to the falls in North Ferrisburgh or downstream through the floodplains of Lewis Creek to the swamp and vast wild rice and Typha wetlands at its outlet on Lake Champlain.

A few miles north of Lewis Creek, I stopped at Adirondack Guide Boat (AGB), owned and operated by the Martin brothers, Justin and Ian. AGB makes both cedar and Kevlar Adirondack-style rowing canoes. The brothers run the business out of a steel building set back from Route 7—you'll see their sign before you notice them. It's a remarkably unassuming place, considering the craft that goes on inside. The shop is small, the office just a desk inside the door. Outside, they have a canoe rack displaying a few lightly used boats for resale. I needed a boat that I could lift on and off my truck with ease, something I could haul down steep banks of rivers, something that tracked well on windy ponds and lakes. The Martins' boats are ideal, and I'd been eyeing them for years. They've managed to stay true to the form of traditional rowing Adirondack-style boats while using new materials and hard-chine designs to make their boats stable. And the boats are beautiful. They have, in side view, the sloping rocker lines of a traditional Adirondack canoe and the straight bow and stern profiles. Ian and Justin have added attractive woodwork, including hardwood gunnels, thwarts and bow stems. They put a tiny brass plate on the mid-thwart so the boat feels christened. When you buy one, you get a pair of cherry oars too.

We'd been talking about my particular needs, and they had a used boat they offered at a steep discount. I could sell it back to them in the fall if I wanted—although I didn't think I would. This was their Kevlar pack boat, about forty-five pounds. While I would have preferred their Vermont dory—they're beamier and you can fish standing—at eighty-plus pounds, the dory was more weight than I wanted. Packs are really solo conveyors, stable and fast. Rowing entails a few inches of hand-over-hand overlap, but you quickly adjust to that. Roomier than kayaks, packs are easier to get in

Lewis Creek in springtime. *Photo by author.*

and out of. And with a rowing canoe, you can take your hands off the oars and they naturally fold into the boat with a forward-motion current, held there by oarlocks with deep pintles and steel rings encircling the oars so they don't slip out and drift away.

New coat of blue paint, new cane seats, cherry oars, cash, handshake and farewell: new boat!

Lewis Creek is well known. Fishing has gone on there for centuries, first by the Western Abenakis and then by early colonists on up to the current day. The Abenaki name for the river is Seniganitegw, meaning "stone works river," in reference to the stone weirs they used to catch fish. Well into the late nineteenth century, white settlers and their kin followed suit, running seine nets at the mouth of Lewis Creek until the Vermont legislature fully outlawed them. Today, the Lewis Creek Association is looking out for Lewis Creek as a partner with the State of Vermont in restoration and management.

There are problems. Lewis Creek suffers from erosion and eroded sediments carrying high levels of E. coli, especially in the upper reaches where pollution sources include a bevy of small dairy farms, logging operations and eutrophic ponds. An abundance of phosphorus from fertilizer runoff has led to nutrient enrichment in the river and in Lake Champlain. Nutrient impacts in the lake are a crisis that the EPA is now forcing the state to deal with. Phosphorus affects every trophic level, including upper-level consumers like fish. It is the limiting nutrient in freshwater systems; plants' growth goes wild with extra phosphorus inputs. Phosphorus loading can lead to blue-green algae blooms, and these can have, along with high E. coli counts, deleterious human health effects and be harmful to fish and natural ecosystems too.

Conservation projects upstream include water quality monitoring stations, and the Lewis Creek Association, State of Vermont and local Trout Unlimited chapter have worked together to stem erosion, using landscape fabric and large stone placement to reduce runoff at particularly offensive gullies. Downstream, where fly anglers are likely to go, the river can be moderately turbid even several days after a rain event. This is floodplain, and the soils are fine silts and highly erodible clays, so the turbidity is to be expected. Erosion in these lower stretches runs from moderate to severe.

However, don't be scared off by a river with problems. What American creek doesn't have problems? Very few. That's why every river needs stewards.

Photo of the author standing with truck and rowing canoe. *Photo by author.*

Lewis Creek is a must-visit place, exceptional in so many ways. The river that meanders through the floodplains feels incredibly wild, and the spring color in May is blazing. This is one of the largest, most intact floodplain ecosystems in Vermont, and it contains rare plants and forest types not found elsewhere. Strange fish, too, like longnose gar. There is a tupelo forest, close to the northern edge of its range, and a yellow oak grove, a species unique in Vermont to Lewis Creek, as well as the unusual red mulberry. The overstory is mostly box elder, brown ash (the Abenakis' source of basket-weaving bark fiber) and silver maple. Also, elm species are found.

During my walk, the floor of the forest was covered with unspooling ostrich fern. The trees' new, unfurling leaves in early spring were electric green overhead. Orioles and tanagers were singing. Marsh marigolds bloomed in tight yellow masses, and blooming as well were bunches of early yellow, purple and white violets. One steep bank by the river was covered in the large bells of white trillium, a showy wildflower that we "eastern shore" Vermonters don't see too much. These soils are mesic—rich in calcium and other macronutrients, the benefactor of nearby Paleozoic limestone outcrops, impregnated with the fossil shell remains of marine animals like the murex, *Maclurea magna* and very weird fossilized bryozoa. The suite of wildflowers, understory and overstory trees reflects that richness. Gardiner Island, a limestone block at the mouth of Lewis Creek, is host to the aforementioned yellow oak community and was once a long-standing fishing and hunting camp for the Abenakis.

I parked on Lewis Creek Drive, a short string of a road that passes two homes and then dead-ends at the concrete abutments of the old bridge. The first home on the river there—on the lower side of the road, with small fields and a large lawn that stretched down to the river—was the original bridge keeper's house and was for sale. The family was out working on brush beside the road, and I spoke with the grandmother. She told me her daughter was selling because the house was too big to take care of. Did I want to buy it? I reached into my pocket. No, I said. But it's historical, she said. It's the old tollhouse. A great spot for someone, maybe, I said. I liked the house actually; it had a uniquely Vermont entryway, DIY covered and fully walled-in, that connected the road edge to the house proper, built by a Vermonter who wanted to take one step from the car into the house and no more.

What about the fishing? I started downstream and walked toward the lake. Lewis Creek is well known among local anglers, and you can find postings online. Bob Shannon, fishing guide and owner of the Fly Rod Shop in Stowe, described the steelhead fishing developing there after the state heavily stocked it with smolts from a California strain of steelhead rainbow trout in the 1950s. The most popular time to fish for them is probably the last two weeks in April and the first in May, but it's best to keep your ear to the ground to get the timing right, as I did not. Much depends on water level. Nymphing with beadhead flies is the preferred method. Bob recommended a Raven float system. He went on to implicate black Kaufman Stones, Copper Johns and egg patterns. Focus, said Shannon, on the deeper, slower-moving water. The Middlebury Mountaineer, an outfitter in Middlebury, also puts up fishing reports that include Lewis Creek, and it's a good idea to check in with those. Otter Creek, Little Otter Creek, Lewis Creek, the Middlebury River, the New Haven—these are all the home rivers of Middlebury and Otter Valley anglers and the outfitters at the Mountaineer. Both Shannon and the Mountaineer can provide guiding services.

Following the steelhead, and overlapping some, are smallmouth bass. They come upriver in great numbers and size. Hit it right and you can have a twenty-five-fish day. I met Neal, a younger angler from Burlington. He'd had one small steelhead the day before. His observation from past years was that by the time bass came in, the steelhead had mostly moved out. And the bass fishing could be outrageous close to opening day on June 1.

After walking a mile or so downstream, I turned around and walked back up and east of the Route 7 bridge. The section above the bridge is just plain gorgeous. An easy, informal trail follows this meandering river through flat to rolling abandoned farmland—classic Lake Champlain Basin countryside, with the spine of the Green Mountains visible to the east. Beaver signs, muskrats in evidence and very attractive trout water, deep on the corners—a river of riffles and pools. I could blink and think I was in Montana fishing a meadow somewhere.

I did see a few of the plus-sized smallmouth bass in the river too. One was a story I'd just missed, although the man showed me the phone shot: his wife, a fish and their daughter. They were fishing with worms in a deep pool before a ledge just downstream of the bridge. The man's wife had just caught and released a four-pound smallmouth—a Mother's Day present, the husband told me. Farther upstream, in the luxuriant grasses of the old meadow section, three spin fishermen were casting plugs into a pool where the river turned, sight fishing to several large bass. Another had a big, treble-hooked bass up on the bank and was laboring over it with the wrong tools, like a surgeon's nightmare—a grim outcome, and a big meal for the minnows, I think, or a rule breaker's meal out of season. There was a fly fisher, too, another quarter mile up, but aside from that and migrating yellow warblers, Lewis Creek was empty.

There's a lovely book about Lewis Creek called *Lewis Creek Lost and Found*, by Kevin Dann (Middlebury College Press, 2001). Dann, a historian of the late nineteenth century, intertwines his research into the lives and work of three prominent nineteenth-century men born in the watershed—each of whom explored Lewis Creek, though in different ways—with his own knowledge of the natural and cultural history of the place and time of Vermont. Dann aims in part to celebrate these forgotten people, "local heroes," some of our earliest conservationists. Cyrus Pringle (1838–1911), "the prince of plant collectors," knew the plants of Lewis Creek better than anyone (and he collected in many distant realms, too, particularly in Mexico). His botanical collections are housed at the University of Vermont's Pringle Herbarium, but little has been written about his secretive personal life. Rowland Evans Robinson (1833–1900), an author and illustrator of stories of thinly disguised local people and places, including Lewis Creek, captured the manners of speech and thought, values and attitudes of the rural century before. And John Bulkley Perry (1825–1872), whose writings contained ideas about geology and religion when those two fields of practice and inquiry were not yet fully teased apart by the march of science, technology and cultural memory loss.

From a fisher's standpoint, it's Robinson in whom we have the most interest. Robinson wrote in his journals a lot about fishing, trapping and duck hunting along Lewis Creek in the middle part of the nineteenth century. His story characters—he places them in the nearby mythical mountain town of Danvis (a nineteenth-century version of Wisconsin's rural Lake Wobegon)—run into seine netters and dicker with them for part of the catch. They camp on Gardiner Island; they fish for perch and pike, hunt blue-winged teal, "duskies" (black duck) and wood duck and collect arrowheads. They encounter Abenaki fishers and hunters, runaway slaves and French Canadian muskrat trappers. These stories and many others were published in magazines like *Field and Stream* and *Atlantic Monthly* during the mid- to late nineteenth century. In his home life, Robinson worked to outlaw seining, a practice that was depleting fish populations throughout the Champlain Basin. The first laws banning seining went into effect in 1879, with a window during which seining was allowed on Champlain tributaries (October 1 through November 15). But those early laws during the days of the first fish commissioners had no teeth. There were no enforcement provisions, and even if there had been, there was no one to enforce them.

Robinson "corresponded frequently with the state Fish Commissioners, both to inform them of infractions and to urge them to ask the legislature for tougher laws."

In *Lewis Creek Lost and Found*, Dann has a deeper purpose than to show early examples of fisheries conservation activism in Vermont. The swamps, marshes and floodplain forests of Lewis Creek were a sanctuary for the dispossessed and the marginalized—the humans among us pushed out of the well-lit American social circle. The exiled by virtue of their indigenous heritage, the color of their skin, their sexual orientation, the twang and slang of their dialect, their gender or their country of origin—French Canadian immigrants, the Abenakis, African Americans, runaway slaves—all suffered from the fear, hatred and outright violence of the "white" European community. Who's to say which century has been cruelest, human on human? You'd think a place like down-home Vermont would have avoided the worst. But that's not the case. Dann's Lewis Creek is a kind of vanishing point where the marginalized went and, in Robinson's view, were equals again—they could rediscover their own and a common humanity, in witness of and a part of the timeless cycles of nature and the sanctuary that a swamp and a dark floodplain river can provide. Deeper still, Dann asked questions about the journey of the American soul at the turn of the nineteenth century. America was busy then conquering the physical world; while equally fast, the spirit world—particularly human beings' age-old quest for and mysterious connections to landscape in places like Lewis Creek—was slipping away.

Isn't reconnecting to the mysterious power of water and fish partly why we go fishing?

Chapter 5

CASPIAN LAKE

Tuesday, May 15, 2018

I came early in life to fly fishing, but much later in life to fly fishing with lead line. Some would not call fishing with lead line fly fishing at all. I had to attend a workshop in my sixties to find my way into this simple practice of rowing or paddling or motoring very slowly across a Vermont lake while dragging lead line with a Gray Ghost attached. Slow fishing, like slow food, has its adherents. I am now one. Fish can grow big in lakes and live longer than in treacherous rivers that dry up, heat up or freeze solid. As far as good fishing in late April to early May goes, just after ice-out, salmon, lake trout and other trout come up to the surface for colder water, move closer to shorelines and tributaries and can be caught there in pursuit of small baitfish, including spawning rainbow smelt.

Why cold water floats on the surface is all about the physical and chemical properties of H_2O. Water warming in the spring reaches thirty-nine degrees and sinks because it is densest at about thirty-nine degrees. Why? I have no idea. As water warms and sinks, it's displaced by colder, less dense water floating on top. When the entire lake reaches thirty-nine degrees and there is no longer colder, less dense water to float on the surface, surface waters warm and the situation flips, with warmer water floating on top of colder, denser water. Lake trout, whose ideal water temperature hovers at around forty degrees, go back to the deeps once that happens, but for a magical few weeks, you can catch them on top—along with salmon and other foreign-sourced trout, like the lovely rainbow and brown.

A large Willoughby River/Lake Memphremagog steelhead, circa 1958. *Steve Bojalian, with permission.*

True oligotrophic lakes (highly oxygenated, low organic matter) are rare in Vermont and mostly found in the Northeast Kingdom (**NEK**). Willoughby Lake, at 308 feet deep, and the Averill lakes close to the Canadian border, each more than 100 feet deep, fit the description, and there are many others.

Many fly anglers I know restrict their preferred practice to rivers and streams. I get it, and I have spent much of my fishing life seeking out rivers. But limiting yourself to flowing water is a mistake in Vermont. Some of the best trout fishing here, particularly by mid-season when many rivers have warmed (if you're still targeting trout, that is, and not bass or pan fish or, better yet, pike), is in the still water of lakes and ponds. Find a copy of Peter Shea's *The Atlas of Vermont Trout Ponds* (Northern Cartographic, 1987) if you can. There is also excellent information online. Check out the Vermont Recreation and Adventure Travel Directory (http://www.voga.org/fish_pond_web.htm) for data on all ponds and lakes. Depth charts can be found on the Vermont Department of Environmental Conservation's website.

The list of good trout ponds and lakes to seek out is long in Vermont, and it's an excellent project to get to know many of them over time. But if you're targeting lake trout, *Fishes of Vermont*, by Richard W. Langdon, Mark T. Ferguson and Kenneth M. Cox, notes about twenty-five lakes in Vermont where lake trout can be found. While natural reproduction takes place in many, almost all are supported by some level of smolt stocking. See Vermont Fish and Wildlife's annual fishing regulations magazine, with its fishing regulations; maps; and lakes, ponds and rivers by name, available species and location. Stocking numbers, dates and locations can be found on Vermont Fish and Wildlife's website.

Caspian Lake—in the north-central part of the state, north of Route 2 in the town of Greensboro—is known for its thriving and naturally reproducing lake trout population. Tom Jones, a fisheries pathologist and avid sportsman, told me that the lakers there are plentiful but tend to run short. Is there a relationship between the two? I asked. Probably not, Tom told me. The important factor is food supply. Right about now, the fish are on the food sources in shallower water—minnow species, rainbow smelt. This is the time to go, he said. So I called Jon Vara, an old friend and hands down the most entertaining fishing partner I know, who lives about thirty minutes south of Caspian in the town of Cabot (home to Cabot Creamery). I spent the night there, and we got out of the house at 5:00 a.m., Jon's canoe strapped to the top of the car, and drove the half hour to Caspian Lake.

The drive to South Wheelock from Cabot is through countryside as hardscrabble as it is lovely. The green of the fields in May and the shadbush flowering white make every modest house into a small kingdom. All the spring shades of pink and pale green and brown in the blooming trees give autumn a run for its money all across Vermont, but it seemed particularly true that morning. There are working farms, dairies, small vegetable operations, sheep and more. The places along the road are a study in contrasts: neat and not so neat, full of life and abandoned looking, a patchwork blend of poverty, wealth, thrift and anti-thrift—happy, well-tended lives on the surface and lives on the edge for everyone to see. The drive north gives the impression of driving through an inexplicable transition zone, from a rural something to a rural something else. Hard to comprehend. This is our rural reality, in which most people get by through some combination of ability, hard work, luck, alchemy and a helping hand; others are born into hardship and stay there. Life isn't fair.

Melanie Finn, a resident of the Northeast Kingdom, calls herself a perpetual outsider. She's white, though was born in Kenya; was a journalist who has covered war zones, though is a peace activist; and now lives in the NEK with two children and her husband. Her recent novel set there is called *The Underneath* (Two Dollar Radio, 2018). She described her book as a considerate exploration of violence—both personal and social. It's particularly hard today, she said during a recent reading, to see the children who are products of the opioid crisis. Addiction isn't only a rural problem. But rural life can compound difficulties because of the social, physical and emotional isolation. It's also true that rural people know how to adapt. Innovation goes on despite fewer government resources (although, on a per capita basis, this perception and assumption of fewer government resources is not always the case). It's always good to know where you are when you fish somewhere far from home, and in the case of rural Vermont, where you are is not often where the tourist bureau wants you to think you are.

But poverty is also a relative term. There's the town center of Hardwick, always surprising, always a reminder of the century before. What some houses may lack in paint, the town business owners make up for in pluck. Downtown—with its late eighteenth-century and early nineteenth-century wood-frame and brick buildings, including Jeudevine Memorial Library, a beautiful red stone structure dating back to the 1880s—has a handful of local businesses that you wouldn't find anywhere else but here. Hardwick has the Galaxy Bookshop, a thirty-year-old community hub that's surviving in the age of Amazon, I believe, because there is a widespread shared ethic in Hardwick and surrounding places that buying local is a good thing. And the farms in Hardwick are some of the most innovative in Vermont. There's a cooperative spirit in Hardwick. Then there's the Village Restaurant, perched above the banks of the Lamoille. The diner was under construction (damaged by Tropical Storm Irene), but the breakfast was undamaged; waitress and cook were trading friendly barbs. And there was the view of the Lamoille River, with its covered walking bridge just downstream. In Hardwick, much still feels right with the world.

When we got to Caspian, the lake was just waking up, undisturbed but for the sound of one distant motorboat. Our canoe felt as stable as a flat-bottomed jon boat. Jon's other canoe is like trying to stay upright on a wine barrel…can't be done. Not to cast blame, but Jon's high center of gravity can be an issue, as well as his sudden movements, and we've tipped more than once. Actually, I do blame him.

I was finally trolling with lead line. There were two colors out, each one thirty or so feet in length and designed to sink about five feet deep. Connected to the end of the lead line was forty feet of Trilene and, to that, a red-and-white streamer designed to look and swim like a rainbow smelt. Then we were just paddling.

Fishing with Jon is one long conversation. He talks. I listen. We settled into a very slow paddle across glass that was less like fishing and more like an Irish fishermen's net-mending circle. Jon pointed out that each Irish fishing family had a unique wool sweater pattern so that when a drowned body washed up on shore, they could tell which family it belonged to. A practice, he said, that sadly endures. That sweater factoid (I don't know that it's true, but Jon is often a trustworthy storyteller) got him going on a theory of wool pants—Swedish army surplus wool pants. You can buy them online at thirteen dollars for four pairs, he said, and they take a long time to wear out. Jon is living proof, since he puts on a pair of these same pants every day and figures he has a lifetime supply at his age (sixty-five), for about thirteen dollars. Welcome to Jon's version of life in Vermont.

On books, Jon is well read. He brought up a question and theory that he's floated before about diminishing fish sizes in places like this. To paraphrase: Isn't it true that the more aggressive fish—in terms of chasing down and capturing bait—are going to grow the fastest and largest? That there is a great advantage to being aggressive and to growing large? That as a survival strategy, the quick and aggressive strike—bite first, ask questions later—works? Until people started putting bait on sharp hooks, and then the wary fish survive and the aggressive fish are caught and removed from the gene pool. This is a question of fish population dynamics that I can't answer. But it stands to reason that in a productive wild fishery with high rates of fishing pressure and fishing success, if there's a size-limit regulation in place—at Caspian you can legally harvest only two fish over seventeen inches—you would expect to see downward pressure on fish sizes. I have no idea. But, Jon continued, it's got to be more complicated than that. Food supply, the gene pool, water quality, fishing pressure. Learning. Slow-growing lake trout. You should tell your experts, he advised.

We argued and slowly trolled the shorelines near tributaries, sure that fish were going to take at every turn. They did not. It could be that we needed to up our game. Or pay more attention and talk less. Some locals, I was told, like to fish at Caspian using a method called "yanking," whereby the angler holds onto the lead line and jigs as he goes. They fish shallow. They fish deep. They catch fish. I imagine they're a quiet sort and that yanking is their substitute for talking.

We managed to get back to the car just as a pounding rain came down. One of the problems of lake trout fishing is not catching. But you don't stumble into fishing success necessarily the first time out on a new lake, I told Jon reassuringly.

"Not us anyway," he said.

Chapter 6

THE BATTENKILL

Saturday, June 2, 2018

Batten Kill, Battenkill, BattenKill. Whichever the proper spelling, I don't know why I'd waited my whole life thus far to visit and fish a mythic place so important in the national annals of fly fishing. A place crowded with the ghosts of fishing giants—whether expert anglers, fly tyers, rod builders, artists or literary men (and some women, most notably author Dorothy Canfield Fisher)—who refined the sport of fly fishing while promoting it too. The Battenkill still has a lot of class. Its best-known angler, Lee Wulff, father of the catch-and-release ethic in America, lived with his family on the river for twenty years (1940–60), fished, wrote and helped advance the river's brand, while traveling and fishing nationally and establishing his own. What's not to like? I chalk up my own avoidance to old-fashioned provincialism—the Battenkill is a long drive away. But perhaps I was put off by the tales of famously difficult brown trout, too, and by the reputation of the Battenkill as traditionally snooty and not welcoming of ignorant bumpkins.

There are several famed personages in this southwestern corner of Vermont. Ira Allen settled with his family on the banks of the Battenkill in Arlington in the late 1700s. His more famous brother Ethan's wife and family lived for a time with Ira's family there. Ethan is best known as the founder and leader of the Green Mountain Boys of Revolutionary War fame. Ira, among other exploits, founded the University of Vermont and put the first dam on the Mississquoi River flowing into Lake Champlain in

Swanton. Both were real estate speculators during the time Vermont was still a British colony.

The artist Norman Rockwell and his wife lived in a home off West Arlington green by the Battenkill for many years, beginning in the 1940s. There, Rockwell painted many of his iconic covers for the *Saturday Evening Post*. His paintings epitomized the purity and innocence of American rural life—back in a time when rural was beginning to fade in much of urbanizing America—using locals from his community as models. And there's Charles F. Orvis, the country's best-known fly fishing entrepreneur, who began his eponymous fishing tackle company in 1856 that, over time, became wildly successful. His brother, Franklin, built the Equinox House around the same time (now the Eqinox Resort, it has changed hands and names multiple times since Franklin's ownership but is still the reigning heart of old Manchester Village). The Battenkill's reputation as a fishing destination was boosted in proportion to the success of the nineteenth- and early twentieth-century tourist hotel trades in the upper parts of the Valley of Vermont. Charles was only too happy to sell fishing tackle and fishing dreams to his brother's hotel guests. Railroads were in on the promotional act too. In fishing, the truth is one thing and myth the other. As John Merwin pointed out in his book *The Battenkill* (1993), "It's a lovely stream that's now more rich with angling tradition than with trout."

That may be true. The original native brook trout—likely in the two- to six-pound range and plentiful at the time of European settlement in the 1640s—are long gone, prey to settler appetites; massive land clearing for sheep pasture, timber and dairy cows; and the assaults of quarrying, dam building and industrial development on the tributaries and main stem in the nineteenth century. Those industries and their dams are gone today. And brook trout are alive and well and on the increase—just not the lovely, fat, twenty-two-inch natives of old. Battenkill brookies in our era, according to John Merwin, rarely exceed twelve inches in length, and most don't live beyond three years of age. They occupy the river mostly in and above Arlington, while brown trout dominate downstream.

Brown trout stocking became a regular activity in 1926 on the Battenkill. In *Fishes of Vermont*, we learn that browns were introduced into the Battenkill in the early 1920s, and by the early '30s, browns were thriving and growing to gargantuan size—a good example, I think, of what happens when you introduce a new predator into an ecosystem and everything goes berserk for a while, until a new balance is reached. Browns ate and ate and grew fat. Brown trout breached the twelve-pound mark, thanks in part to fish

Left: Charles Orvis. *Courtesy of the Orvis Company.*

Below: A nice wild brook trout on the "kill." *Photo by author.*

food—stocked trout, no doubt, but also a rich moveable feast of insect hatches. John Merwin believed that the fabled reputation of the river, originally promoted as part of the region's appeal to new urbanites seeking an Arcadian respite, was partially based on the memory of those giant browns from the 1930s.

Much has changed due to "human actions," and yet the Battenkill is a river that perhaps could be equal someday to its reputation of old. That's an exciting thought. It's got great stats. Spring fed, cool and nutrient rich, the Battenkill's waters can be fished all summer. Battenkill trout have been wild born and raised in the river since the 1970s, when stocking ceased. These fish, especially the browns, are famously stingy, but, hey, that's why we love to try for them. There's great access to fishing on the Battenkill, too, and there are special regulations in place designed to protect the quality of the fishery and the increasing numbers of large fish in the system. Finally, the Battenkill's surroundings are a place of substantial pastoral beauty: the river, the valley, the sentinel mountain ridges. The rural aesthetic values are remarkable, especially on the New York side of the border, where, as John Merwin wrote in 1993, time seems to have stood still. That was twenty-six years ago as of this writing. The valley is still stunning. Sunderland and other small villages pressed up into the Green Mountains—churches, graveyards, greens, small town intersections with no blinking light. Change continues at a slow pace (although there is a nice little craft brewery with a tasting room called Argyle in the old railroad station in Greenwich, on the New York side—I tasted the Caddis Cream Ale, among others).

Today's conservationists are working hard together to remake the Battenkill, this time with a commanding new set of technologies and much citizen involvement (and not in image only).

For a tour of the Battenkill, Doug Lyons is exactly the kind of friend you want to make—like the brother of the girl you wanted to date in high school. Serious and studious, Lyons knows the Battenkill through forty years of encounters, and he's been a good friend to the river all that time. He first came here with his father in the mid-1970s, and he kept coming back. He's been a member of the local Trout Unlimited (TU) chapter board and currently serves as a board member of the Battenkill Watershed Alliance. Lyons has been gathering data so he can put together a book of his own that picks up where John Merwin's book left off. A lot has changed in twenty-six years. (Lyons's book will dwarf my cursory treatment of this epic river, and I highly recommend it, when it comes out, based on my tour of the river with Doug.) Merwin (he passed away in 2013) may be best known for

Doug Lyons fishes a Battenkill pool. *Photo by author.*

his collected writings of Lee Wulff (*The Compleat Lee Wulff*), his founding of *Rod & Reel* magazine and his editorial work during the early years of *Fly Fisherman* magazine. He relocated to Dorset, Vermont, in the upper reaches of the Battenkill in 1975.

Bridges are such excellent places from which to stop and gaze. Lyons and I met in Manchester at the Orvis parking lot at 6:00 a.m. After a ten-minute drive south into Arlington, he pulled us over on the lower Richville Road next to a bridge in a place the locals call Oscar Johnson's Meadow. Lyons wanted to frame the physical setting and the problems the river has faced. Looking across Oscar Johnson's Meadow, Lyons remarked that more and more landowners are working with conservation organizations to let buffer strips of shrubs and trees develop on their banks, like those here. Not only are buffer strips good for the river because they provide shading and cooling, food production, cover habitat and pollution filtering, but they're also good for the landowner too, providing flood relief, bank stability and reduced erosion and sediment, deadly to the gravel substrates that aquatic insects need.

We turned a 180 to get our broader bearings. Lyons pointed out the distant ridge of the Green Mountains to the east and the bit of the Taconic range we could see to our west. Out of the bulwarks of these two ranges, the Battenkill's waters arise north of us beyond the village of Manchester, where an east branch and a west branch come together to form the main stem. The main stem of the Battenkill runs about fifty miles to the Hudson River. So the upper half of the Battenkill is in Vermont and the lower in New York. This is a river you want to spend many days on, a river that suggests you buy two state fishing licenses.

Much later in the day, we'd visit the east branch to do a little fishing and see an impressive planting designed and installed as part of an Eagle Scout project. But while the east branch contributes to the flow by half, Lyons explained, and is important for brown and brook trout spawning, it is less consequential to the quality of the fishery than the west branch (cut off by a dam and a waterfall in Manchester). The bedrock underlying the Taconic Mountains on the west side of the valley, and the bedrock beneath much of the valley, is limestone. Called a klippe by geologists—a mass of isolated rock—the Taconics are a key water recharge zone for the Battenkill. Water falling on the Taconics percolates down into the broken rock and fissures of limestone bedrock and discharges out of the springs on the valley floor at average air temperature, around forty-seven degrees. West branch waters are colder, richer in the macronutrients needed for plant growth and have a higher pH. The water stays cool enough in midsummer to support brook and brown trout and keep out pike and bass. Without the spring-fed, enriched waters of the west branch, there likely wouldn't be a wild trout fishery sustained in the Battenkill.

Leaning on the bridge railing, we gazed down the river. The Battenkill flowed quietly below, stained lightly with tannins but otherwise running clear over a stony bottom. I didn't see any fish below us. Lyons pointed out the vegetated banks, the trees overarching and shading, the river muted on this overcast day. That's where the fish were. Here and there, downed trees projected into the channel, clogging up and netting other woody debris. These downed trees—once often removed by enthusiastic tubers and kayakers—are proof of progress made with the recreational floating community. This is excellent trout cover now, Lyons said, a sign of real improvement here. Ideally, a stream's got plenty of woody debris and other cover like this—submerged stones, dead falls and shrubby banks—on 30 percent of its shoreline, he added, whereas in the mid-1990s, only 5 to 7 percent of the Battenkill could claim that kind of cover. Trout numbers had crashed by then; 6- to 10-inch fish were just disappearing.

Flatlining. Monitoring studies showed that where there had been upward of one thousand fish per mile, by the 1990s there were fewer than five hundred. Catch rates and size classes were down too. The only good news was that there were any fish at all.

We had a big public meeting in Arlington back in '94, Lyons said. No-kill test waters had been introduced (stocking brown trout had ended in 1972 and brook trout in 1975). One of the problems that soon became apparent was the public's lack of awareness and understanding. "The facts," Lyons told me, "were far from it." The audience, we all, were in the dark, he added, in the absence of good information. There was plenty of blame pushed around too, and the ordinary divides among a diverse fishing (and floating) public were evident. Luckily, the meeting and the ensuing restoration work had the steady hand of Ken Cox, Vermont Fish and Wildlife fisheries biologist, on the wheel. The U.S. Forest Service, the Natural Resources Conservation Service (NRCS) and the two states began working together. Between 2000 and 2006, scientists gathered data on geomorphology and hydrology, riparian zone plants, invertebrates, water temps, water quality, pesticides, brown trout genetics, cover and spawning habitat and trout population studies. As they worked to put the big picture together, it became clear early on that a lack of trout habitat was the limiting factor.

From the bridge at Oscar Johnson's, we traveled downstream, stopping here and there to talk about easements given, decent access points, habitat improvement projects and the river's special regulations. The Battenkill has been catch and release since 2016; bait fishing is allowed. I voiced my opinion that this was an example of positive, inclusive regulations. Doug wasn't so sure.

We fished…here and there. I'd tell you where precisely if I knew. Doug knew. If I lived here or fished here often, I'd come to know. Fly fishing constructs in your head a map of a river that is a blend of geography, animal intelligence and obsession. The head's natural GPS does all the work. In fact, actual GPS units on a river are a buzzkill, eroding our innate inner compass. You're on a river after all. And the river knows where it's going—to the sea.

Generally, we were not fishing to rising fish. At fish stop number one, Doug suggested something nymphy and sulfury in size 16, so I tied on a little green beadhead nymph. Doug is bug literate. There wasn't a place we stopped to fish where he wasn't turning over stones to see the life there. In early June, he said, it's the sulfurs and then march browns and various caddis. He saw a size-10 cream variant mayfly, the largest mayfly on the river. In the evening, he'd planned to go with a friend downriver into New York to fish a brown drake hatch—a size-10 mayfly. His chief tip to me was stealth. Fishing the Battenkill requires it, he said. I was using a sink-tip line and a 5-weight Sage rod. Casting across and down actually yielded a surprisingly fine brook trout that I really hadn't expected to catch, so low were my lowered expectations. Average catch rates, from creel studies, are something around 0.5 fish per hour. That hasn't changed in years. Not great, but not terrible either, and catch rates are averages; on a good day, there could be considerably more action, and an expert angler with a lifetime of experience like Doug would expect to better the average often by a factor of two or three.

At our second stop, we found a few fish rising daintily under the brushy cover of the far shore. Here, the river ran between high banks with overhanging limbs. Doug told me there'd been a deep channel running along one bank but that it had shifted into the center of the run after Irene in 2011 (Irene is such a primary reference point for Vermont river people). Here, I believe, were a few of those famously reluctant brown trout; we got the flies where they needed to be. It would have been picturesque if the fish had shown any interest in eating my fly and pricking itself on it. Nothin' doin'.

Our next fishing jaunt was at a narrow metal bridge, where a father in high rubber boots and two children were out walking a dog. There were fields on either side and a small house in the distance. We greeted them—Doug knew them by name—as we walked down the bank, into the river and upstream.

It surprised me that there were so few anglers out on the water. On a Saturday morning in early June on the Battenkill? That seemed wrong. Late May's hatches actually see a lot more interest, Doug said. This time is a bit of a lull. So we had this long, deep pool two hundred yards upstream to ourselves. Doug had had recent success here with a brown trout in the thirteen-inch range. We didn't scare up anything like that. But he did catch a pair of small brown trout in riffles on the way back down to the car.

Driving along the Battenkill—it's such an accessible river—and stopping to see the restoration work, or to try for a fish, is to come away at the end of the day with a series of still photos that when put together give only an impression of the whole place—fish, graveyards, clear and cold tributary streams where trout make their redds, mountains and people included. We spent much of the afternoon in New York, driving the Camden Valley, a major tributary, and then Eagleville Road by Eldridge Swamp below Shushan, visiting the town of Cambridge for a beer, an antique car rally and some lunch at a deli (according to Doug, its bacon hamburger is the best in the world). We stopped at the famed Grocery Pool, a favorite of Lee Wulff's. We spoke to an angler getting into the water at the access just above and then watched several anglers fishing Spring Hole below and above a metal bridge. We drove down through the gap of the Green River, a crystal-clear tributary essential to brown trout spawning. In the fall, Doug said, you can stand on a bridge there and count the spawning redds. The dirt road along the Green is potholed and one car wide, but it pops you out near where the Green enters the Battenkill. Twin Rivers. Near there we got out of the car and surveyed the river habitat amendments that the U.S. Forest Service had made. We turned off into a graveyard and got out to look down at the "Cemetery Run," where much woody debris has been added. After improvements, fish increased there by a factor of twenty, according to shocking studies. Big, big changes occur when woody debris is added, Doug said. Much of this work is letting nature do what it wants to do.

After all the data gathering, the groups began the work together of remaking habitat and measuring the results. The U.S. Forest Service, Vermont Fish and Wildlife, TU Southwestern Vermont, Orvis, the Batten Kill Watershed Alliance, the National Fish and Wildlife Foundation and others began remediating banks, anchoring heavy root wad "shelters" into them. The root wads provided sheltering habitat immediately. During the Twin Rivers restoration project on the Lesko property, twenty-four were added, along with fifty-nine rock structures with submerged wooden slabs. The bank structures deflected flow into the center of the river, deepening channels. Like great wooden nets, they trapped debris floating down the river. Over time, eddy action deepened pools and undercut banks behind the new structures. Pool habitat increased. Banks that had been denuded were planted, and erosion along those banks slowed. The results were pretty spectacular.

In 2016, fisheries biologist Ken Cox summarized the projects on the Battenkill, comparing pre- and post-project trout per mile, based on shocking data before and after improvements. In pool habitat prior to improvements, they had measured a mean of 197 trout per mile, looking at two years of data (2005 and 2006). In riffle sections, the pre-treatment mean was 263. After improvements, the mean for the years 2007 to 2016 for pool habitat was 646, while riffles averaged 333 per mile. Not only did these sections of river (roughly three miles) see vast improvements in the numbers of fish—and numbers of large fish specifically—but a real shift also occurred in the quantity and quality of pool habitat. Fish were taking to the new habitat in big numbers.

Along with habitat work came new regulations protecting large fish. Cox's report pointed out not only that the presence of greater numbers of large fish increased fishing quality for the angler but also that large fish, which are particularly vulnerable to angler harvest, benefit the overall health of the population. They have higher fecundity, contributing larger egg size and egg counts. Fry survival is higher too. Large fish strengthen the gene pool. Some of the new regulatory structure is aimed at closing down fall fishing in important spawning tributaries like the Roaring Fork and the Green River. Much more work is needed, Doug told me—funds for continued habitat improvement work, including redoing some of the oldest amendments that are failing.

What else do they all need to do here? We were making our way north back toward Manchester now, passing through a resort community the likes of whose stonework and manicured gardens I'd never seen before. President Lincoln's wife lived in Manchester for some time after the Civil War. That home, called Hildene, is now a museum. The high and mighty do indeed still hide out in this part of Vermont. I've known a few of them. But we were headed to the Pig Farm, a decidedly non-elite-sounding place, and a public easement, high up on the main stem, for some late afternoon exploring. One of the most complex issues affecting water quality is the town of Manchester itself. Most rivers see the heaviest amount of urban development downstream. The reverse is true here, Doug said. Manchester, with its growing area of impervious surfaces—paved roads, roofs, parking lots, new outlet shopping centers—sends a lot of untreated and warmed runoff (not sewage runoff; Manchester was sewered back in the 1950s) into the river. Pollutants and warmed water have a huge impact on overall water quality, an issue that affects everyone, not just trout and anglers. Good fishing, and not just fishing mythology, has almost always been good to the economies of these rural places. John Merwin was right about that. The Vermont portions of the Valley of Vermont around Manchester and Arlington saw big benefits from the influx of fishing tourism going back to the later years of the nineteenth century. You could argue that Manchester overdid it in the factory outlet department. On the other hand, development brought jobs and has been highly concentrated and contained.

The Pig Farm, contrary to its name, is actually a fine-smelling place, protected by easements and accessible for the intrepid fisher. Here, the main stem of the Battenkill is a rushing stream ten feet wide, draped in tree limbs and crowded on either side by bushes and deadfalls. A great explore. I did catch and release a brook trout there—the size you'd expect—but what I remember best are the schools of just-hatched (from egg sac fry) brook trout fry, thousands of tiny black squiggly lines moving together in the still water of a small oxbow, where the translucence of the water and the bright light of the near-solstice sky lit the stones three feet down. The trout school was like a moving pointillism—a little living etching of black lines moving, nearly invisibly, toward some unknown shore.

The future is looking bright for the Battenkill. Habitat restoration and a brand remake are in progress. Much of what is needed is already there: clean, cold, nutrient-rich water; good science; and a cadre of citizen anglers and citizen conservationists who care. I'm coming back to the Battenkill.

Chapter 7

LAKE MITCHELL TROUT CLUB

Friday, June 6, 2018

A funny e-mail mix-up happened earlier this spring that had the happy result of me meeting Jon Vincent of Norwich, Vermont, and getting an invite to fish a morning with him at the esteemed Lake Mitchell Trout Club, in Sharon. I've always been curious about private trout clubs. There are no fewer than three within a fifteen-minute drive of my home in Taftsville. If the same local density were to be spread evenly across all Vermont counties, then Vermont would have many dozens of private trout clubs, which it does not. I know of one other nineteenth-century club, the Lake Mansfield Trout Club in Stowe, founded in 1899 by two fishing buddies, Orlo Luce and Mark Lovejoy, and still in operation. Each of the three clubs close to home was built around the turn of the nineteenth century: Lake Mitchell in Norwich in 1899, the Lakota Club in Barnard in 1891 and the Meccawe Club in Bridgewater in 1900.

My host, Jon, a retired architect and a lover of bamboo fly rods, had done some research into the early years of the Lake Mitchell Trout Club. I asked him why so many clubs seemed to have had their start in the 1890s. Jon's theory is that it was during this final decade of the nineteenth century (the Roaring Nineties) that American businesses, lawyers, doctors—professional men—had made enough expendable money to spend on recreational and social gathering places like trout clubs. Of course, a lot of developments were occurring in fisheries management during those years. The first hatchery in

Vermont, the Roxbury Fish Culture Station, was built in 1891. In the 1870s and 1880s, private citizens had been encouraged to raise and stock exotic species on their own. Before the formation of the state's fish commission, it was kind of a free-for-all. The townsfolk built trout ponds to provide fish to the marketplace and to stock private ponds. The trout clubs were something different. The public hue and cry for better fisheries management was on the rise during the last decade of the century. Atlantic salmon in Lake Champlain were on the brink of extirpation. Native lake trout had been extirpated from Lake Champlain by 1900. Private clubs could promise decently good fishing at a time when the common two-pound brook trout was long gone from most local lakes and streams. Stocking was increasing. The first rainbow trout were stocked in Lunenburg, Vermont, in 1886 and the first browns in Bennington County in 1892.

Private trout clubs had a large social function too. Originally, the owner-members of Lake Mitchell came from East Coast urban centers and would spend a week or several summering with families in tow. To get to Lake Mitchell, they took a train to White River Junction and then boarded horsedrawn wagons to the lake. Jon pointed out that the front steps of the Lake Mitchell lodge were, in fact, four to five feet above ground level—wagon floor height.

The lodge at Lake Mitchell is not a pretension—no mansion in the woods—but it isn't plain either. It's three stories tall, built in the cottage style of the day; unprepossessing though elegant, with a wild garden on the side that's protected by a handmade sapling fence. The caretaker lives with her dogs in the caretaker's cottage, fishes, takes care of the garden and grounds and does the cooking for special club events. The interiors of the lodge are spacious, with dark, heavy hardwood furniture, high ceilings, a large mahogany dining room and a long table that the caretaker was setting for the annual meeting. I didn't ask Jon to place the architecture, but it looked Victorian, as opposed to the Lakota's Adirondack style and the Meccawe's nineteenth-century schoolhouse (with no electrical service). Each private club sits on a hill with a commanding view of their fishing lake and the surrounding hills.

The socializing that goes on at the clubs has always been at least as important as the fishing. Adults can let their hair down and be kids again. The Lake Mansfield Trout Club Coral Society sang "The Trout Club Song," an ode to friendship and fishing both. The Meccawe has Calvin Coolidge's floppy hat. He was a member. The Lakota has a pair of deer heads with antlers locked in a deadly embrace, a telling gift made to the club by Teddy Roosevelt. The Lakota also has a possibly unique example of the rare Hummingbird fly, some tyer's flight of fancy. We can think of the trout clubs as a snug and private version of Vermont's well-loved summer cottage communities, at places like Lake Elmore, known as tight-knit, family fun–oriented getaways with decades-old traditions and intergenerational family connections that have an informal order. Mansfield is next to the Long Trail. There is a swimming deck. While trout fishing has always held a great centrality at these clubs, they also serve as private social retreats in an increasingly busy outside world.

As far as fishing at Lake Mitchell goes, for nonmembers like me, it takes an invite. Jon Vincent rowed and recommended flies. I flogged and dragged line. Lake Mitchell, like the other clubs, provides a small school of aluminum rowing boats, life jackets and oars. All this makes fishing so easy. You arrive, assemble your rod; your boat's waiting for you. Inside a small shed, you can clean and refrigerate your catch if you don't release it live. Members keep track of their catches in a ruled notebook inside the lodge.

Perhaps you will figure out how to win an invitation too. In the meantime, fish one of the many trout ponds that the state stocks. Go with a few friends and you'll have an instant private club of your own. Furthermore, in Groton State Forest there's Seyon Lodge State Park, a public trout club–like place. The cost is $20 for a half day, or you can buy a Frequent Fly Anglers pass for $125 (a fraction of the cost of a membership at one of the private clubs—although without all those clubs' membership benefits). They provide the squeaky rowboats, and it's fly fishing only, all catch and release.

The e-mail mix-up that got me up to Lake Mitchell? I'd written to an outdoor writer named Vincent Freeman, praising an unusual piece he'd published on gun control (actually an attack on the NRA). Outdoor writers don't usually dish out gun politics that I agree with. I ended up sending him a copy of my book *Lost in the Driftless*, which had created a bit of a stir in Wisconsin. Weeks later, I got an e-mail from a Jon Vincent with his comments on my book, including a few corrections. Of course, my brain turned them into the same person. I didn't realize Jon Vincent wasn't columnist Vincent Freeman until the day I met him and we fished Lake Mitchell. Oh well. I never heard from Vincent Freeman, but Jon Vincent became a new friend. How many people have the last name of Vincent, or a first name Vincent for that matter? There's Vincent van Gogh, Norman Vincent Peale (*The Power of Positive Thinking*) and Phil Vincent (inventor of Vincent Motorcycles). That's not that many Vincents.

Chapter 8

THE LOWER CONNECTICUT RIVER

Friday, June 8, 2018

Where to begin a chapter on fly fishing on the Connecticut River? The Connecticut is 407 miles long with a watershed of 11,000 square miles. In northern New England, it provides much of the boundary between Vermont and New Hampshire, joining Quebec (Canada) and the northern U.S. border to the coastal port of Old Saybrook, Connecticut, and linking the intertwined histories of the Abenaki and the colonists, both French and English, by warfare and disease, by trade, by fish and by genocide. The Connecticut is—all of its blockages (there are eleven main-stem dams, mostly power generating, and numerous tributary dams) and drowned miles included—figuratively speaking anyway, the aorta of New England.

For the purposes of a Vermont fly fishing book, I've broken the river into three short chapters. Fishing opportunity isn't so different from north to south, in many ways. You can find northern pike and perch and walleye and bass, even trout, as you get upriver to Lebanon, and the upper river has a thriving destination trout fishery controlled in part by the Murphy Dam and its tailwater, large northern lakes, remote brook trout ponds and bogs and rambling wild streams. The river has numerous backwaters and adjacent wetlands, too, and there are ponds behind dams and large reservoirs. At least three dams have productive, cold, tailwater trout fisheries, and there are falls and canoe access points, making the river truly a lifetime's worth of fishing explorations. But let's start by looking at shad fishing in southern Vermont.

The primetime fish story on Vermont's southeasternmost stretches in late May is shad. Shad are a river herring that, along with alewife and blueback herring, made prehistoric spawning runs measured in the millions of fish—together with a much lesser number of Atlantic salmon, measured in the tens of thousands. (The low numbers of salmon during the colonization years surprised me. I'd heard stories of salmon so thick that colonial farmers speared them to feed their dogs; that you could cross the river on the backs of spawning salmon—more fiction than fact.) Shad make it as far north as Bellows Falls. Salmon reached Beecher Falls, just south of the Canadian border. With dams that began going up in the late eighteenth century, salmon were quickly extirpated from the basin. Under its first commissioner, Spencer Baird, the U.S. Fish Commission initiated a salmon fry stocking program on the Connecticut in the 1880s, but that proved unsuccessful. Then again, in the 1950s, the U.S. Fish and Wildlife Service began a program of stocking smolts from fish of New Brunswick, Canada origin. Stocking efforts and the construction of fish passageways continued, with a narrowing of target areas for stocking and a switch to fry stocking. In 1971, the U.S. Fish and Wildlife Service began stocking salmon fry in the White River (grown by the federal hatchery in Bethel). By 1994, all of the fry released were of White River hen salmon origin. But still the program could not manage to produce returns large enough to establish a viable population.

Thirty years ago, my reference point was Atlantic salmon, not shad. We moved to the town of Wilder, Vermont, in the Upper Valley during the peak years of the federal Atlantic salmon restoration program. I had worked at one of the federal Atlantic salmon hatcheries in Milan, New Hampshire, for a few seasons, so I was aware of the basic challenges—to both growing Atlantic salmon and establishing viable populations back in the wild. The year we arrived in Wilder was the same year the fish ladder at Wilder dam opened for business. It was front-page news, and we all went down to the dam with our kids for a look through the new observation window. I remember seeing a large smallmouth swim by. We wanted to see one of these majestic salmon, and we were hopeful that it wouldn't be long before Atlantic salmon were spawning once again in rivers like the White River, the Ammonoosuc, the Passumpsic and the Nulhegan.

While salmon restoration on the Connecticut and Merrimack Rivers turned out to be unsuccessful after nearly sixty years of effort—despite failure, the effort provided a huge amount of data for future restorationists—scientists were not able to discern with certainty why the effort failed. Some thought it was downstream passage. The restoration effort had focused on upstream passage in the early years,

Decomposing shad litter the shore toward the end of their spawning run on the Connecticut River. *Photo taken below Vernon dam by author.*

but downstream passage proved to be equally important and even more perilous for salmon. Some pointed to the range issue. Connecticut River salmon were at the southern edge of the Atlantic salmon population's range—was climate change and warming water affecting them? What about commercial fishing pressure? Others believe that the fundamental barrier was genetic. Once the Connecticut's genetic stock was gone, it was gone, and another river's salmon wouldn't take. Of course, failure was disappointing, but perhaps salmon had robbed the focus away from where it needed to be all those years? The river herring.

Shad are an excellent game fish. Through the centuries, they have been a well-loved and important food fish too. In studies that analyzed bones found in Abenaki middens, shad are well represented (Atlantic salmon are all but absent, although these bones appear to degrade faster). Shad were a staple of early settlers. Sometimes called "poor man's salmon" or "Gill pork" (after the poorly faring community of Gill, Massachusetts, that could not afford to buy the real thing), shad were taken in great numbers by just about everyone. George Washington was a commercial shad fisherman.

(For a great read on the place of shad in the American story, see John McPhee's *The Founding Fish*.)

Shad still make heroic runs, though at dramatically reduced numbers. Shad fishing in Vermont is strictly catch and release, which plays well into the fly angler's playbook. You can go south across the border into Massachusetts and down to Holyoke to fish over a much greater number of fish and even take a few home for the table if you want. You'll need to learn to bone shad before eating shad, unless it's shad row you're after, in which case the fish body can go into your compost pile or under a hill of corn seed—a practice much older than the Massachusetts Bay Colony.

Fishing for shad and catching shad are two distinctly separate phenomena. McPhee, an impassioned shad angler, reports on his many hours of striking out. He also notes that slightly turbid water is best, that very clear or very muddy water will curtail strikes. In northern rivers, "they hit best in low light, overcast days, in light rain, early in morning, or just before sunrise."

I like fishing below Vernon Dam. There's a recreational park below the dam where you can park, put in a canoe or fish from a small point just south of the dam. The fishing can be great, and the surroundings are post-industrial interesting. You always meet someone or something of interest below Vernon. I like drifting downstream a mile or so and then dragging a sinking line back upstream. Or I stand on the small point below the dam. Early morning is best. I have graduated from a lightweight spinning rod to a fly rod with sinking line and then to a sink-tip line. I've used shad darts with spinning gear, shad flies and a fly rod and shad darts with a fly rod. They all work. Sometimes they don't. My leaders run short at seven feet, but the shad don't seem to mind. The shorter leader gives me a little better line control in a fast current; the sinking line or sink-tip line puts my fly lower faster for a long drift at depth.

American shad are our largest river herring. Adult shad weigh between three and eight pounds. Like their cousins, alewife and blueback herring, shad are anadromous, spending most of the year in the ocean then running up freshwater northern rivers like the Connecticut in spring to spawn. (A separate race spawns in southern rivers in winter, and like all Pacific salmon species, 100 percent of these die after spawning.) In the Connecticut River, shad spend on average thirty-nine days in the river during the spawning run. They lay their eggs and fertilize them when waters reach roughly fifty-eight degrees Fahrenheit, and then the adults do the return trip.

Shad are made for long-distance travel. The body, eighteen to twenty-two inches long, is ovoid in profile. They have a small head with an expansive back and wide sides that slim down to a narrow, deeply forked tail. Like one big bicep, they're jacked with the stores of fat on the side needed to make the spawning journey. They have large silvery scales, their armor against the many insults they face in their long migrations. Silver in schooling fish has an important survival value; it reflects the surrounding environment. Reflection, like the invisible car in that James Bond film, allows fish to become nearly invisible, and that helps them evade predation. Fish scales also function as part of a fish's lateral line system, used to detect the direction and strength of water flows around them. Thanks to microscopic hairs in the channels of the lateral line system, fish are delicate sensing devices, like swimming antennae. The hairs turn the mechanical motion of water into electrical signals. Their lateral lines give them the power of what has been described as "distant touch," or seismo-touch. It's the lateral line that shapes fish behavior, whether that fish is an ambush predator like northern pike or a migratory fish like American shad, which has to navigate one hundred miles of fishways, falls, changeable flows from dams and hot-water plumes from nuclear power plants in order to spawn.

Unfortunately, river herring are severely reduced across their northeastern range. Dams, other power plants, habitat loss and the disruption of freshwater and marine ecosystems from climate change are all factors. Marine fisheries in particular are imperiled by warming ocean temperatures. According to Ken Sprankle, a fisheries biologist with the U.S. Fish and Wildlife Service in charge of protecting and restoring migratory fishes in the Connecticut River watershed, rising ocean temperatures are having clear effects on species' ranges. Some are shifting north out of range in southern New England (lobster), while others are becoming newly dominant (black bass). Storm event frequency and intensity, precipitation patterns and warming temperatures affect the timing of migrations in spring and the absence or presence of prey species. Today, Sprankle said, they have to practice triage and focus primarily on species, like shad, that are in trouble but not at the extremes of their range. Salmon, sadly, are no longer the target, but shad are, as well as shortnose sturgeon, nearly extirpated in the century before and now just beginning to show up again above Turners Falls.

Key to conserving a species is understanding its natural history. Sprankle's work includes piecing together the story of shad migration. He described processing about 1,300 shad in the lab annually. He records ages by looking at otoliths—ear bones. He also looks at scales. Scales, like tree rings showing annual growth, show the number of times a fish has spawned. Since shad can live up to ten years and spawn many times, improving return rates, and expanding upstream habitat by reducing the stress of migration and mortality, in both upstream and downstream trips, could have a profoundly positive effect on shad populations.

The challenges are great for shad, particularly at Turners Falls, Sprankle said. Three separate fishways there create a significant barrier to migration. During strong water releases, it can take shad up to a full day to make it up just one of them (a mile-long canal leading up to the Cabot Station fish ladder). That may be as far as it gets. An agreement could come out of the current Federal Energy Regulatory Commission (FERC) relicensing process to replace failing fishways at Turners Falls with the type of elevator at Holyoke Dam, which works well. Only about 5 to 10 percent of the shad that make it as far as Holyoke, Massachusetts (south of Turners Falls), make it to the Vermont border and beyond. Turners Falls is the deadly gauntlet.

Shad in the Connecticut River now are measured in the hundreds of thousands, down from 3 to 5 million. Some forty to fifty thousand make it as far as Bellows Falls. But there's hope. The nuclear plant at Vernon closed in December 2014, and the thermal plume created by it is gone. Vermont state fisheries biologists had completed a study and a report on the impacts of the Vernon thermal plume and were preparing to submit it for FERC review just prior to the power plant announcing that it would soon close. (The state's role in FERC relicensing is significant: under the Clean Water Act, it's the state that issues a water quality certification.) There is also the potential that FERC relicensing will result in improvements to the fishways and consistent flows on the Connecticut. If we're successful in the next few years, future generations could experience huge increases in river herring in the Connecticut River over the coming decades.

Meanwhile, we can fish for shad and release the fish we catch. The scaly shad, so well suited to the migratory task, continues to delight, and we can imagine what fishing more than 500,000 shad at Bellows Falls might be like in the future.

Chapter 9

THE FAMILY FISHING FESTIVAL

Saturday, June 9, 2018

Teaching children and families how to fish has been a sideline interest of mine for a few years. I volunteer for Let's Go Fishing, an educational approach run by the Vermont Fish and Wildlife Department that pairs volunteer teachers with school groups, summer camps, state park programs, local trout fishing derbies and the occasional free fishing day or fishing festival. The department hosts ice fishing festivals (very popular and very cold) and wildlife fests. It also provides workshops for adults who want to learn something new about fishing (this year: a workshop on lead-line fishing, another on fly fishing for carp and a third on catching brown bullhead—thought by some to be the best-tasting freshwater fish in Vermont, although I'd vote pike). In an age that's increasingly stressful for families and oriented toward technology, fishing as a gateway to nature and to native pleasure seems like a no-brainer. But how to get kids started? How do you hook 'em? Help them catch a fish! It's almost that simple. What better chance to catch that fish than in a fish culture station? That's what brought me up to the Ed Weed Fish Culture Station on Lake Champlain. The Family Fishing Festival is a free fishing day statewide too.

Ed Weed raises fish strictly for Lake Champlain and its tributaries. According to hatchery personnel, the total annual fish produced there approaches several million in fry, smolts and catchable-sized trout, salmon and walleye. That's a lot of fish. Rare and endangered lake sturgeon eggs work their way through the fish culture system as well. Grand Isle is a strategic spot for fish culture. Lake Champlain, at 124 miles long and 490 square miles of water, was designated by the U.S. Congress for a brief time in the 1990s as the sixth Great Lake, a designation that helped lake restorers when it came to funding research aimed at repairing water quality and restoring lake trout, salmon and other native fishes, while supporting coordinated bi-state and bi-country planning.

Champlain has a varied and sometimes tumultuous cultural and natural history, from post-glacial times, seventeen thousand years ago forward. The lake is an important center of tribal culture, kinship and present-day society for the Abenakis, who trace their ancestry to bands of hunter gatherers who came across the Alaskan land bridge twelve thousand years ago.

Lake Champlain contains about eighty of Vermont's ninety-two fish species and is economically the most important destination fishery in Vermont, with a growing reputation for world-class bass fishing and a very respectable increase of its lake trout, walleye and salmon fisheries—not to mention its less sought-after fish, including longnose gar, pike and freshwater drum. There are immense challenges to restoring these fisheries. A bevy of historic forces brought disruption, change and loss, including overfishing, pollution, habitat destruction, the introduction of nonnative species, the development of shorelines, the loss of wetlands, the construction of dams and historic weirs, seine fishing, urban and agricultural runoff and increasing erosion from timbering in the hills. All the more reason to educate our children. I see the Ed Weed Fish Culture Station and all hatcheries as raising children as well as fish.

When I arrived at Ed Weed and parked my car, a line of parents and their children had already formed at the registration desk under a pop-up tent near the station's entrance. Below the registration booth and the station itself, the land drops down. On either side of the road, many small pavilions had been set up with activities designed to engage children in the world of fish and fishing. You could make pieces of art; learn about fishing laws and fishing ethics; learn to spin cast and catch a plastic fish (backyard bass) and then learn how to identify the species on the back of the plastic fish; construct a pond ecosystem out of pieces of felt; learn to fly cast, learn to set the hook; and watch volunteers fillet and deep fry the fish you caught. Eat those fish. *Let's Go Fishing* had established a punch-card system so that each time a child learned to set a hook, tie a knot or build a lure, they got a punch. Earn ten and you were handed a rod, a reel set, a container of worms and a blue stringer, and you could go fishing for rainbow trout in the station's pond. The pond at the bottom of the hill, with its thousands of hungry brook and rainbow trout, was the main attraction. Our job was to circle the pond and help untangle line, fix reels, bait a hook and provide some instruction, some moral support and encouragement. Each child could catch up to two trout and keep them if they wanted. After catching the fishes, they could go to a photo station and get a high-quality digital print of themselves and their fish to take home.

You meet a very pleasing diversity of families. I found myself explaining to children who spoke English, who then translated in Chinese to their parents who did not, what was needed when it came to catching an American trout. This felt to me, on one level, like teaching English as a second language. On the other hand, it is also true that we volunteers were the ones getting educated. The whole affair involved diverse populations—there were new Vermonters; new kinds of families; old-school rural people who knew their way around fishing quite well, thank you, and didn't need help; low income; high income; families of color; and the very old in wheelchairs and some wheelchair-bound youth. Everyone was catching fish, the common denominator.

By 10:00 a.m., the pond was ringed with small children and their families. Most of the kids would catch at least one fish, and many would catch two. Not all wanted to keep their fish. I helped them release dozens back into the pond, which must have had three thousand fish in it. Many wanted a photo, and many more wanted to eat that fish for lunch, which they did; Fish and Wildlife's fish fillet and fry station was pretty darn cool.

It went like that until closing time at 3:00 p.m. Ed Weed had made a kind of happy aquatic edible fish zoo for a day, a hands-on one. What struck me most was the moms—as many as there were dads—jumping in to bait hooks, take fish off lines and encourage their children. One recent marketing study shows that in a generally flat market of new youthful anglers in Vermont, there's an upswing in women taking children fishing. Good on that.

One reason (among many) for society to invest in fishing is that it nurtures the family. Mostly we get the bad news. Children who have to cope with a drug-addicted parent, who suffer through a broken home, neglect or outright abuse on some level through no fault of their own. Who endure poverty and not enough to eat, who suffer through an ugly divorce, homelessness or an untreated illness because families don't have healthcare coverage or because rural families in particular don't know where to turn for help. It's very easy to fall through the cracks in rural America, Vermont included. Fishing is a kind of out, a kind of ruse, a workaround. Rural life can be isolating. To a child with a good family, fishing can be a joy. A rod, a bobber, a hook and a worm—they mean a good day on the pond. In a stressed-out, dysfunctional family, fishing may be the best escape. It did occur to me that children, with their green spongy minds, catch on so fast. So adaptable, even to hardship. It's we adults who may need that fish even more.

Driving back down the state to the east and south, I stopped at the bandstand on the South Royalton Town Green, where the Greater Upper Valley Trout Unlimited chapter was awarding prizes for the White River Open Fly Fishing Tournament, a contest I'd had to forgo. The White River Open is an annual trout fishing event that raises money for the projects of the chapter—everything from work in classrooms to teaching vets how to tie flies and stabilizing river banks with plantings of dogwood and willow. I knew some of the anglers, which included a smattering of fishing guides—the pros—and the rest of us. There were a handful of boys with their fathers, as well as a few girls and grown-up women too. The fishing seemed like it had been good on the river this year. Smiles all around. One father-and-son duo had only caught lots of smallmouth bass in the lower river; others had hooked into big fish and lost them. They'd had fun but did not win a prize. A few had found pockets of recently released hatchery fish and caught a few dozen. Many collected trash and earned a few extra points that way. The winner of the largest fish category went to one of the guides. The prize was an $1,800 handmade bamboo fly rod donated by the maker of Gove Hill Fly Rods, Brian Ganley. C'mon now, that is one outsized first prize!

Next year, I'm going to participate so's to win that bamboo rod.

Chapter 10

THE WHITE RIVER

Monday, June 11, 2018

There are as many ways to write about fishing as there are ways to fish. That became obvious recently when I went online to see what other writers had written about fishing the White River. At one end of the spectrum was the "fishing is incredible here" school in magazines, where hefty wild brown trout are caught frequently and described dancing across the surface of the sunset water. There are wild brown trout in the White River and some stocking of browns, although precious few are actually caught, according to recent creel surveys. The White, to characterize it, is a rainbow river. Happily, a surprising and increasing number of these are wild, although stocking is an important foundation to good fishing as well. The White's tributaries have some of the best wild brook trout fishing around, and feisty brook trout can be found in the upper reaches of the three main branches as well. At the other end of the writing spectrum are the grumpy naysayers who blog that the fishing is all downhill, the rivers too warm and crowded with floaters and what's the use, I'm moving to Wyoming or dying soon anyway. The truth is that fishing in the White River is not going downhill. It's actually pretty good, and thanks to data-driven stocking policy, wild trout management, vital habitat-improvement work by multiple partners working together and water quality improvement work, not to mention changing angler practices and reliable sources of cold water, the White is better than holding up—it's improving.

Personally, I love the White River as much for the river itself as for the part of rural Vermont it flows through, a land of hillside farms, mountain ridges, long open valleys planted in corn (also other grains, if talking Third Branch) and small towns where change is slow. The White is the state's fourth-largest watershed at 710 square miles, and it penetrates deep into the Green Mountains in the center of the state. Those mountain headwaters are its saving grace. The streams that flow off them supply the White with cold water, provide spawning habitat for brook and rainbow trout (and fewer populations of wild brown trout) and, during drought and increasingly warmer summers, provide refuge from waters that can get into the seventies in the upper river and eighties down low. I've generally stuck to the main stem and the upper reaches of the Third Branch, which flows from Roxbury down through Randolph to Bethel. The fishing for both stocked and wild rainbows—and, higher up in the watershed, wild brookies—can be quite nice. Or you might get skunked. But in addition to fishing the main stem, exploring the pools, places, the wild tributaries up through the small towns of central Vermont never gets old. And there's far more river than any one of us will ever get to know.

What do the biological data tell us about fishing the White River? Two recent studies point to some interesting and mostly positive fishing trends. The first was an assessment of wild trout spawning activity in the White's most promising tributaries. The study looked at some twenty spawning tributaries and compared the most recent data with past data going back forty years. The study found that "overall, wild trout populations are relatively stable with evidence of widespread, successful natural reproduction." The second study was a creel census, or angler study (both projects managed by state fisheries biologist Bret Ladago). Creel censuses provide an inside look at who's fishing and what they're catching. Conducted during the 2017 fishing season, it compared data from a 2001 census of the same reaches. Surveys were conducted along thirty-seven miles of the main stem, from Rochester downstream to Hartford. The river was segmented into three reaches. From the interviews and creel data (in certain reaches today, most of the fish caught are released, so creels are thin in these places), researchers were able to estimate catch rates, species caught, release and harvest rates, rates of angler effort and terminal-tackle usage rates. The studies also compared water temperatures. The year 2001 was a severe drought period, while 2017 had normal, slightly above-average flows and one two-hundred-year flood event. Interestingly, 2017 was actually cooler than 2001.

A few "global" observations are worth considering. While overall angler effort on the river dropped from 2001 to 2017, angler effort within one section of the middle reach (B1) and one section of the lower reach (C2) actually increased by more than 50 percent. Summer temperatures were relatively cool in 2017 compared to 2001, but still, main-stem temperatures exceeded seventy-five degrees in places in midsummer. In other trends, catch-per-unit effort for rainbow trout has remained about 0.4 rainbow trout per hour since 1995. Also, there is a steady decline in the proportion of trout harvested by anglers, which has "decreased dramatically since 1971." More than 90 percent of the fish caught in the middle reaches of the White were released in 2017.

Where to fish? Fishing in the upper river and its main tributaries just above Rochester and down Stockbridge, a distance of about ten miles, is for the explorers. This reach neither gets the attention of many anglers nor has it been stocked for several years, in part due to low angler effort (less than sixty hours per mile) and in part due to the damage sustained by the Roxbury Fish Culture Station during Tropical Storm Irene (the hatchery is being rebuilt this year). Access can be a little tricky. Still, for the intrepid angler, the upper stretches can be full of discovery.

The most promising for fly anglers is the middle reach, described in the study as a 10-mile section from the Route 107 bridge in Bethel upstream to the Route 100 bridge in Stockbridge (near Ted Green Ford). The upper and lower sections of this reach are stocked with nine- to eleven-inch rainbow trout, and they grow up to seventeen inches during the season. Sandwiched between the upper and lower sections is a 3.3-mile special-regulations section, from Lilliesville Brook to the confluence of Cleveland Brook, managed for wild trout, with no stocking. Fishing there is limited to artificial flies and lures, with an eighteen-inch minimum length limit instituted in 1994. While earlier studies show that special regulations have not resulted in larger fish and higher catch rates (than adjacent stretches), catch rates remain respectable at 0.436 trout per angler hour, and there is plenty of spawning habitat for wild fish throughout the entire middle reach (Lilliesville, Locust Creek, Cleveland Brook, Stony Brook, Little Stony Brook and the Tweed River). Overall, angler effort for the entire reach was estimated at 323.3 hours per mile, and the fishing skews strongly to fly anglers (68 percent). About 94 percent of the fish caught were released in 2017 throughout the 10-mile stretch. My experience of this part of the White is that it never feels crowded; there are plenty of pools along the river road (which runs parallel to Route 107 along the opposite bank). The report discusses the potential of the entire 10-mile middle reach, Bethel to Stockbridge, to be managed someday as a wild trout fishery: "Considering the high frequency of catch and release angling, the prevalence of artificial fly and lure use [81 percent of anglers in the 2017 study] and the abundance of cold, productive tributaries within reach B, the entire 10.8 mile section may be a candidate for wild trout management in the future." That's an exciting prospect. The report goes on to suggest the limitation of the existing special regulations water. "The current 3.3 mile section may be inadequate too, as these fish likely migrate seasonally within the entire reach and connected tributaries to seek thermal refuge, to spawn and feed."

On the lower reaches of the White, reach C, the 2017 study looked at trout fishing success between Royalton and Hartford (15.7 miles). These stretches get more angling pressure from all types of anglers—lure, bait and fly—with bait anglers in the majority at 42 percent. Rainbows were the only trout species reported caught in this reach, and an estimated 15 percent of these were wild (no fin clip), ranging in length from nine to seventeen inches. And here's a surprising statistic: a total of 3,111 trout was estimated caught in this reach, and only 12 percent of the 510 anglers interviewed accounted for 94 percent of the rainbows caught. Of the two sections in reach C, the lower one (Sharon to Hartford) is a good bass fishery, and the highest trout catch rates are in this reach as well. Lure and bait anglers have the highest success rates here and together make up a majority of anglers, but fly anglers are well represented in the mix (39 percent) and do well too. Favorite spots include pools below Broad Brook in South Royalton and the drops and pools around the island half a mile up from the West Hartford Bridge. Almost any pull-out on Route 14 has ledges and pools that can hold fish.

This year, closing in on the summer solstice, I made a beeline up to Bethel and beyond, to the upper section of the middle reach described in the creel survey (this section is stocked twice in May, and that does significantly improve the angler's catch-per-unit-effort prospects). I brought a friend, Steve Hoffman, who was just getting back into fly fishing. His most recent frame of reference in the fishing world was commercial seine-net fishing for salmon with his Alaskan brother-in-law. I told him not to expect salmon in the White River, although there was a time....

We fished here and there along River Road in the special-regulations water. Then we drove upstream to the pools below the Blackmer Boulevard Bridge, right near the intersection with Route 107, and had there what I would describe as a typical evening on the White in mid-June. The hatches started an hour or so before dusk and continued until it got too dark for us to see. It was midweek and we were the only two fishing miles of river. A bank beaver was slapping its tail a hundred feet downstream. A few bats came out—good to see, given that bat populations in Vermont have been devastated by white-nose syndrome. A barred owl began calling. My friend caught his first rainbow of the season, a nice eleven-inch fish, probably stocked a month or so earlier. He harvested it. Between us we caught a half dozen more; most were seven- to nine-inch wild rainbows, and we released all but the first. Back at the truck, nearly full dark, we cracked two beers. The moon came up, and the temperature dropped into the low fifties. All around us were miles of White River worth exploring. Long pools at the dogleg where Blackmer Boulevard comes into Route 100; Stony Brook, damaged in places by Irene, very lightly fished; and pocket water and deep pools along the White River Golf Course a few miles away. And in Rochester, the West Branch.

The White is much more than its main branches and their wild and stocked fish. I think of it like a set of lungs or an ancient maple tree. You can't know a lung until you explore the tiny branches out to the alveoli—so much like high-elevation beaver ponds connected by tiny tributary brooks. You can't know a tree by its trunk alone. So while I'd point you to the very handsome waters up the main stem upstream of Bethel, the White also connects to such seldom-explored landscapes as the Chateauguay, the Roxbury State Forest, Brandon Gap, Middlebury, Appalachian Gap, Lincoln Gap, the basins of the Long Trail, the tributaries that feed the Tweed River, the West Branch, the Vershire highlands, the hills of Sharon, Chelsea, the hamlets of Lost Nation, Granville Notch and Gulf Brook, Randolph, Brookfield's Floating Bridge and tiny Roxbury, which quickly drops you into the upper reaches of the Dog River. There is the picturesque mountain town of Rochester, cut off for a few days by Tropical Storm Irene, and dozens of healthy wild brook trout streams coming out of those hills. Local angler Ron Rhodes, a river steward with the Connecticut River Conservancy, prefers these kinds of places and their native brook trout. It's why he's spent a good part of his professional life removing dams and other migratory blockages to tributaries of the Connecticut. He told me to grab a few topo maps and go exploring.

If you're new to the White River, not to worry; armed with a Delorme *Vermont Atlas & Gazetteer* and Northern Cartographic's *Vermont Trout Streams* (bring your magnifying glasses to read the maps), as well as your state fishing regulations magazine, you can explore on your own. Topo sheets and satellite imagery are best if you are hoofing it into beaver ponds. Better yet, hire a guide to get situated. The trout fishing in the main stem is best through June and then again in September and October. Almost all the fish I've caught in the White over sixteen inches have been in the lower river in the fall, when they seem to be on the move. Searching for wild brookies in the tributaries can be good all summer long and into the fall.

Up and down the White River, biologists are gathering the data, and citizens in the watershed are working to restore the river together—not to some vision of world-class angling greatness, necessarily, but, over time, back to itself. To high-functioning, connected and integrated aquatic ecosystems, where anglers can find clean, cold water and the fishing can be pretty fine.

Chapter 11

THE WINOOSKI RIVER

Tuesday, June 12, 2018

There's a Hindu parable about six blind men and an elephant. Everyone knows some version of it. When an elephant comes to the blind men's town, they attempt to describe it. The catch is that each only gets to handle one part. The man on the trunk describes an elephant as a thick snake; another has the ear and describes the elephant as a type of fan; the one on the leg describes a pillar-like beast, a tree trunk–like animal; the one who gets the tail calls the elephant a living rope. No one with a small piece nails the elephant entirely (and that's the point of the parable). I think of the Winooski River as a kind of landscape-scale elephant. Simply too large to get your hands around. I have family and friends up and down the river, from Jericho to Cabot, and have fished lots of the corners over the years. I've lived by it in Burlington and had offices in Montpelier overlooking the North Branch, and I still don't know the elephant.

Partly, that's because there's a lot to know. The Winooski, at more than one thousand square miles, is Vermont's largest sub-watershed. And it's diverse, beginning at Lake Champlain and flowing through several of Vermont's most urbanized environments, including Burlington, Winooski, Montpelier, Barre, Stowe, Waterbury and the smaller towns of Northfield, Waitsfield, Warren, Marshfield, Cabot and Plainfield. And yet most of the Winooski watershed is lightly settled, deeply rural and hardly known by anyone these days. Parts of the watershed, like the east side of the Worcester Range, still look like they did when the Abenakis were the only humans.

Since colonization, it's been a working landscape of farms and forestlands. There are numerous brooks where wild brook trout thrive and wetlands and riverbanks where beaver dominate. As if to serve as a reminder of what was going on throughout the watershed in the eighteenth and nineteenth centuries, there are more than one hundred small tributary dams dating back to the early years of the Industrial Revolution, many nonfunctioning and blocking aquatic wildlife passage, as well as causing other nuisances like elevated flood potentials, polluted sediment loads, the threat of dam failures and warm-water sinks. Some make electricity. The main stem has dams too, notably the Winooski One Hydroelectric Dam, owned by Burlington Electric, with other power dams in Bolton, Waterbury, Moretown, Stowe, Montpelier, Cabot and Marshfield. And there are hydraulic issues with these, including fluctuating flows and severe and untimely withdrawals. The Winooski feels more diverse, more complex, as watersheds go in Vermont, although Otter Creek is arguably even more complicated when it comes to aquatic ecosystems and biodiversity. With Lake Champlain on one end and Vermont's highest uplands at the other—including Mount Mansfield, Sterling Mountain, Mount Abraham and Camel's Hump—there's as much vertical landscape worth exploring in the Winooski watershed as there is horizontal.

My first fishing foray on the Winooski this summer, as often has been the case, was with my brother-in-law, Wayne Ellis, as guide (and personal conservative political commentator, if I let him stray too far). A Jericho resident and IBM engineer, he's fished for years from Richmond up into the trophy section beginning in North Duxbury. He has many tales to tell of large brown trout, some of which I now suspect to be true. Although our politics are about as different as a can of worms and a pair of Simms waders, we are strangely alike—nearly the same age to the day and simpatico when it comes to trout fishing—and striped bass fishing, for that matter. Any kind of fishing. Blood is thicker than water, and fish talk is more engaging than talking politics. Actually, we've simply learned over time what not to talk about. And that's sad in a way.

We met at 6:00 p.m. in Jericho, headed to the community market in Richmond for some dinner and beverages to bring along, crossed the river in Richmond and headed east on the river road. It was a gorgeous evening, and the river was looking good—somewhat down, but the temperatures were right. And I was seeing several large trout in our future.

Wayne's plan had us fishing the trestle section at the downstream boundary of the trophy stretch. This was out of the ordinary for us. Usually

A large Winooski fallfish, *Semotilus corporalis*. Fallfish are natives in the minnow family, but contrary to their family name, they can grow as large as twenty-four inches. *Photo by the author.*

we pop into the river at Richmond, closer to his home, and walk upstream from the bridge, casting over early summer evening hatches and yearling stocked brown trout. That's fun, and there's a long sandbar that gets you out into the middle of the river, so the aesthetics are excellent too. Wayne's a grandfather now, so if his four-year-old is in tow, he'll take him to the town landing to catch perch. But tonight, it was that train trestle section that held the most promise. The trestle crosses at a particularly interesting part of the river, where it flows around a few small islands, creating what is close to a shallow braided channel that drops into deep pools. The pools were clear and, with the temperature in the mid-sixties, just oozing visions of large

Fishing the Winooski River trestle section with brother-in-law Wayne Ellis (shown in the far view on the left bank while the Amtrak train crosses the trestle). *Photo by author.*

trout. And if the fish proved uninterested, there was always the train. An Amtrak passenger train comes through around 8:00 p.m. and makes a pretty picture up on the trestle.

What about the name Winooski? It's an Abenaki place name, referring to the location of onions—wild leeks, or ramps, so plentiful along streams and certain rivers in May in Vermont. For centuries, before dam building, the Abenakis made fishing camps at Salmon Hole near the Winooski's mouth at Lake Champlain. I imagine they made weirs and caught all the salmon they needed. For a time, the name Winooski River (the river and the settlement) was replaced by the name Onion River. Historians think that the name switch was marketing related, engineered by the clannish and scheming Allen brothers. Ethan Allen is enshrined in our statehouse as a founder of Vermont and leader of the Green Mountain Boys, a Revolutionary War militia. It turns out he was also a pretty guileless businessperson who owned real estate up and down the Winooski Valley. Or the name change could have been orchestrated by English settlers who didn't like or trust the French or Abenakis and made busy doing away with Abenaki and French place

Higher in the watershed are several ponds and reservoirs, including Wrightsville Reservoir, well worth a float. A study of the upper watershed that assessed more than 100 tributary streams and 34 ponds found healthy populations of wild brook trout in most of these streams. Vermont Fish and Wildlife Department manages these as wild trout fisheries and does not stock over these wild fish. Management priorities in these wild places include: improving connectivity by removing those dams and dealing with the hundreds of culverts assessed (some 940 that are not fully passable by trout and other aquatic organisms); enhancing riparian vegetation—planting shrubs and trees to maintain cool temperatures for trout, filter pollution, prevent erosion and provide food and shelter; acquiring key lands that include headwaters, riparian zones and access to streams; prevent erosion and nutrient pollution from fields and roads and restore natural hydrologic regimes; improving habitat complexity by increasing woody additions; and, finally, stemming the spread of undesirable invasive species.

One of the most iconic reaches of the river is downtown Montpelier, Vermont's capital city. The reach has its small and loyal fly anglers. A classmate of mine, playing college fishing hooky, caught a twenty-two-inch rainbow in downtown Montpelier one fall. Four major tributaries to the main stem converge in Montpelier, and the river through the city has riffles, pools and some interesting structures, like bridge abutments, although there isn't much riparian vegetation. Stevens Branch on the east side of town and the Dog River, which comes in just below the I-89 underpass (across the street from the historic Green Mount Cemetery, worth a visit to see remarkable nineteenth-century granite statuary from Barre's Rock of Ages Granite Quarry), are both wild trout fisheries that contribute wild browns and rainbows. Vermont Fish and Wildlife supplements these wild fish with stockings of brown and rainbow trout. Montpelier is one of New England's finest small cities and the smallest state capital in the country. The statehouse, with its gold-leaf dome—atop of which stands a statue of Ceres, the Roman goddess of agriculture (removed, restored and replaced this year)—is often cited as having the prettiest backdrop of any statehouse in the country (Hubbard Park, with its surprising stone observation tower at the height of land, built between 1915 and 1920).

I have not mentioned the fine work of the Friends of the Winooski River ("Friends" for short). As far as I know, they are among the first such groups in Vermont and are quietly, highly effective. The Friends have been involved for more than twenty years with a range of projects, including dam relicensing processes, improvements to aquatic passage, dam removal, floodplain easements and river cleanup. Recently, the Friends and the Vermont River Conservancy (VRC) began working together to create a new river park at the confluence of the North Branch and main stem of the Winooski. As part of the VRC's Face the River program, the park is being designed with access for all in mind. Steve Libby, head of the VRC, told me that the park, which has a steep bank to the river, would serve the gambit—from families with a canoe and young children to anyone with mobility issues, including elderly anglers with arthritic joints.

Chapter 12

LAKE CHAMPLAIN

Saturday, June 16, 2018

Volunteering at the annual Lake Champlain International Fishing Derby, a fundraiser for lake restoration efforts, one morning in June, I began to feel transported back to an earlier time. Haggard groups of anglers started coming into our check station on Apple Island at 9:00 a.m. to tally their catch and then return to their boats to try to better it. They'd been up all night, and they came in bearing large, living fish. Our job was to keep the fish alive through the weighing, measuring and team validation process. We set up a large, oxygenated aquarium for fish that needed a nursery. As for successful releases, I don't have the data—most releases were handled by the anglers themselves—although our station seemed to do pretty well with the patients left behind. One thirty-seven-inch northern pike we couldn't revive came home with me under a few bags of ice.

Some of the early morning fish were the most interesting and unusual. A large bowfin, an eight-pound sheepshead (freshwater drum), several thirty-inch-plus northern pike and many four-pound and larger smallmouth bass came through, as did large specimens of largemouth bass, lake trout and salmon. Surprisingly, we had no walleye. The cutoff for walleye was twenty-five inches. We thought we might see a few of greater size with the first boats. Large walleye, we'd heard, move from deep water into shallows to feed at night.

No walleye, but the night fishermen brought something else. Call it the whiff of neo-indigenousness. They reminded me of something I'd read about the first anglers here ten thousand years ago, hunting and fishing bands from the Archaic period, ancestors of the Western Abenakis, People of the Dawn Land. These people fished during the Champlain Sea period (when retreating glaciers created a temporary inlet of the Atlantic Ocean at the end of the last ice age), using log ships that extended their range far to the north. By the time they turned south again, toward home, they were loaded with dried fish, seal flesh, oil and walrus. They caught much larger fish than we see today and more of them. What's long lost for most of us, though not all, is the subsistence piece, relying on our catch to live. For the Abenakis at Missisquoi, or the Nulhegan band or Abenaki tribal groups in southern Vermont, subsistence hunting, fishing, trapping, herbal medicine and the related crafts of forage, farming, the arts of basketmaking and dance endure to this day.

There were the centuries of the Abenakis' disappearance when they intermarried, moved, melted into the landscape and became invisible to survive prejudice and outright racism. Or they became nomadic again, transient hunters, fishers and guides, generally invisible except to themselves. George Perkins Marsh, in his report to the legislature on fish declines in Vermont in the 1850s, besides suggesting some of the root causes of fish declines and recommending fish culture as a way to address those declines, made the point that fishing and hunting gave vitality to rural life and were foils to the softening effects of urbanization. For the Abenakis, it's much more than that. Fishing is a part of their cultural continuity, their survival story and their identity. I wish Marsh, the great man, in his great book *Man and Nature*, or in his study of fish decline in the 1850s, had noted the presence and the significance of the indigenous people, their lost lands and nearly lost language and their importance in the long story of fishing. Today, the Abenakis don't have to disappear to survive, but there is still the long hard road ahead to restore bountifulness and culture, to gain federal recognition and to achieve the return of lands. The metaphorical big fish.

That we have large specimens of native cold-water game fish (and nonnative) in the lake, including lake trout and landlocked Atlantic salmon, is kind of a minor miracle and mainly a tribute to fisheries science and restoration management in Lake Champlain over the past fifty years. The suppression of lamprey eel using chemical lampricides beginning in the 1990s is about half the story. Adult lamprey parasitize lake trout and salmon, attaching to them with suctioning, rasping mouth parts that kill or weaken the host fish. The other half may be fish culture and the stocking of cold-water and cool-water fish, begun systematically in 1972. Without lamprey suppression and annual contributions of fry and yearling fish from the Ed Weed Fish Culture Station in Grand Isle, lake trout and salmon—and possibly walleye and lake sturgeon—would disappear.

There are other nonnative cold-water fish populations alive and well in Lake Champlain, including steelhead trout and brown trout, both naturalized with wild populations supported by stocking. Lake Champlain supports cool-water species, although walleye appear to be in decline in many of their ancestral rivers. Walleye are reared at the Ed Weed Fish Culture Station, too, along with Atlantic salmon and lake trout, and are either stocked by the hatchery staff or sent as fry to a private nonprofit walleye association, where they are reared to larger size in private ponds and then returned to the agency for stocking. The Bald Hill Fish Culture Station also grows walleye for water bodies in the Northeast Kingdom. Warm-water fisheries are healthy, and angling interest, particularly for small- and largemouth bass, is growing in Lake Champlain. In all, there are eighty-seven fish species in Lake Champlain. Fifteen of these are considered nonnative, late arrivals. Another sixteen are listed as threatened or endangered.

Fly anglers have a lot of fish to choose from and many places to explore, rod in hand (587 miles of Lake Champlain shoreline on the Vermont side of the lake). There are island state parks you can walk or paddle to, convenient Vermont Fish and Wildlife access points and preserves and thousands of acres of properties in public nonprofit domain (including the South Hero Land Trust, the Lake Champlain Land Trust, Vermont Land Trust and the Vermont River Conservancy).

My knowledge base when it comes to fly fishing on Lake Champlain is scant, but there are ample resources online. Plenty goes on from shore and offshore in boats. There are charter captains catering to fly anglers. My personal points of reference are Hog Island and Shelburne Bay (my wife grew up on the bay, and our children caught their first perch from her father's dock). At its southern end, Shelburne Bay has a large boat ramp and public access points from shore popular with anglers. There are walking trails from the Shelburne Bay access that get you up into the LaPlatte River—an excellent natural marshy area and spawning place for carp and other warm-water species. The Harry Clark Trail heads north from the access point along the shoreline toward Shelburne Point. Shelburne Point (private) is a well-known spot for trolling salmon. You might try running a crab imitation fly along the rocky bottom there for sheepshead (although I've found the best way to find sheepshead is with a mask and snorkel). We've caught large- and smallmouth bass casting around that shoreline. Hog Island in Swanton, where a sister- and brother-in-law own a camp on Maquam Bay, is just south of Missisquoi Bay, and the deeper waters farther offshore attract many boat anglers all summer long. From the Sandbar Wildlife Management Area north to Maquam is the so-called Inland Sea. There's a Vermont Fish and Wildlife boat access at Hog Island, and the iconic Hog Island Market there may buy your catch and then sell it into the restaurant market. Missisquoi National Wildlife Refuge manages much land around the mouth of the Missisquoi River and Swanton, a center of Abenaki culture, and extending across the grasslands of Hog Island. Its visitor center on Hog Island is well worth a visit, and small-boat exploration is excellent at Missisquoi. New England's only black tern colony is found there, and efforts are underway to reestablish muskellunge, so far with limited success.

Maquam Bay and Missisquoi Bay are shallow and highly eutrophic now from fertilizer runoff (phosphorus); their bottom sediments are colonized by Eurasian watermilfoil and water chestnut. The fish communities at Missisquoi have been nearly completely transformed over the past 150 years. Once the center of commercial harvests of white fish and walleye (a highpoint of 68,500 walleye harvested in 1902, and nearly 300 million eggs harvested in that year by the U.S. Fish Commission for fish culture purposes), Missisquoi Bay is now dominated by nonnative white perch. Fly rodding for them has its loyal following. Other than lake trout, salmon, bass, walleye and pike, you might target other native fish like sheepshead, longnose gar or burbot (said to be very good eating). Targeting carp and catfish might be interesting too.

Maybe, though, the whole idea of targeting individual species will soon fall by the wayside when it comes to managing aquatic systems? When I graduated from the University of Vermont in the 1970s, the fields of fisheries and wildlife management were in the early stages of a major transformation, from a focus on managing individual target (generally "game") species to thinking about whole ecosystems and managing for diversity, resilience and ecosystem health. We still may be in that transition. I'm not sure. Whether we are or not, there are new atmospheric, aquatic and terrestrial dimensions to restoration work, as well as social and economic. The targets have shifted and broadened to include entire suites of plants and animals, most with no discernible economic value. But stewardship work involves knowing and protecting them. Success is measured differently today; data sets are much larger. What's at stake feels greater. Diverse communities' history, culture, politics and values factor in. The upside for anglers is that success at the ecosystem level will lead to better fishing, though not necessarily to fishing as we know it today. It may also lead to conflicting views. Managing at the ecosystem level means understanding the role and impact of new arrivals, like the double-crested cormorant. Yes, they feed on fish; no, we can't solve that one with a simple eradication program.

You can see the visible dimensions of the system from shorelines and mountain ridges that overlook the lake. Better yet, if you don't have a canoe, get out on a charter boat or a ferry into the main lake and look around. You're in the middle of a dramatically defined natural basin, with the Adirondacks looming to the west and the Green Mountains rising to the east. Lake Champlain—the Abenakis' *Bitawbágw*, or "the lake between"—is one of the most spectacular landscapes in the country. On its north–south axis, the lake is 125 miles long, river-like at its southern end, where it connects to the Hudson River drainage by the 60-mile-long Champlain Canal, opened in 1823. The main body—the deepest, coldest part of the lake—is 12 miles wide at its widest and more than 400 feet deep. The lake itself is 435 square miles. It has seventy islands, 587 miles of shoreline and two projecting arms, mesotrophic to eutrophic, with various bays, islands and connecting channels. At its northern end, Lake Champlain grows shallow again, projecting into Quebec, its water exiting there via the Richelieu River to the St. Lawrence. The Chambly Canal, opened in 1943, bypasses the rapids of the Richelieu River, making barge traffic possible but cutting off fish passage and leading to the demise of the American eel. The lake's watershed, including the mountainsides you can see, is large at more than 21,000 square kilometers. About 56 percent of the lake is in Vermont, 37 percent in New York and 7 percent in Canada.

The loss of any species is disturbing, disheartening and usually perplexing. Sixteen native fish are listed as threatened in Lake Champlain. The best known and most threatened may be the lake sturgeon. Research is advancing rapidly on the sturgeon's numbers, movements in the lake and spawning habitat requirements. There is a program of fish culture, as well as closures at river mouths during spawning. But most of the threatened species in the lake are small fish, minnows little known except by fisheries biologists. It's the loss of native lake trout that may be most perplexing— or rather the inability of stocked lake trout to successfully reestablish a naturally producing population. Lake Champlain's native lake trout are a longtime research subject, particularly the mystery of the failure of wild lake trout fry—the product of successful wild spawning—to survive to year one. There's no obvious culprit, but given the changes that have taken place in the watershed since the early 1800s, it's understandable that the answers to the question of lake trout collapse and failed reproduction would be both complicated and elusive.

J. Ellen Marsden and Richard W. Langdon's paper, "The History and Future of Lake Champlain's Fishes and Fisheries," in the *Journal of Great Lakes Research*, described the major human-wrought changes to the Lake Champlain Basin since European discovery and colonization four hundred years ago. By the 1860s, much of the Champlain Basin had been deforested for timber, pastureland, cropland (up to 60 percent) and, on the New York side, pulp mills in Wellsboro and Au Sable (also major polluters by 1900 of the lake and rivers including the Bouquet and Au Sable Rivers). The loss of the forest resulted in massive erosion, sedimentation and siltation in rivers and the lake. Marsden and Langdon pointed out that sediments covered the spawning gravels of stream-spawning fishes like Atlantic salmon, brook trout, white and redhorse suckers and lake-spawning fish like lake trout. Sedimentation altered invertebrate communities too, while creating more habitat for larval lamprey eels, which need fine sediment beds in rivers for their early life stages.

Nineteenth-century dams on the eleven main tributaries flowing into the lake had major effects on species like Atlantic salmon, walleye, lake sturgeon, redhorse suckers, stonecat and others using rivers for spawning. While there are natural barriers to fish migration on most of the major rivers flowing into Lake Champlain on the east side, and these blocked passage to upper watersheds, they didn't prevent fish from using the available river sections and their tributaries closer to the lake. Marsden and Langdon described a falls line at an elevation of about forty-six meters above the lake. In the Winooski River, salmon were able to navigate the falls line drop and access upper river sections. Lower river sections "provided unique habitat for smaller species, many of which are rare, including eastern sand and channel darters, mottled sculpin, and stonecat." Surprisingly, there were only two dams built between the lake and the natural falls line: the Swanton Dam on the Missisquoi in 1797 (still in place and blocking all spawning potential farther up into the Missisquoi watershed) and the Peterson Dam on the Winooski.

The majority of dams built in the Champlain Basin and throughout Vermont are not on main stem rivers but rather on smaller tributaries. Zadock Thompson, Marsden and Langdon wrote, estimated a total of 786 sawmills, 373 gristmills and 252 fulling mills (part of the woolen cloth–making process) in Vermont. Today, there are some 463 standing milldams in the Champlain Basin, blocking most of the tributaries and limiting natural reproduction. Nineteenth-century dams on the Richelieu (at Saint-Ours and Chambly) affected the American eel fishery and possibly anadromous salmon. When both dams were rebuilt in the 1900s, the eel fisheries began a steep decline. Anadromous Atlantic salmon (ocean migrants) may have entered the basin via the Richelieu and then used spawning tributaries in New York and Vermont, although historical observations are not reliable and, Marsden noted, "We may never know."

Marsden and Langdon wrote, "From the earliest period of European colonization fishes were harvested from Lake Champlain using shoreline seines, trap nets, pound nets, fyke nets, handlines, spears, and grappling irons. Fishing was largely from shore or in small boats....Lake sturgeon were fished with gillnets in rivers until 1888." The commercial lake sturgeon fishery seems to have been very small. Spawning season seemed to be fishing season, with much of the fishing "concentrated in Missisquoi Bay, the shallow southern end of the lake, and the Lamoille and Winooski Rivers. While some of the catch went to Boston and New York in barrels, more of it was sold or utilized by locals," they noted.

Lake white fish was one of the most important commercial fishes, and they were harvested during fall spawning near shorelines, especially in Missisquoi Bay. But harvests fell over time, and the commercial fishery was closed off and on during the 1880s and closed for good in 1912.

The historical abundance of Atlantic salmon reads like a fairy tale. Marsden and Langdon quoted an observer from 1876 named Watson who described salmon as so abundant and so large that, from a wagon driven into a shallow tributary, men could "spear the salmon with pitchforks, and thus obtain in a few minutes all the fish needed for consumption. Many of the fish obtained would reach twenty pounds in weight." They added (again quoting Watson), "A single seine haul near Port Kendall was recorded as netting about 1500 lbs. of salmon. Salmon were observed to have 'ranged throughout the northern lake, but did not spawn south of the Bouquet River in New York and Otter Creek in Vermont.'" The last Atlantic salmon was reportedly caught in the Ausable River in 1838.

On walleye, they added, "Walleye were harvested by seining in spring on their spawning grounds in Missisquoi Bay and West Swanton....[The] average weight of walleye was .7 kg and the harvest between 1893 and 1904 averaged 38,584 fish annually....A quota of 7000 lbs was imposed in 1961....The commercial walleye fishery was closed in 1971."

On lake trout, according to Marsden and Langdon, "Virtually nothing is known prior to their disappearance from the lake by the 1890s." They suggested that it wasn't commercial harvests alone that extirpated native lake trout. The commercial lake trout harvests were during fall spawning, when lake trout congregated in inshore areas. Since lake trout historically also spawned in deeper waters at offshore reefs, the small inshore commercial fishery alone probably wasn't the only reason for the decline of the fish. Marsden has visited offshore reefs recently and found them covered by thick layers of silt, so the more general loss of spawning habitat due to lakewide sedimentation may have been the driving factor. It's also postulated that the fry of lake trout, since the addition of alewife to the diet of adult fish in Lake Champlain, could suffer from thiamine deficiency, which can lead to "early mortality syndrome." Thiamine deficiency was found in fry hatched from the eggs of lake trout utilizing alewife, although a recent paper looked at that hypothesis and concluded that naturally produced fry in Lake Champlain were not found to be thiamine deficient.

In the face of major fish declines in the mid- to late nineteenth century, legislators began debating the question of closing commercial fishing on the lake altogether to give way to "tourist angling." In some ways, these debates were a version of the same between commercial fishermen and sport anglers today.

Marsden and Langdon pointed out that the effects of the causeways built for roads and railroads between the islands in the nineteenth and twentieth centuries—linking the eastern and western shores of Grand Isle and the other islands—are poorly understood. The earliest causeways were built over existing sandbars, and these may have had no cut-through for water passage, instead acting like coffer dams, fragmenting the lake body in much the same way that a dam on a tributary would block upstream passage. (Currents and sediment flows would have been affected.) The construction of the Sandbar Causeway is thought to have blocked rainbow smelt's access to the Lamoille River and "necessitated a longer, westward journey to reach Missisquoi Bay." Causeways "may have also contributed to the lack of movement between the main lake and spawning sites in the Northeast Arm." While harvests may have played a role in the demise of lake sturgeon (commercial harvests were never very large), declines "are probably largely attributable to the degradation of spawning substrates [settlement of sediments] and dams that blocked access to spawning sites."

The sea lamprey became a serious fisheries management issue soon after the salmonid stocking program began in 1972. High wounding rates on stocked lake trout and Atlantic salmon necessitated a control program that was initiated experimentally in 1990. (Wounding rates were also high in lake sturgeon, and it is now thought that lamprey parasitism was a significant factor in sturgeon declines.)

Sea lamprey, unlike brook and silver lamprey, are parasitic. After spending two to fourteen years in tributary sediments as larval filter feeders called ammocoetes, they become "transformers" in search of hosts. Transformation occurs between July and October. Once they find a host fish and attach themselves, they remain attached for twelve to twenty months. During that time, studies show that lamprey consume upward of twenty pounds of fish, resulting in high rates of host mortality. Wounding rates in Lake Champlain prior to the lamprey control program ranged from thirty-one to ninety-eight out of one hundred fish, higher than Great Lakes wounding rates by as much as a factor of five. The lamprey control program went forward (not without strong opposition by some corners of the environmental community) with the application of lampricides to fourteen tributaries and five lake deltas. Wounding rates have dropped in lake sturgeon, from fifteen to eighteen per thirty fish to just several, and by-kill of other species susceptible to lampricides appears to be low. Still, lampricides can impact other native fish, including sturgeon eggs and fry. Fisheries experts continue to look for alternatives to chemical treatment (dams, electric shock, traps, manual use of rakes) and for improvements in chemistry to more narrowly select for lamprey.

There is an interesting debate among fisheries experts as to whether sea lamprey were native in Lake Champlain or invasive by way of the Champlain Canal, opened in 1823 (genetic analysis seems to point to sea lamprey as native to Lake Champlain). The question is relevant because if they were present for the thousands of years before European colonization, and if lake trout and salmon were also present and their populations generally stable, then maybe that shows that these populations "co-evolved," living together more or less in balance? Marsden and Langdon postulated, too, that lake trout historically may have been present in fewer numbers and so presented less of a target species to adult sea lamprey. Lake trout may also have evolved avoidance strategies. Predators to sea lamprey, both adult lamprey and larval lamprey, would likely have been far more abundant, and from the historical accounts, Atlantic salmon were superabundant in the early settlement days. American eel, known to prey on larval sea lamprey, would have been much more abundant than they are today. Lake sturgeon, northern pike and hungry walleye all would have preyed on lamprey. Maybe increases in lake trout and salmon populations supplied by fish culture beginning in the 1970s and increases in lamprey spawning habitat (delta sediments provided by deforestation and agricultural and urban development) were a perfect storm, feeding a spike in sea lamprey numbers that then necessitated chemical control methods.

Was it the Chinese who first pointed out that there is opportunity in crisis? A system out of balance seeks balance. Anglers are uniquely positioned in the middle of things. As enthusiastic users of fisheries resources, as license and equipment buyers, as participants in fishing tournaments and as an audience of consumers, we make choices that drive policies. In the final section of their paper, labeled "Management Implications," Marsden and Langdon pointed out that progress is being made.

Signs of fish population recovery have been noted. Collection of eggs and larvae indicates that lake sturgeon are spawning in the Winooski, Lamoille and Missisquoi Rivers; stocking of elvers (baby eels) in the Richelieu River since 2005 has resulted in substantial numbers of American eel showing up in warm-water fisheries assessments; and lamprey wounding of lake trout and Atlantic salmon has decreased substantially.

Marsden and Langdon wrote, "Additional activities that are possible, but are politically, socially, or economically infeasible, include removing dams, removing causeways, and removing nonnative salmonids by discontinuing stocking." We could add to this list: working with the farming community in places like the Missisquoi watershed to put an end to the phosphorus inputs that have rendered places like Lake Carmi a "crisis" zone and Missisquoi Bay, once the crown of the walleye kingdom, a wasteland by comparison.

State agencies and universities typically don't take the lead with activities that are possible but "politically, socially, or economically infeasible." Private citizen groups tend to take that work on. Anglers are needed as partners to educate, change the political and social environment, shift the economic paradigm and open up new conversations.

Chapter 13

THE OTTAUQUECHEE RIVER, PART II

If you can clean up the thirty-six miles of streams of this Ottauquechee valley, a showpiece of scenic beauty, a sparkling example of unpolluted water, you will have set an important example for the nation.
—Lady Bird Johnson, at the dedication of the Marsh-Billings House as a National Historic Landmark, 1967, Woodstock, Vermont

Monday, June 18, 2018

While every river is unique, and each town built beside a river has its special traits, stories and characters, it is also true that every river is the same. For example, all fish and other living creatures—including people—need clean water to thrive. The national push for clean water has its roots in the late 1940s with the passage of the Federal Water Pollution Control Act (1948), which led to the construction of sewage treatment plants nationwide. Congress passed other clean water laws built on that foundation (the Clean Water Act, 1972; the Clean Air Act, 1970; the National Environmental Policy Act, 1970; and the Endangered Species Act, 1973). States followed suit. Vermont's signature land use law—Act 250, enacted in 1970—gave the state power to review and assess the effects of large-scale developments, requiring environmental impact statements (EIS) that included impacts on water quality, wildlife and wetlands ecosystems. Since the 1970s, Vermont has passed a host of laws protecting

Sally and David Laughlin in 2018. As early environmentalists, they fought for clean water on the Ottauquechee River in the early 1970s and helped change the way Vermonters thought about their rivers. *Photo by author.*

wetlands, floodplains and river corridors and has recently upgraded water quality standards to check urban chemical runoff and sedimentation from roads. Often, it was local communities and citizens that forced change.

Woodstock residents were the first along the Ottauquechee River to recognize the dire need for urban sewage treatment in the early 1950s. In 1965, voters approved a sewage treatment plant, and construction began with federal grants under the supervision of Tom Bourne, who'd owned and operated a dairy farm called Maplewood on the banks of the river since 1939. Tom had a keen interest in water quality and rivers, and he served on the boards of both the Connecticut River Watershed Council and the regional planning commission. But constructing the plant in Woodstock is where progress ended. For five years, although the plant was completed, most of Woodstock remained unconnected to it. In 1970, the river was as polluted as ever. That's when David Laughlin, a local dentist, and his wife, Sally, an environmental educator, responded to the call. At least two important new organizations grew out of their effort to clean up the Ottauquechee: the Vermont Institute of Natural Science (VINS) and, thanks in part to Tom Bourne, the Riverwatch Network.

The following is an excerpt of an interview I conducted with David and Sally Laughlin about their monumental efforts on behalf of the Ottauquechee River.

> *Tim: How did you become aware of the pollution in the Ottauquechee River back in 1970, when all the drama in Woodstock began?*
>
> *David: My office was right on the river, so every morning, I could see the river running yellow or blue depending on what the dyes in the Bridgewater Mill were that day. I knew the river was in trouble but had no idea how bad it was. And I remember we used to go to the Little Theater in Woodstock, and at intermission, you'd want to go outside, but it stunk so highly with sewage, you couldn't.*
>
> *Sally: The Little Theater itself had been a three-story mill originally but was converted into a small theater. Bridgewater Mill was the last of the operating mills on the river.*
>
> *David: Anyway, Tom Bourne was a patient of mine. Tom was part of the Ottauquechee Regional Planning Commission* [now called the Two Rivers–Ottauquchee Regional Commission] *and the Connecticut River Watershed Council, both. Tom was in my dentist chair one day and said, "David, the river out there is really a mess." Would I head up a committee to study the river's water quality?*
>
> *Sally: As we looked back on it, I think Tom was roping you into a battle that had been going on for a long time.*
>
> *David: Tom had a long interest in rivers and environmental health. He'd been very instrumental in getting a sewage treatment plant for the town. The plant was there, but the select board had never hooked up half of the town.*
>
> *Sally: They had spent millions* [of federal dollars] *to build it but then didn't spend the money to use it.*

David: All the houses and businesses on the Woodstock Green were just straight piping it into the river.

Tim: So Tom roped you in. What was the committee's job?

David: We needed to test for fecal coliform bacteria and then make a case to the town for hooking up to the sewage treatment plant. Sally, at the time, was working with Rick Farrar, a science teacher at the County School [a private high school], in South Woodstock. Rick had a bird banding station going, and Sally was running it.

Sally: Rick, at the time, was doing a lot of experiential education with the kids, including involving them in the study of birds and bird migration.

David: We asked Rick if he could get his kids involved in this water quality testing project on the river.

Sally: Rick had a chemistry lab at the school.

David: He got his kids out there and testing up and down the river. The initial results of the testing were alarming. The Ottauquechee at that time was class D almost everywhere—open sewer. One of my classmates at Dartmouth was Skip Mahady [Frank Gordon "Skip" Mahady], the state's attorney at the time. I was talking to him one day and mentioned what we were doing on the river, and he said he would talk to Martin Johnson in the state water resources department at the time. Martin came down and talked to us and said that he'd like to send an investigator to help us do our studies.

Sally: At this point, Rick, with the bird banding station and the water quality monitoring, had formed the Ottauquechee Valley Environmental Analysis Center. And that became the blanket organization for the water quality monitoring work and the bird banding.

David: And was the precursor to VINS [the Vermont Institute of Natural Science].

Sally: Yes, it was.

David: Anyway, they sent Paul Cummings from water resources. Paul had the authority to get in people's houses and flush dye down the toilets.

Sally: Paul would flush the dye at one end, and David was out there with his camera at the other end taking pictures.

David: That's how we proved our case. The graphics made a big impression. We made the big announcement about the findings of the study, and Tom Bourne got the press there. It was big splash headlines in the Valley News about how polluted the river was. I was also working with the Vermont [Department of] Health, trying to get fluoride into towns' drinking water. I spoke with a Dr. Aiken up there and told him about the river work we were doing. With his help and the partnership of the department, we came up with this plan to create a health and welfare committee for the entire valley, organized under Tom Bourne's regional planning group. We were going to have Rick Farrar be the principal investigator. The idea was to document all sources of pollution. We held a public meeting at the Historical Society [of Woodstock] to introduce the idea and invited the various select boards: Sherburne, Woodstock, Pomfret and Bridgewater were all there. They were just mad as hell. They turned us down flat-out.

Tim: Times have changed. Did the Woodstock selectboard come around?

Sally: The Woodstock selectmen thought they didn't need to do anything. They didn't think these new Clean Water laws were enforceable. It was unbelievable. The Woodstock town manager told us, "We're not going to do anything, and you can't force us to do anything."

David: So that's when Skip Mahady brought charges against the town. We on the committee built the court case and went to court. The town was defiant. It was a two- or three-day trial, with Judge George Ellison presiding.

Sally: David's pictures played a key role. Toilet paper hanging from the pipes and roots of trees on the riverbanks. From Quechee to the woolen mill [in Bridgewater], everything just went straight in. There was no sewage treatment at all in Bridgewater.

Tim: That's nuts.

Sally: At the end of the trial—I don't remember how long the jury was out, but not too long—the jury came out and announced that they'd found the town guilty of polluting the river in violation of the state's new water quality act. The Woodstock select board, led by their town manager, walked out of the courthouse and said the state can't make them do anything. They may have been found guilty, but there was nothing they would do about it. Whereupon Skip Mahady immediately slapped a fine on the town. Ten thousand dollars a day. He threatened to put selectmen in jail.

David: With the fines and the threats of jail, cooler heads ultimately prevailed.

Sally: The town began working on it within two days of the end of the trial, after twenty thousand dollars of fines.

David: Mahady suspended the fines, as long as the town was working seriously on hooking up the town.

Sally: We survived, and [yes, it was a tipping point], *after the whole affair, we asked ourselves, "How is it that a town select board can think it was okay to dump raw sewage into a river?" That's when we decided we needed to found an environmental organization where people—especially children—would learn at the basic level about the requirements of the environment and why that couldn't be done.*

Tim: It seems like you were right on this cusp back then. I guess we call that a tipping point today. Did it feel that way then?

David: You think about the environmental movement, [which] *has been so incredibly successful—if you polluted that river now, there would be such an outcry.*

Sally: But back then, nobody knew.

David: A lack of understanding had led to selectmen who honestly believed that the [new] *water quality laws were some silly rules Montpelier had come up with and they didn't need to pay attention to them...once we won the thing, we had a dinner party at the house. Rick, Tom, Skip, June*

McKnight were there—the core of what became the first Vermont Institute of Natural Science (VINS) board.

Tim: To debrief and celebrate.

Sally: We all agreed that what we had to do was make sure people didn't get through childhood without having a basic understanding of the environmental facts of life.

David: It took a year or two for VINS to get up and running. [Sally Laughlin was director of VINS from 1974 to 1992. The first major project of VINS was ELF (Environmental Learning for the Future), an in-classroom program for children, taught by VINS-trained volunteers. By 1992, ELF was reaching eight thousand children annually. Sally went on to begin statewide programs to monitor and recover threatened species. She also served as chair of the Vermont Endangered Species Committee and was instrumental in working with government agencies to establish new laws protecting non-game wildlife.]

Tim: What were those early years of VINS like?

Sally: Well, the first summer we were able to use space in the old schoolhouse in West Woodstock, where Farm and Wilderness [a summer camp] *had space. When they came back in the fall, we rented space in the old* Elm Tree Press *building next to the Prince and the Pauper in downtown Woodstock. That was only a six-month lease. Every time we moved, we had a whole library to carry with us—we'd inherited the Vermont Environmental Center library in Ripton. They had government funding for a few years but no local support. When they went out of existence, we got the lovely library they'd put together. Plus a lot of books Rick Farrar had had.*

Tim: When did you start doing work with rare and threatened species— peregrines, loons and terns?

Sally: Very early on. The mid-1970s. We did our first loon survey— David and I went around on a loon survey—in 1974. We had chicks on just two lakes. The problems were human disturbance and the abrupt changes in water levels on lakes with water containment. Amazing how wonderfully quickly loons responded to management. Today there are over ninety nesting pairs statewide.

Tim: And peregrine falcons?

David: As far as peregrines go, we had Heinz Meng, a researcher on captive breeding from Cornell, come speak to our bird conference [for years an annual event at VINS]. *A great guy who got us going in Vermont. We worked with the U.S. Fish and Wildlife Service's reintroduction program and had our first hatching from Cornell on a hack site in Groton State Forest. There was an enclosed box for the falcon on the cliff, and food was sent down a tube from above so there was no human exposure. Eventually, the door was left open and the falcon would fledge, coming back for a while for food until learning to feed itself.*

Sally: A wonderful site—a cliff overlooking a pond—but very difficult to climb up there. We had barely enough money to hire one person that summer. The rest of the crew were volunteers. Betty Jillson would take her vacations up there and spend two weeks on that site. We had many volunteers do the same...an incredibly successful hack site. One of our banded birds, a female named Ruby, appeared in Montreal with a male bird and they were observed mating. They made a nest on a scrape on the Sun Life Building, twenty-six stories up, for six years.

David: I remember watching from the street Ruby take a pigeon that the male had killed but was unable to carry up to the twenty-sixth floor. Ruby flew down, rolled and the male dropped the pigeon to her. [Males are one-third smaller than females.]

Tim: It must be tremendously satisfying to you both to see progress made over the years.

Sally: Peregrine falcons have recovered completely since those early days and are no longer on the threatened species list. The loons have recovered completely. And ospreys. There were no ospreys on the first Breeding Bird Atlas [conducted by VINS] *twenty-five years ago. They're practically common today. Bald eagles are nearly commonplace. Improvements to water quality in our rivers and lakes is very connected to the return of these species.*

David: It really is astounding, the progress that's been made since 1970. People are so aware now, compared with where we were.

Tim: You were running VINS during the time of acid rain? Another success story. Were you involved?

Sally: Yes, indirectly we all were. The work Hub Vogelmann was doing on spruce declines. We all knew about it. Eventually, we came to know *the causes* [coal-burning power plants to the west and rain that was one hundred times more acidic than surface waters in the Northeast].

Tim: You were pioneers in the area of using volunteers in the field—your banding programs, wildlife monitoring work, using volunteer educators in schools. Today we call that citizen science. Chris Rimmer, who worked with you at VINS for thirty years and now has his own organization called the Vermont Center for Ecostudies [spun off from VINS in 2009], continues to employ hundreds of volunteers in the field, and so does his staff, many of whom worked with VINS for years. Why is it important to build citizen scientists through real research experience in the field?

Sally: Fieldwork with volunteers was a way to educate and inspire people, as much as a way to get conservation work done. Kids and adult volunteers became very passionate and stayed with us for years after experiences banding, taking part in a Christmas bird count or monitoring loons. One example of citizen science I'm particularly proud of was our Breeding Bird Atlas project. VINS used volunteers to gather data for the first Breeding Bird Atlas to be published in North America. We couldn't have done it without many dozens of volunteer birders making their observations. Thanks to that volunteer corps, the methods we developed are now the standard. Chris Rimmer and his science colleagues, partners and volunteers have taken citizen science to a new level—what they are doing now in Vermont and as far afield as South America, using new technologies, hundreds of volunteers and new ways to share data. With long-term studies of Bicknell's thrush, forest birds, mountain ecosystems....It's heartening. [The Vermont Center for Ecostudies completed a second Breeding Bird Atlas several years ago, twenty-five years after the first.]

Tim: What VINS has always been particularly good at is working with children, beginning with the ELF program for the elementary age. Why is that important?

Sally: The biggest challenge is an uneducated electorate. I never thought I'd live to see the day when the Endangered Species Act would be weakened, the EPA taken apart. Obama said elections have repercussions. That's for sure. You have to begin with the children.

David: It goes to show that there is still a large percentage of the population that doesn't have a basic understanding of how the world works.

Sally: We've done so much work over these decades to clean up polluted rivers, to restore species. The work can be undone so quickly.... We have this environmental protection infrastructure that works well, that's taken fifty years to build. Now it's being unraveled. If we elect a decent government again, the social programs can be restored. The environmental losses cannot be.

Chapter 14

THE ROD MAKERS

Thursday, June 21, 2018

There appears to be quite an uptick in interest in cane rods, not only in the collection of antique bamboo rods and in the selling and buying of them online but also in fishing with split bamboo. For some, that translates to restoring and using an old rod that they may have inherited or purchased. For others, it means building a rod themselves or buying one from one of today's growing number of bamboo rod makers. I met one such rod builder, Brian Ganley, at Trout Unlimited's White River Open Fly Fishing Tournament earlier in June, that friendly fishing contest and fundraiser for TU's educational and conservation programs (see chapter 9). Ganley had donated one of his rods as first prize in the contest for the largest fish. I thought that was generous of him. Quite a beaut of a rod, too.

Ganley lives on a dirt road, off a dirt road, off a dirt driveway in a corner of Thetford, Vermont, called Gove Hill. Beside the door to his shop was a load of ash firewood. He'd been clearing a corner of a woodlot for an upcoming solar electric installation. Friendly and warm, Ganley opened up about his passion for fine bamboo rods. He was quick to point out that he builds cane rods to be put to use, not put behind glass. His day job is engineering lighting systems for commercial buildings. An engineering mindset lends itself to the meticulous and artful construction of a cane rod. A perfectionist, he's demanding of himself. He knows rod builders out there who will put out a rod with flaws, and he knows others who spend forty hours on a tip section then snap it in two because there's a flaw, perhaps too small for the rest of us to see. That's the camp Ganley's in. His rods run from $1,000 to $1,800, depending on whether he makes you one or two tip sections. He has more orders than he can fill. Given the hours he puts in, the high prices don't translate to high profits. Not yet.

Cane rods, he told me, aren't just aesthetically pleasing, they're also easy on the arm. You can cast all day. Light in weight, they load without the same level of effort you put into synthetics. A well-made cane rod should last for generations and never lose its value. I asked him how long it takes him to make one. A well-made cane rod, he said, may take sixty to ninety hours to build. "Yeah, I'm probably making less than minimum wage," he added.

The first thing that strikes me about cane rod building is the bamboo itself. Bamboo is a type of grass. It's hollow and has nodes just like the switch grass we spend the summer pulling out of the garden or the ornamental bunch grasses we baby. But that's where the similarities end. Bamboo from the Gulf of Tonkin in China grows fast, straight and tall. Ganley buys it in bundles of ten stems, each twelve feet long. Stored in his rafters, the stems look less like grass and more like the fat bass sections of church organ pipes. These are grasses on steroids. The advantages of bamboo's fast growth are the long distance between nodes and the straight, tight grain. Tonkin bamboo's strong, flexible fibers are key to the flexing properties needed in a fishing rod.

Ganley checks (splits) the cane when it comes in to control and prevent random splitting as the cane naturally dries. Later, he'll carefully split out fine strips. We look at these in cross section. Each has an inner white pith layer that has to be removed, leaving the dark material he calls the "power fibers." That's the tight, straight grain that Tonkin bamboo is known for. There is a surface enamel on this layer that has to be sanded away so the fibers can accept glue and lacquer, and the nodes—the grass joints—are sanded flat. They present a challenge. One of the tricks of the trade is staggering them; each is an interruption in the flex pattern of the rod and a potential weakness.

The strips, pith removed and shorn of their protective enamel coat, are then planed to sixty degrees, arranged into bundles of six, tied, dried and glued. Now he's got two hexagonal, un-tapered, proto-rod sections. They will become, after many more hours of shaping—all by hand plane using a very expensive and accurate-to-the-thousandth-of-an-inch jig—the straight, finely tapered sections of a new fly rod. The jig, or form, may be the most expensive tool in the shop, but making a cane rod depends on it. Made of

Bamboo rod maker Brian Ganley, owner of Gove Hill Rods in Thetford, Vermont, standing in the doorway of his rod shop. *Photo by author.*

two finely calibrated pieces of hardened steel, like a pair of wide levels set up on edge, the form creates the negative space that precisely fits the shape the rod will become. That space has constant depth and a constant side angle but a diminishing width. Set screws micro-tune that width. The top of the tip section of a 3-weight, seven-foot rod might be something like 0.08 inches, Ganley said. During the planning process, he checks that measurement constantly, using a depth gauge to see that he gets it right.

    Sometimes, he told me, you end up with a tip section that simply won't straighten. So it's back to the starting point. In fact, he had one and showed it to me. Lining it up to my eye, I could see the slight bend that wouldn't go away. Fire starter, he said. Even if the tip is arrow straight, the work isn't over. The sections need lacquering, drying, the application of wraps, setting guides, the sanding and installation of nickel silver ferrules from Germany, a reel seat and a cork grip. He'll apply six coats of a color preserver for the wraps and six coats of poly and more fine sanding before that cane rod's ready to be put to use. That's a fishing rod that will last for one hundred years, assuming you don't step on it (hence the extra tip section).

We took some of his rods out into the yard and cast them. They cast beautifully, both on gravel and on lawn, into the wind under an afternoon sun surrounded by pines. Wonderfully balanced. The desire for a well-made cane rod—I think I suddenly got it—is simply the logical extension of a fine-tuned sporting aesthetic: You remove anything you can that isn't as close to perfect as you dare go.

Late in the day, I drove up to Post Mills, an unincorporated community in the western reaches of Thetford, on the banks of Lake Fairlee—itself a pretty decent trout fishery (good pickerel and bass fishing too). Orvis was making fine bamboo rods down in Manchester beginning in 1856. The other large, commercial cane rod maker in Vermont of the period was Captain Thomas Henry Chubb and his T.H. Chubb Rod Company, making his rods here in Post Mills, getting his water power from the upper reaches of the East Branch of the Ompompanoosuc River.

Chubb was born near the Charlestown Naval Yard in Charlestown, Massachusetts, in 1827. He moved to Galveston, Texas, with his family in 1836; his father had gone to Texas a year earlier to fight in the Mexican-American War. Later, both father and son fought for the South in the Civil War, after which Thomas and his wife, Isabel Mason, moved north on the advice of Isabel's physician. It's likely both were suffering from malaria (although, apparently, being Confederates from the South didn't help smooth their transition to Vermont).

Initially, Chubb and a business partner named William Marston bought an old linseed oil mill in Post Mills and began making wooden rake and pitchfork handles, all built by waterpower. But they couldn't compete on rake handles, so, having seen a rod builder in Boston who made ash and "lancewood" rods (many trees go by the common name "lancewood," but most are either southern hemisphere or tropical), they set up shop for rod making. They thought there'd be a growing market for fishing rods as soldiers came home from the war and settled back into civilian life.

At first, Chubb and Marston had bad luck. In 1869, just as they began making rods, the factory flooded. They rebuilt it, and business in rods picked up nicely—right off the bat they had upward of $30,000 in orders and soon had a business with fifty employees. Six years later, the new plant burned. Chubb then bought out Marston and rebuilt again, running the T.H. Chubb Rod Company until 1891. Chubb is known in the rod-making world as an innovator who held patents on many modifications, rod-making tools and rod-

Thomas H. Chubb fishing rod factory in Post Mills, Vermont. In the 1920s, the rod factory was owned by the Montague Rod Company, at the time the largest maker of split bamboo rods in the world. *Courtesy of the Thetford Historical Society.*

making techniques. He's particularly known for his innovations of the reel seat. When a second fire burned him out, he sold what was left to the Montague City Rod and Reel Company, at the time the biggest cane rod builder in the world. By 1920, T.H. Chubb Rod Company, under Montague City Rod and Reel, was making twenty-four thousand rods per year.

I have a Montague Redwing cane rod, as well as a handful of other rods that have come down from family members. The Montague rods came from both my Vermont wife's side and my Virginia grandmother's side. My wife's father's ancestors were among the first settlers of Glover, Vermont, and the Downeast reaches of Machias and Cobscook Bay, Maine. Her grandfather owned the Montague Redwing—a three-piece, 8'2" rod—and fished mostly from a canoe on Northeast Kingdom lakes, including Shadow Lake in Glover. His other rod was an Orvis "Special"—7'6", made in Manchester, Vermont, in 1946 by Cal Skinner. This is an early Bakelite impregnated rod (before the patent was issued). It's missing one snake-eye guide but otherwise is in beautiful shape. Jon Vincent (my friend from the Lake Mitchell Trout Club and a bamboo rod enthusiast) assured me that "restoring" it would mean simply removing and rewrapping the frayed guide wraps and replacing the missing snake eye. Varnish the new wraps and I'd have a very fishable rod again.

On my side of the family are the rods from my maternal grandmother Belle Hart's attic. They were owned by her second husband, Harold Hart, from Kenosha, Wisconsin. Harold worked for the Nash Motors Company, founded in Kenosha. (My generation, anyway, probably remembers Nash Motors cars. Nash eventually morphed into American Motors, but during World War II, Nash-Kelvinator made forty-four thousand one-ton, two-wheeled cargo trailers for the U.S. Army; air-craft engines, propellers and R-6/Hoverfly II helicopters for the U.S. Air Force; and rocket engines for the U.S. Navy.)

I believe Harold and my grandmother, who was head receptionist in the Service, Supply and Procurement Division of the War Department, met at the War Department before the outbreak of the war. They had a mutual friend in John Hancock, a navy captain higher up in the War Department (also a fly fisherman), who, we think, introduced them. The courtship between my grandmother and Harold undoubtedly involved some fly fishing. She was an old hand at crabbing and oystering—squirrel hunting, too, she claims—having grown up on a tidewater farm in Virginia.

I love Harold's and Belle's old rods—mostly the stock South Bends, now in terrible shape—because they remind me of them. If I ever restore a rod, it will be one of theirs.

Chapter 15

THE WALLOOMSAC RIVER

Tuesday, June 26, 2018

My wife, Delia, begins her Long Trail journey. For me that means the start of my Long Trail chauffeuring and resupply service. First job: To the trailhead in North Adams, Massachusetts, for a drop-off of said Long Trail hiker. Our plan was to meet again in five days at Stratton Pond, north of Stratton Mountain (the peak on which the Long Trail was conceived by James P. Taylor in 1909). I thought I could fish for the brook trout I'd read could be found there and thus truly make a Vermont taxi service into a Vermont fishing excursion. We walked together about a mile up the trail, and then I turned back to head north for a brief fishing stop at the Walloomsac River in Bennington, Vermont.

A fishing summer—one designed to get me out to "foreign" waters—I have come to realize, is an exercise in discovering my own state, and not just its trout and other catchable native fish on a fly, but also its social, cultural and landscape variety. I am geographically challenged, and I've lived here for thirty-one years, not including the college years. I can count on one hand, for example, the number of times I've been to Bennington. And I'd never visited the Bennington Battle Monument, I'm ashamed to say—yet another reminder of my own provinciality. Finding a river, donning waders and rigging up, on the other hand, can be an excellent way to rediscover where you are in the wider landscape. The Walloomsac offered the chance to see Bennington from a new angle of view.

Urban rivers, whether in Vermont or Manhattan, have their own unique set of problems. For years, we've treated them badly—as sewers, as convenient places to dump trash, as power plants or as neglected industrial sites. Beginning in the eighteenth century, rivers and streams in Vermont were sources of power and industry, so we dammed them and allowed sediments and chemical pollutants to build up in the ponds behind them. Generally, cities ignored the state of their rivers. But knowledge, awareness and perceptions of value began to change in the middle of the twentieth century. Many cities began rethinking their relationships to their rivers. Some made the river the focal point of major redevelopment efforts. Providence, Rhode Island, comes to mind. The Providence River was one of the most paved over (literally) and heavily polluted rivers in the world, thanks in part to the Providence jewelry industry. Today, the river's been uncovered and cleaned up. Parks, walkways, pedestrian bridges and public art gardens connect the river to the heritage of the city. Providence's WaterFire events attract millions of people and dollars annually.

The big shift in Vermont began around the early 1970s—as exemplified by David and Sally Laughlin's work in Woodstock—with cleanup efforts sometimes as straightforward as hauling trash out of rivers and extending all the way to federal and state laws mandating sewage treatment plants and improved water quality. That work goes on today.

But it's one thing to remove trash and another to restore a high level of water quality to an urban river; creating a trout fishery is yet another whole rung up the quality ladder. Cities' high degree of impervious surfaces—roads, parking lots and rooftops—send warmed, polluted water into rivers, and urban rivers are often hemmed in by shopping centers, highways and industrial buildings, making access a major challenge. Sometimes there are toxic soils and polluted river sediments needing removal or burial. Rivers too frequently show up on the EPA's Superfund list (the old Bennington Landfill is a Superfund site). On the other hand, abandoned nineteenth-century industrial sites—mill complexes, dams, power stations and waterworks—even when there are brownfields involved, can create exciting public redevelopment opportunities that include fishing. Development and environmental restoration can go hand in hand.

Some of the most successful trout stream restoration efforts have been part of urban river restoration projects (State College, Pennsylvania's Spring Creek comes to mind). The Walloomsac has a dam recommissioning project that shows how a well-designed, environmentally sensitive hydroelectric project—in this case, in an urban industrial setting—can provide green energy (not contributing to greenhouse gas emissions) while improving fish habitat and water quality, as Bill Scully, who oversaw the recommissioning of an old power dam in Bennington, noted. The Vermont Tissue Paper mill dam on the Walloomsac River in Bennington (just upstream of the Walloomsac's Quality Trout reach) was recommissioned in 2015. Before recommissioning, the industrial site suffered from contaminated sediments: dioxins, PCBs, semi-volatile organic compounds and heavy metals. Some 17 percent of the time, the reach below the penstock was dry. As the result of a Federal Energy Regulatory Commission (FERC) licensing process and green engineering, the new operation provided new tourism resources, added recreational features, improved fish passage, improved grid resilience and computer-managed outflow optimization to maximize in-stream aquatic habitat. The project removed all contaminated sediments and turned the ephemeral reach into a permanent reach with dedicated bypass flows—all of this on top of creating new local jobs and providing renewable energy from non–fossil fuel sources that help Vermont achieve its long-range emissions objectives. While the conservation community I've been observing is busy removing dams that block fish passage, in some cases (possibly many), rebuilding a dam with careful attention paid to FERC relicensing processes or a recommissioning process, with climate change considerations included, can do as much good as an old dam removed.

The state's trophy fishery in the Walloomsac is highly regarded—if you believe all the videos on YouTube—attracting anglers from well beyond Vermont. And the trout fishing there, to the delight of many of us diehards, is year round. Doug Lyons (of the Battenkill) told me the Walloomsac has both wild and stocked brown trout. At the Silk Road Covered Bridge, where I was headed, I was likely to find fish stocked by the Bennington Fish Culture Station. The Bennington hatchery is the largest and one of the oldest fish culture stations in the state. It grows only cold-water species, including some of the two-year-old rainbow and brown trout stocked in trophy waters (the Walloomsac's trophy section runs from the New York border to the Henry Covered Bridge crossing and Murphy Road). It's the hatchery's fish that populate much of the Otter Creek watershed, including the Neshobe, the Middlebury, East Creek, the Clarendon River and the Castleton River. Wild brown populations have been documented in some of the tributaries of the Walloomsac here in Bennington, including South Stream and Jewett Brook. These can be accessed via the Walloomsac Headwaters Park and Natural Area in Bennington. There are also many records of large rainbow and brown trout in the non-trophy urban stretches of the Walloomsac.

Fishing upstream of the Silk Road Covered Bridge was quite lovely. The river was wadable well upstream through a ponded section. There were some plastic chairs beside the river on one spot and a few old tires sticking out but also good riparian habitat on both banks and some woody additions in the river. Trout were rising. And beaver, of course, had been busy there. As for fishing pressure, there were two women with their young daughters bait fishing below the covered bridge. Nice to have that company, but I walked upstream a few hundred yards to give them room.

Very picky fish, in fact. Their colors were stunning, remarkably bright for hatchery fish. It's good to be seen if you're a trout; the release mechanism for aggressive behavior in trout is visual. Flashes of bright color help them maintain their position in the stream and their chances to spawn—although the size of the fish is the greater determiner. On the other hand, if you're too visible from above, the osprey may get you, hence the trout's two-toned skin, dark on top and bright on the sides.

Walloomsac River brown trout. *Photo by author.*

From the Walloomsac, I drove thirty minutes north to meet Doug Lyons for another try on the Battenkill. He'd e-mailed me saying he was hoping and expecting to find a green drake hatch. When I arrived at around 8:00 p.m., he was fishing from the bank downstream of the bridge at Benedict's Crossing (metal bridge/dirt road/farmland). The river is a long, slick pool there with a backdrop of green fields and a small farmstead just down the road. No sign of green drakes, although the fish were dimpling the surface there, feeding on tiny emergers. Another angler was casting flies from the edge of the river downstream. Behind him, more open pastureland.

I went in above the bridge and began casting to wild brown trout rising around the tails of riffles. I hooked a few fish and hooked a few trees. A lefty like me casting upstream on the left side of a river at dusk can be dicey. The moon, two days off full, rose above the trees and provided lots of night light, and the temperature dropped—really dropped—down into the forties. I was in a T-shirt and shorts.

After dark, a few big green drakes, *Ephemera guttulata*, finally came out of their old selves. Doug switched his fly and began getting light hits.

The fishing that evening turned out to be light, but there is something compelling about seeing these big light-colored mayflies fluttering about on the wing under a full moon and a Maxfield Parrish blue sky. These are the kinds of evening conditions that the Irish poet William Butler Yeats had in mind when he wrote these famed lines in "The Song of the Wandering Aengus":

> *And when white moths were on the wing,*
> *And moth-like stars were flickering out,*
> *I dropped the berry in a stream*
> *And caught a little silver trout.*

While his trout turns into "a glimmering girl / With apple blossom in her hair," my trout remained trout and remained in the river. By 9:00 p.m., the Connecticut angler had quit and was standing on the bridge. He opened up about his love of the tailwater section of the Farmington River, his reliance on emerger patterns and his disdain for wading—he catches all his fish while standing on shore. I'd never thought about that preference before…or had this conversation with another angler. Consider not wading? Huh. Maybe I should consider. But it seems limiting. Too cold to think, anyway. Two-hour drive home…a very good day for an Uber-fishing taxi driver.

Chapter 16

THE CONNECTICUT RIVER

Sunday, June 29, 2018

I like to recommend to fly fishing friends a float on the reach of the Connecticut River from Wilder Dam south to Sumner Falls in Plainfield. Not only is there excellent bass fishing, but you also never know who you're going to run into. And you might catch a trophy rainbow. Twenty years back, there were almost always homeless men tenting in the woods down in White River Junction. The homeless population swelled in summer—I think to be near the VA hospital—many of them middle-aged men, and some living on the fringes. Some were quite good anglers, fishing for dinner off the old train trestle or along the banks. I got schooled in fishing more than once there—and also hit up for spare change for "a cup of coffee." There are still many unclaimed bits of floodplain forest here and there, forgotten little corners, comfortable and private encampments in summer, bitter cold in winter.

One place I recommend putting in (there are others, such as Watson Park a mile up the White River and Wilder Dam on the New Hampshire side) is an unmarked fishing access on the New Hampshire side. If you turn into the Hannaford Supermarket parking lot in West Lebanon (coming from the Vermont side, take Exit 20 off I-89 and turn left onto Route 12A), there's a deeply potholed dirt road on the left that takes you down to the mouth of the Mascoma River. You'll get the sharp odor, for a bit, of the Lebanon Wastewater Treatment Plant nearby, so you'll know you're going in the right direction. This is a popular spot with locals who fish the deep hole at the mouth of the Mascoma. There's an informal, hardened put-in here for launching small boats on trailers, although it's rare to see engines around here and anything with much draft can't go downstream.

This place, a relatively intact mature floodplain forest, is a study in contrasts. A few hundred yards away are the shopping centers and big-box stores that are the Upper Valley's shopping central in sales tax–free New Hampshire, while across the Mascoma River is a forest in recovery—a twenty-acre wedge of land behind Kmart, nearly under the I-89 railroad bridges. Once the site of an asphalt plant and gravel dredging business in the 1960s (the Mascoma River delta deposits), the land behind Kmart has surprising reminders of its industrial past, including piles of old asphalt and pieces of industrial equipment. The vegetative type there is a mix of invasive plants and early successional native tree species. A tangle. There has even been a small wetlands mitigation project carried out there, where the developer—as recompense for the loss of a wetland he filled a mile away—excavated an acre or two of land to several feet below grade and planted native wetland-loving shrubs.

Over time, the entire wedge should revert to the native floodplain it was. Planting native trees and shrubs, facilitating natural flooding and some additional strategic excavating to allow for more flooding is helping that change along. The city got ahold of the land when it was gifted in the mid-'90s to the Upper Valley Land Trust by Tom Bascetta, past owner of Lebanon Crushed Stone (see the location of Bascetta Park in David Delorme's *The New Hampshire Atlas & Gazetteer*). The gift came with a small commercial site in the Kmart shopping plaza. In an act of creative genius, the Upper Valley Land Trust (founded in 1986) gave the gravel-mining piece to the City of Lebanon and then swapped the commercial lot for a four-hundred-acre property around a natural pond in Lyme, New Hampshire. For the price of a small endowment, the Mud Pond parcel went to the Town of Lyme. You'll find similar stories—sustainably managed timberlands conserved, public access protected, rare species and critical habitat conserved, trails created, farms conserved and natural areas put under state, town or land trust stewardship—up and down the Mascoma and Connecticut Rivers, thanks to the Upper Valley Land Trust and other conservancies, including the Nature Conservancy and the State of New Hampshire.

Just as I was arriving for an evening float to Sumner Falls, I met an older guy on his way out. He told me that the previous night he'd had a bass on every third cast. I didn't doubt him. This stretch can be amazingly productive. Tom was pulling out an ancient aluminum boat with a nine-horse Mercury engine. Every year, he told me, he repacks the bearings on the wheels of that trailer. He also said he was a retired heavy-equipment operator, as his father had been—they used to fish here together when they were still scooping gravel out of the Mascoma River delta. More often than not, favorite spots are multigenerational, but this one is changing, as there isn't a mining operation here or any mills upstream. The Mascoma was a working river in the nineteenth century, with five power-generating dams between here and the Lebanon Green fewer than five miles away. The mills are long gone.

After Tom left, a car with New York plates drove in and four millennial-aged people—two women and two men—got out. Busy night. Three were dressed very stylishly; the fourth, less so. I figured he was the local guide because he opened the trunk and took out four new fishing rods wrapped in plastic. There is a hidden story here, I thought. I watched them set up the rods and bait the hooks. The last I saw they were laughing, standing on the bank, casting into the mouth of the Mascoma…waiting for a fish. They looked like my children's urban friends. My kids grew up in Vermont and then moved to big cities far away where jobs were. I've got one in New York, one in LA and, until recently, one in Portland (Maine) then Boston. Different worlds. It's always good when they come home, and it was great to see these four here visiting this backwater place, hacking around with fishing. And to see people of color. The White River is aptly named in Vermont, the whitest state in the country at over 95 percent Caucasian. New Hampshire is not too far behind. The lack of diversity means we miss out on a dialogue and cultural dynamism that cities have and that Vermont's society and economy need. The flashes of overt racism, anti-Semitism and violence against minorities in Vermont are just plain disgraceful. (As to why Vermont is so white, it's complicated and not easy being non-white here. Check out the March 2017 episode of the podcast *Brave Little State*, by Angela Evancie and Rebecca Sananes, called "Why Is Vermont so Overwhelmingly White?")

There are small signs that demographic patterns may be changing. Young people are staying and moving up from the cities to rural towns like Peacham. White River Junction has JAGFest, its own black repertoire theater group and expanding immigrant populations, although most of that growth is in the Greater Burlington area. Nationwide, demographics are changing; we are becoming more multi-hued, less Eurocentric. About 50 percent of us are non-white now, and maybe that's going on in Vermont too? The reality is that our Vermont's population is projected to continue to decline through about 2040. This does not bode well. The sociologists tell us that in-migration is a function of "push and pull." To reverse the out-migration from rural places like Vermont to urban places, there has to be a motivating force pushing people out of urban areas and a pulling motivation toward rural areas—motivations such as jobs, safety, healthy air, clean water, locally grown food, affordable housing, family connections and good schools. We have those. And we have a temperate climate. Will we begin to see an influx from the West, where wildfires are on the increase? From coastal areas prone to increased flooding? Will we become a home for climate change refugees as well as refugees seeking asylum, a better life? What does this have to do with fishing? Catching dinner and/or being able to recharge your batteries on a stream with a fly rod or bait are primal needs that do relate to family, community and landscape. The pull of Vermont is the sense that Vermont is a place that is safe outdoors and welcoming, a place that has jobs and affordable housing and a place that can provision the stomach and the soul both. Our Vermont Fish and Wildlife Department seems to be well aware of the connections. That's good.

The float to Sumner Falls is about 6.5 miles from West Lebanon. I launched at around 7:00 p.m., planning for two hours on the river—longer if this turned out to be one of those hungry fish nights. I brought a fly rod rigged with a floating line and a box of dry flies in case I ran into rising trout. And I brought a spinning rod. When I'm handling this boat on a river and moving fast, I spin fish. Casting plugs for bass is just a lot less complicated when I have to navigate around rapids or shallows. Drowned trees on the bank come up fast. On the other hand, if fish are rising, or if I row up into an eddy to fish the bottom of a riffle, I'll use the fly rod. I use small Rapalas and bright poppers when I spin fish for bass. Small crankbaits with a single hook instead of a treble too.

Down river. There are usually fish around the mouth of the Mascoma; you can often see them if the light shines in just so. Below the interstate bridge above the island, and then around the island, look for rising trout on early summer and fall evenings. I didn't see any this time, but some very large rainbows are caught here.

I picked up my first smallmouth on the left bank on the back side of the island and then another in a riffle below the island. I've often caught bass out in the riffles, sometimes at midday. Otherwise, they're in close to the banks. Then, rowing down the right side—which has been riprapped for a road that accesses one of the river's largest gravel operations—I picked up a third. You'll be seeing that gravel pit, unless it's hidden behind trees, for the next three miles.

Gravel mining is one of the legacies of the last ice age. When the river was dammed to the south by glacial moraines from the retreating glacier, it formed glacial Lake Hitchcock. Rivers flowing into Lake Hitchcock dropped their loads of sands, gravels and silts, and these created deep deltas, kame terraces and, in a few places, eskers. Lebanon Municipal Airport sits up on an ancient delta made by a much grander Mascoma River. The massive gravel deposits downstream on the Vermont side are the remains of the White River delta washed into terraces. The lined landfills of Lebanon are also built out of the pits of mined delta gravels.

The next really fishy spot is a tributary called Blood Brook that comes in from the New Hampshire side. At the mouth of Blood Brook, there's a riffle and, below it, a pool, another good rainbow spot. Big rainbows run up Blood Brook in the spring as far as the falls about a mile upstream, and I bet they find some refuge there in hot weather (just below the falls is a well-loved swimming hole protected by the Upper Valley Land Trust). If you're on foot, you can park at a small New Hampshire Fish and Game parking area on Route 12A at Blood Brook and walk into the river to fish that riffle. In a boat, you can come back up into it from downstream and fish the pool from below.

Around mile four, another small island came into view. There's a little rapid up above it that's worth fishing. The island has one of the few fine sandy beaches on this stretch of river (and a lot of poison ivy on the north end). We often pull in there. Grab lunch and swim. In the early 1990s, the Upper Valley Land Trust, working with local groups, including conservation commissions and schools, began putting together a trail of canoe camping spots on the river. This island was one of the first on the map. Today, the trail, including primitive camping spots and access points for paddlers and anglers, stretches from the Canadian border to south of Lebanon. In the northern reaches of the Connecticut River Paddlers' Trail, there are camp spots nearly every five miles. The Vermont River Conservancy (VRC) is the informal coordinator of much of this, holding easements and, in some cases, owning land outright. (You can find maps and information online at the Connecticut River Paddlers' Trail website.) There are similar efforts underway on the White River (see the White River Partnership), and stitched across the northern tier of New York, Vermont, New Hampshire and Maine is the 740-mile Northern Forest Canoe Trail (the VRC is its managing partner in Vermont).

Almost directly across from the sandy island is the mouth of the Ottauquechee in North Hartland. I rowed under the railroad bridge there and poked around this small basin where the Ottauquechee comes in. I picked up a fish on the right side just under the railroad bridge and then rowed up to the base of the dam. Originally, this was a bobbin mill, but I think it went through many iterations. This entire region was a center of industry and industrial innovation in the nineteenth century. Think of the Connecticut Valley as the Silicon Valley of the nineteenth century. Windsor's American Precision Museum interprets that history well, and so does the Hartland Historical Society's museum.

Back out on the river, I fished down the left bank, but the fishing is generally thinner through here and stays spotty until you get to Sumner Falls. So, I zipped along and imagined the farms I couldn't see, hidden below the banks of the river. The working farms on the banks have some of the best soils in the region. Farms on the New Hampshire side—Edgewater, Riverview and McNamara Dairy—supply area markets and restaurants with vegetables, syrup, apples, annual and perennial flowers, berries, bottled milk, cream, butter and more. On the Vermont side, the valley is considerably wider. There are two large dairies here and a number of small hobby farms with animals—horses, sheep and llamas.

In the mid-1980s, both states created funding mechanisms for protecting important farm, forest, natural, recreational and historic sites. New Hampshire's Trust for New Hampshire Lands and the Land Conservation Investment Program, a partnership between the state and a private organization, funded projects up and down the Connecticut River. State government provided the funding and oversight, and the nonprofits did all of the project development, from working with landowners and towns to selecting the most important lands for conservation. On the Vermont side, around the same time, conservationists teamed up with advocates for affordable housing and historic preservation and worked with the governor and legislature to create the Vermont Housing and Conservation Board. Rather than pitting affordable housing needs against land conservation needs, groups lobbied together for an annual appropriation, with decisions on how to spend the appropriation left up to a statewide board to apportion. It continues to work well.

One of the early Upper Valley Land Trust projects was the purchase of development rights on the first large dairy you come to after the sandy island, Green Acre Farms, at the time owned by Ruth Shumway. Further along on the New Hampshire side, the Trust for New Hampshire Lands bought easements on large working forest parcels and farmlands bordering the river. Both states had the power to require wooded buffer strips along the river to reduce erosion, as well as corridors for public access. The Nature Conservancy worked with Plainfield's Conservation Commission to protect the critical habitat for rare plants and animals, including an insect called the cobblestone tiger beetle, a plant called milkvetch, a Campanula species and several other rare species found at Sumner Falls. Traces of floodplain forest, with the rare hackberry, and northern reaches of river birch are part of the mix. During the campaign to raise funds for the Nature Conservancy land purchase, the Town of Plainfield adopted the cobblestone tiger beetle as the official town insect during town meeting. You could buy T-shirts emblazoned with tiger beetles and endangered species of freshwater clams.

I made Sumner Falls just as the full moon was coming up behind me, the roar of the falls rising in front. You do need to make sure you pull out of the river on the Vermont side before the falls. There's a park there (no camping) with places to park a car. The portage is well marked. Don't try to shoot the rapids at Sumner Falls. People have died. But after you pull your boat, do check out the river for rising fish. Sumner Falls is one of the best-kept fishing secrets in this part of the state, with bass, walleye and trout all available. And don't forget to pay homage at the stone commemorating the youth from Cherryville, Maine, who lost his life in a log drive. If you look, you'll find it on the drive out to Route 5.

Chapter 17

STRATTON POND

Sunday, July 1, 2018

One of my goals this fishing summer is to visit some of the more remote walk-in ponds along the Long Trail and Appalachian Trail in the Green Mountains for some off-the-beaten-path brook trout fishing. (The trails are co-located through the southern portion of the state and then divide midway up, with the Long Trail continuing north and the Appalachian Trail turning east to the New Hampshire border.) Stratton Pond seemed like a good candidate. It's about a four-mile walk in from the trailhead on Kelley Stand Road, with only four hundred feet of elevation gain—nearly a flat walk. I could have done an in-and-out in one day, packing the pack rod and a few flies, a bag lunch, water and a headlamp and gotten the gist of fishing at Stratton Pond (never trust a fishing writer to tell you the 100 percent truth). But my wife was hiking the Long Trail— or, I should say, the Long Trial—and we'd made plans to resupply her at Stratton Pond. So I packed for an overnight and carried, in addition to the ten pounds of food she needed for the next segment of the Long Trail— or, I should say, the Lawn Trail (though the trail is most often described as a "green tunnel")—balloons, birthday cupcakes, new silver earrings, a birthday card, original poetry (pretty darn good rhyming, if I say so myself) and a bar of dark chocolate.

Arguably, the biggest conservation story in Vermont over the past eighty years is the formation of the Green Mountain National Forest

(GMNF) in April 1932. While the Forest Reserve Act of 1891 provided authority to the federal government to set aside forest reserves, it was the Weeks Act, signed into law in 1911 by President William Howard Taft and authorizing the government to protect lands vital to navigable stream flows, that led to the creation of the GMNF. Much of the inspiration for the Weeks Act was the 1910 fire season in the Rocky Mountain West. About 3 million acres burned, and there was significant loss of life. The GMNF is 400,000 acres of forestland and includes thousands of historic settlements and Abenaki archaeological sites. Its creation was in response to unregulated logging and the despoiling of forested ecosystems and watersheds in Vermont. The job of the GMNF today is to "restore, protect, and manage" these watersheds, forests and historic resources. Wild trout are very much in the sights of foresters who manage the national forest today, and most of the major fish passage and habitat improvement projects are partially funded by the U.S. Forest Service. It's partly to its credit that we have the cold-water resources we have in Vermont—that we have wild trout.

The idea for a Long Trail was conceived in the mind of James P. Taylor in a tent on a blustery day on top of Stratton Mountain in 1909. Not one to waste any time, by 1910 Taylor had formed the Green Mountain Club and begun, with a handful of members, cutting the Long Trail. Construction of the Long Trail inspired Benton MacKaye in 1921 to imagine a similar though multifaceted project in social engineering that would link trails, recreational areas and residential communities all along the peaks of the Appalachian chain, connecting Maine to Georgia. MacKaye was a forester, philosopher and visionary regional planner ahead of his time. He was an early critic of urban sprawl, and like George Perkins Marsh before him, he sought balance between the urban and the wild. He saw trails, mountains and wilds as vital to the human spirit. His ideas and energy gave birth to the Appalachian Trail. Later in life, he helped found the Wilderness Society.

So, in this august place where the Long Trail and Appalachian Trail are one and where we could celebrate the vision and accomplishments of Taylor and MacKaye, my wife and I had a birthday party in the wilderness, complete with birthday cupcakes, candles and balloons.

I have to say, thinking back now, that we couldn't have chosen a better place to put our tent. We'd found a flat spot well off the trail. The forests in the shadow of Stratton Mountain are quite mature mixed hardwoods, with a few southern species we don't have farther north, including large

Unnamed beaver pond south of Kelly Stand Road, Green Mountain National Forest, southern Vermont. *Photo by author.*

specimens of tulip poplar that overtop much of the canopy of yellow birch, beech and sugar maple. Good water was a five-minute walk away, and just below us was an ancient beaver meadow—perfectly round, perhaps one thousand feet in diameter and looking as green and lush as any springtime cow pasture, with the hub of a broken-down beaver lodge in the middle. After dinner, we walked through the meadow and found the remains of a circular oxbow to the nearby stream. Four-inch-long brook trout were cruising this oxbow, with its black peat bottom, and rising to the occasional size-22 fly. Those darn critters are real survivors. We observed them for a solid hour.

To fish Stratton Pond, leave the balloons, birthday cupcakes, large bar of dark chocolate and the other birthday presents at home and hoof it in for the day. In other words, don't go on your partner's birthday unless he/she wants to. Stratton Pond is entirely hemmed in by forest, and wading along the edges is treacherous. A roll cast is a necessity almost everywhere, and unless you can rip a forty-foot roll cast, you're not going to get to rising fish. A float tube might work at Stratton Pond, but then again, you've got the weight of that to carry for four miles. Go light. I would recommend bringing a lightweight spinning rod and a handful of daredevils. On the way home, swing down and fish Grout Pond with your fly rod. Grout is a drive-in pond with wild brook trout.

The following day, bidding my wife farewell, I walked out and then into the unnamed ponds south of Kelley Stand Road. In the intense heat of midday, in this deepening drought, I didn't even rig up.

Chapter 18

THE METTAWEE RIVER

Monday, July 2, 2018

The Orvis Flagship Store in Manchester, Vermont, is worth a field trip, particularly when the American Museum of Fly Fishing is open next door and you can double up on the visits. There are big leather couches to sit on at Orvis and greatly enlarged photos of the early days along the staircase wall, when Orvis was mostly a tackle company and everyone—men sporting tweed caps and women in long hiking dresses alike—seemed to own a state-of-the-art cane rod. On a hot, dry day, the air conditioning at Orvis feels awfully good. After cooling down, you can trudge upstairs and purchase flies, rods and fly fishing gear of all kinds at the north end of the second floor. They post water temperatures and flows for all the major streams in southwestern Vermont on the wall behind the checkout counter up there, and the staff are knowledgeable anglers and helpful. Other than the north end upstairs, the store is mostly clothing.

No one in the fishing business on July 2, 2018, in Vermont could be too happy about the weather and what was happening on the creeks. Summer was tipping into a severe heat wave and drought up and down the Green Mountain chain. July would prove to be the hottest on record in much of Vermont. Fluke? Evidence of climate change? No and—in the context of shifting weather patterns—yes. When I told them I was headed to the Mettawee for a little scouting, the angling staff dolefully pointed to the low flows coming off the Taconics into the Mettawee, as well as the heat of the summer drought in the water. Not much going on, and maybe better to leave the trout alone? I hear you. I still asked them to advise me on fly selection, on what hatches could be coming off the Mettawee in the evening, and they obliged, suggesting I buy the Copper Johns. Buying flies based on professional recommendations is the cheapest way I know of purchasing a little hope.

Freshwater anglers, particularly fly anglers—many of whom are so carefully attuned to water temperature, quality and flows; riparian habitat; the presence and absence of insect larvae, insect emergence and adult insect hatches; the time of year; the weather; the wind; the light of day; and time in general—may be America's most engaged observers of rivers and their environs. In this they share a trait with the nineteenth century's George Perkins Marsh. Arguably, the heart of Marsh's book *Man and Nature* is a meditation on the relationship between woods and waters, as well as an argument for the restoration and stewardship of forests. (What's so great about Marsh is that he became in short order essentially a fisheries restoration expert, although his primary method—fish culture and replenishing depleted stocks—was somewhat ill informed. But who can blame him? It was 1850.)

Marsh's insights and thesis into what happens to the flows coming from springs and streams—and to the force and frequency of floods, the absorptive quality of soils, the temperature and humidity of the atmosphere and the impact of sedimentation when forests are destroyed and soils washed away—were so important to him because he'd first begun to observe these relationships as a boy in Vermont. He wasn't a scientist, per se, but these were homegrown observations. Because he watched his forests come down. He witnessed massive deforestation; he saw the population of Merino sheep on his hillsides explode and the movement of logs down his river multiply. Marsh put two and two together. Much later in life, during his long residency and travels in Europe, his early observations were confirmed by the hundreds of books and scientific treatises he read—from Pliny the Elder and Alexander von Humbolt to John Evelyn's *Sylva* (1664) and the writings of William Harrison in *Holinshed's Chronicles* (1577), to name a very few. They were confirmed, too, by what he observed as an adult and by the scientists he met.

Besides being a foreign diplomat, Marsh was a traveler and a polymath with a lawyer's knowledge of argument to a biochemist's take on water quality. First and foremost, he was a curious synthesizer. What he did so well was assemble the jigsaw puzzle of human insults and depredations on nature. While he borrowed much from the Europeans, the birthplace of his original insights was Vermont, its woods and waters. In the middle of *Man and Nature* is a 166-page chapter called "The Woods," taken up mostly by what happens in the world when you remove them. The next chapter, less long, is "The Waters," about what happens to them when you remove the woods.

It's easy, as well, to imagine Marsh as an early version of the scientists studying climate change in all its manifestations today. In *Man and Nature*, again, with a focus on forests, he marches right up to a declaration of their role in determining the amount of carbon dioxide in the atmosphere but stops short—not because he doesn't suspect it to be true, but because "not enough is known." He wrote, "It has even been supposed that the absorption of carbon, by the rank vegetation of earlier geological periods, occasioned a permanent change in the constitution of the terrestrial atmosphere."

Marsh also observed, in a lecture to the Agricultural Society of Rutland, Vermont, in 1847: "It is certain that climate itself has in many instances been gradually changed and ameliorated or deteriorated by human action. The draining of swamps and the clearing of forests perceptibly affect the evaporation from the earth, and of course the mean quantity of moisture suspended in the air.... Within narrow limits too, domestic fires and artificial structures create and diffuse increased warmth, to an extent that may affect vegetation. The mean temperature of London is a degree or two higher than that of the surrounding country."

What a genius, huh? The other minor miracle is who came to occupy the Marsh homestead after Marsh was gone. Frederick Billings, who, with his family, took up residence in the Marsh home in 1869 overlooking the wide floodplain of the river, was Marsh's heir apparent, following where Marsh left off by buying up denuded hill farms and replanting the forests Marsh watched cut down. Billings made his fortune during the gold rush managing claims and settling disputes. Later, he bought a one-twelfth interest in the Northern Pacific Railroad. Billings, Montana (1923), is named after him. He served as president of the Northern Pacific from 1879 to 1881 (nearby Yellowstone National Park was formed in 1872 under President Grant; the railroad was a major promoter of the park). Billings took Marsh's *Man and Nature* and his personal role to heart, buying up Marsh's twelve-thousand-volume library and creating a home for it at the University of Vermont. He made equal contributions in the dairy industry.

THE METTAWEE'S HEADWATERS ARE in the Taconic Mountains, including Danby Mountain, Dorset Mountain, Mount Aeolus, Mother Myrick Mountain, Woodlawn Mountain and Mettawee Peak in the towns of Dorset and Rupert. It's a wide teacup of heavily forested Taconic highlands, with many small brooks filled with brook trout, contributing to the flows of the Mettawee. The Taconic Mountains are underlain by limestone bedrock, and the area, particularly the towns of Danby and Dorset, are well known for their marble and limestone quarries. The deep caves at Danby, now closed, provide the right temperature, humidity and air circulation for roosting and hibernating colonies of six species of bat, including two federally endangered species, the Indiana bat and the eastern small-footed bat.

Significant land conservation efforts have taken place over the years in the upper watershed of the Mettawee—notably in the 3,200-acre Merck Forest and Farmland Center, a nonprofit educational organization. George Merck began assembling small farm parcels in the 1940s, when much of the area was pastureland and the soils were depleted. In the headwaters of the Mettawee, within the Green Mountain National Forest, the U.S. Forest Service has been adding woody debris to streams to create scour pools and improve eastern brook trout habitat. Lower down and outside of the forest, in Dorset Hollow, Trout Unlimited (TU) has been working with landowners and partners to improve fish passage, including Vermont Fish and Wildlife; the Natural Resources Conservation Service (NRCS), which can provide funding for fish passage and other work on privately owned lands; and the Poultney Mettawee Natural Resources Conservation District. Erin Rodgers, TU's Western New England project coordinator, described to me six barriers to fish passage in the few miles of Dorset Hollow that they've set their sights on. The main stem here parallels Route 30 and passes through neighborhoods that are at high risk for flooding. Improving fish passage has the added benefit of reducing flood risk. Working with landowners this year, summer crews replaced two undersized and perched culverts and built a rock ramp and step pools around an old weir. Three barriers remain, including a pair of dams and a bridge with a concrete bottom, now perched much of the year four to five feet above river level. Removing each of these in coming years, she said, means opening up hundreds of miles of cold-water tributaries and their healthy populations of brook trout to the waters of the main stem, as well as wild rainbow trout to the headwaters—a wild reunion in the making for more than one hundred years.

One of the most impressive and important conservation projects in the state of Vermont has been taking place across the past twenty-five years in the broad valley of the Mettawee River, west of the phalanx of the Taconic Range and Dorset Hollow. The Vermont Land Trust (VLT) began working with these farming families—including some eighth-generation farms—in 1986, with a first purchase of development rights, thanks to a John Merck Fund grant in that year. Perceiving that farming needed groups of families and blocks of farmland working creatively together to succeed, VLT got funding for a community organizer (Jackie Lapan) to begin reaching out to farm families in 1988. It took years of listening and meeting, learning about the stressors and the needs of farmers and slowly gaining farmers' trust.

Joan Allen, who took over from Jackie, told me that some of the conversations went on for ten years before farmers were ready to protect their land. Joan, like Jackie, learned farming on the job, with help from a local advisory committee, and had to overcome the typical biases—she's a woman and she wasn't a Vermonter. Eventually, Joan protected half a dozen farms and several thousand acres of land along the river. She worked with early adopters like Shorty Stone (Stonebroke Farm), the Leach family (Woodlawn Farm) and Gabe Russo, a top-notch farmer and consulting forester. The easements placed on these farms not only removed the option of future subdivision and suburban or commercial development forever, but they also gave the state some say in how these farms are managed. While VLT and the Vermont Housing and Conservation Board were more narrowly focused on protecting the working landscape back in the 1980s and 1990s, today "ecosystem services"—such as flood prevention, habitat inventory and protection, wildlife corridors, fish passage and pollution buffering to protect water quality and the protection of natural communities—get equal attention. Joan, who went on to spend a dozen years at the Nature Conservancy, sees more cooperation today among agencies and has witnessed changes in approaches, whether its within NRCS (once a big proponent of riprapping) or the Nature Conservancy.

River access, while it was often a "right" acquired by the land trust and state agencies along with farmland, was rarely required of the farmer. Actually, granting public access was often a voluntary act, left up to farmers. Thanks to groups like the Vermont River Conservancy (VRC), the state is getting access through projects once devoted to the protection of farms and farmland soils. VRC is a private group now willing to become involved in public-access management. Joan's latest project is a collaboration between Vermont Fish and Wildlife Department, the Nature Conservancy and VLT to protect the 1,100-acre Johnson farm in Canaan. The Johnson property includes six and a half miles of river frontage on the upper Connecticut River, with a new put-in for trout anglers; a new 623-acre wildlife management area; and a 600-acre working dairy farm.

I remember how struck I was seeing the Mettawee Valley for the first time in the fall of 1975 and how foreign it seemed from the metro Burlington area that was school and home. I had put out my thumb in Burlington one mid-September noontime to hitch a ride down to Rupert to see my girlfriend (now my wife, hiking the Long Trail), who was working at Merck Forest at the time. I was completely ignorant of the fact that to choose the rural Route 30 rather than Route 7 meant that I would be, literally, walking my way down between short lifts. I remember the Mettawee Valley so clearly because I got a bunch of rides there close to dusk, each about a mile long, from farmers getting to their late milking. The valley was full of standing corn, migrating geese in the sky overhead and small farms where laundry was hung off front porches. When I walked into Merck Forest at around 11:00 p.m., I recall the extreme thirst—nobody carried around water bottles back then—but also the images of the Mettawee Valley's early golden evening seared into my brain. Today, the valley from Pawlet to Rupert is much as I remember it.

My recent visit to the Mettawee Valley began with a longing look at Dorset Quarry, back in Dorset Hollow—a popular swimming hole today. There must have been one thousand people lounging on the lawns and rocks and in the water, using all manner of floating apparatus. That's the place to be on a blistering Fourth of July weekend in Vermont. Even the fishing guide I ran into at an East Pawlet convenience store was headed to the river with two lawn chairs, a six-pack and his girlfriend. Not a fly rod to be seen.

I drove northwest on Route 30 up through the valley to Pawlet and got into the river at the School Street bridge. There's a parking access there. I got out and walked upstream. Even in the extreme heat and drought, the river was cool and shaded, bounded by a steep wooded bank with some housing on one bank and farmland on the other. There was low flow but plenty of pools and riffles. This section is within the special-regulation waters that begin at the Route 153 bridge in North Pawlet and continue to the town of Dorset sixteen miles away. No tackle restrictions here, but there is a ten- to fourteen-inch slot limit—all fish within that size class need to be returned to the stream—and a bag limit of two fish, only one of which can be greater than fourteen inches.

The Mettawee is a wild rainbow stream with no stocking. It's got some of the same characteristics as the Battenkill in terms of cold spring inputs, higher pH and nutrient richness. I'm curious about sediment runoff and the nutrient contributions from farms, but I don't know how that is going. Much of the river corridor itself is lower by fifteen feet from the contours of the fields, and the bank near where I stood was heavily vegetated.

My impression is that public access feels limited. While I didn't see a single "No Trespassing" sign, the river does disappear beyond wide meadows. Bridges occasionally cross the river, and they make a convenient jump-in place. But the river meanders widely through the valley, and some local knowledge would be useful. I have read that many landowners allow anglers access. I think that is true.

Chapter 19

MILLER POND

Tuesday, July 3, 2018

Each summer, I try to make a trip or two to Miller Pond in Strafford, Vermont. This is a sixty-three-acre state property in a remote corner of one of Vermont's prettiest small towns, managed by Vermont Fish and Wildlife. (If you're visiting for the first time, be sure to run up into North Strafford to see the famous town meetinghouse and stop at the store in South Strafford for a soda.) The pond has a big parking lot and a concrete boat ramp. The low foothills and woods surrounding the pond in this part of the piedmont, with the Green Mountains far to the west, make for a nice evening float. The pond is about thirty feet at its deepest. The fishing recommends a visit here too. The state puts several hundred two-year-old trophy trout here, along with yearling rainbow trout. The *Hexagenia* hatch around the Fourth of July is pretty reliable, and it's a hoot seeing those Hexes pop up around dusk and watching trout (bass and bluegills too) coming up to any fair presentation.

For whatever reason, I also associate Miller Pond with eating trout. So often, I'm releasing what I catch, so it's nice to take a meal home. We fly fishers tend to release upward of 90 percent of the trout we catch, and we generally are looking for sport and sustainable populations of wild trout rather than a summer meal. But this summer, I've been giving fish to a friend, Sylvia, who's using a stovetop smoker to experiment with new trout recipes. Trout flesh, she writes, is tricky because the flavor is subtle. An avid gardener and seed saver, she gathers herbs and greens in season from her garden to complement the fresh-caught fish. Her garden is no ordinary garden. I don't know anyone else who grows saffron or dry-soil rice varieties. She's got a solar greenhouse, and a walk through her garden in June is like entering the old world. As far as eating trout, the old standby—trout in a hot oiled frying pan—works for her too, but she does get fancy.

Eating local fish is not only about trout. Consider the bluegill. The time I've spent fishing in the Midwest has taught me that there is no end to peoples' enthusiasm for eating bluegills. A product called Fryin' Magic is popular in Wisconsin and Michigan (you can buy it online), and bluegill fillets dredged in Fryin' Magic and fried in a pan get my vote for one of the best entries at a fish fry. Several dozen wild brook trout dredged and fried in Fryin' Magic work well too. Deep-fried smallmouth bass is always a treat. It seems as though the old-fashioned fish fry—when friends spend a day catching a mess of fish, whether crappie from a lake, brook trout from a backyard brook or horn pout—is less common today, as fishing and hunting for sustenance and/or subsistence is less common. Tonight, I was hoping that between my friend Steve Hoffman and me, in his strip canoe, we could ride on the success of our White River outing and come up with a half dozen fish for Sylvia's fish smoker—and get a whiff of the old subsistence ways.

Part of the appeal of Miller Pond is the diversity of the angling community here. There's a balance of fishers harvesting fish and others letting fish go. You're likely to see a bass boat with two guys casting lures, and there are often families with kids fishing with worms on hooks and red-and-white bobbers near the ramp. Miller Pond, well out in the boondocks of Miller Pond Road, gets serious fly anglers too. It's a great spot for a kayak. There's something for everyone. You don't have to know fish names in Latin or what *Isonychiidae* are. You just have to know what you love. It's the kind of place parents take their kids for a first fishing venture.

One such parent is Thomas Ames, who, together with his ten-year-old son, was introduced to fly fishing by a friend who took them out here to Miller Pond back in the 1990s. While Tom's son had a great time, it was Tom himself who got completely taken up by fly fishing for trout. I think it's safe to say that *Hexagenia* had something to do with it. Over the next handful of years, Tom—a professional photographer with his business roots in the marketing world of Madison Avenue, where he worked on some ground-shifting products like Apple's IIe computer and the original Sony Walkman—schooled himself not only in fly fishing technique but also in the natural histories of northern New England hatches. He became one of New England's top authorities on and photographers of aquatic invertebrates.

Writing his first book, *Hatch Guide for New England Streams*, Tom told me, taught him how to fly fish (although he also told me he had a lot of mentors along the way). Based on the success of the hatch guide, he published two more books on the insect life of eastern streams: *Fishbugs* and *Caddisflies*. These two books are coffee table–sized. Each contains his superb photography and engaging prose. His books go far beyond entomology to cover all aspects of fly fishing. Contrast Tom with the guys you meet who fish with worms and go off exploring beaver ponds and brook trout streams west of Norton Pond in the Northeast Kingdom and you get close to the full spectrum of Vermont trout anglers.

Who are Vermont freshwater anglers, anyway?

Fishing and hunting are important parts of Vermont culture, even if numbers are down since the 1990s. We hunt and fish for sport and social connection, and many hunt and fish for food. Vermont is a working landscape, with a long history of farming, logging and wood-products industries, as well as tourism. We are among the most rural of states in the country, with a population of roughly 626,000. About 85,000 of us in-staters buy fishing licenses each year. Add to that the roughly 35,000 nonresidents who buy either annual or limited-day licenses. While the highest number of anglers in Vermont come from urban centers, Vermont's rural towns have higher per capita numbers of anglers. For example, in 2014, Burlington (on Lake Champlain, in Chittenden County) had the highest number of anglers in the state with 2,057, yet that's only about 4 percent of Burlington's population. The northwestern counties track the highest (Franklin, with a 19 percent license buying rate, tops out the state), showing that fishing continues to be popular in spite of the shrinking and aging of many of Vermont's rural towns. The present-day indigenous Abenakis are particularly well represented in Franklin County, and many still practice subsistence hunting, fishing and farming there.

By county, there is remarkable continuity in Vermont. Between 9 percent and 12 percent of us buy licenses and go fishing annually across all counties. That means that whether you live in downtown Burlington or under the shadow of Mount Snow, you can always find people who fish living nearby. And they tend to know their local waters. One of the best strategies for anyone who wants to learn how and where to fly fish in Vermont, aside from hiring a guide (and I strongly suggest you do if you are new to Vermont), is to connect with other anglers. If you are new to the state, you'll get a big headstart on where and how to fish by making new friends. Take a lesson at the Orvis Company in Manchester. Groups like Trout Unlimited have chapters in every region of Vermont, and there are other watershed groups, like Friends of the Winooski River, and river-specific angler groups that welcome your participation.

The majority of anglers in Vermont are between the ages of forty-two and sixty-four, with the highest concentration in the mid-fifties. Because we're an aging population—37 percent of Vermonters are currently above the age of fifty, and that percentage is growing—and because recruitment of young anglers is less than those aging out of fishing, Vermont has seen a slow decline in license sales over the past twenty years. Three statewide surveys with identical methodologies showed a 30 percent decline in resident fishers between 1990 and 2010, as well as a decline by nearly half of nonresident anglers. On the plus side, this means few crowded streams and more fish for smaller numbers of anglers. On the downside, funds for the protection of fish and game and for the development and management of recreational fishing come in large measure from revenues generated by license sales and taxes on the sale of sporting equipment. Fewer anglers means less funding for the managing agencies being generated by users and less money going into the pockets of local businesses—guides, restaurants, motels and shops that cater to anglers. One-third of the Vermont Fish and Wildlife Department's budget (about $7 million) comes from hunting and license sales.

But all is not lost. Nationally, expenditures on equipment have been on the rise on a per capita basis, according to the 2011 National Survey of Fishing, Hunting and Wildlife Associated Recreation (11 percent growth in expenditures between 2001 and 2011). These reports are generated every ten years and linked to the national census. They are reliable indicators of the general pulse of the national interest. And it seems that interest in nature-based recreation, including hunting and fishing, is growing nationally. Outdoor experiences are sought more than ever by an increasingly urban America. How to address the issue of an aging state when it's harder than ever to pull young people away from their technology du jour? Maybe fishing is a way.

There are other hopeful trends in the world of fishing in general and fly fishing in particular. According to recent surveys, 30 percent of all Vermonters say they fish, whether they are active or not in any particular year (and whether or not they purchase a license). We Vermonters have at least a mental perception of being anglers on some level. That may be symbolic or wishful thinking of some kind (either that or evidence of blatant poaching), but it means a lot of us carry memories of early fishing ventures deep in the reptilian brain. We also have a strongly favorable opinion of the Vermont Fish and Wildlife Department (according to recent studies). Another positive sign: While women make up 12 percent to 20 percent of the current angling public in Vermont, they are increasingly fishing into their forties with children and grandchildren in tow. Fly fishing is seeing an uptick in active women anglers, and organized trips catering to women anglers are increasing nationwide. One of the most poignantly hopeful women's angling organizations is Casting for Recovery, which brings women cancer survivors together on the stream. It was founded in Vermont and now resides in Montana, although programs are still held regularly in Vermont. Ice fishing as a family activity is also hot these days.

Fishing (and hunting) has always been about forging a love of nature through relationships. Families are changing, and so is the institution of marriage. Vermont was one of the first states to pass a law allowing for same-sex marriage. Vermont prides itself on being a welcoming state. Fishing is relationship building. We fish as children because an older family member takes us fishing and teaches us. We pass that down. While that role may have been mostly under the purview of husbands, uncles and grandfathers in the past, mothers, aunts and grandmothers are stepping into that role more and more.

Another positive culture shift going on is a growing awareness of locally caught fish as healthy food. We have a burgeoning local food movement. Young people are taking up organic farming. We have perma-culturalists growing two-hundred-year-old varieties of plums and pears, and we see hoop houses going up that are reminiscent of Abenaki bark lodges. We have farmers who grow ring-necked pheasants for the high-end restaurant trade. There is a growing interest in organic ice cream. There is a parallel interest in wild-crafting foods; the number of mushroom foragers and ramp hunters is growing, along with the perception that fish caught at a local pond are healthy and affordable food (children and pregnant women, especially, need to be aware of consumption guidelines for freshwater fish). This doesn't mean that trout fly anglers are suddenly going to begin to keep and eat their full limit of trout. Highly unlikely. Catch and release is a cultural tattoo, learned and inked on beginning in the 1970s. The catch-and-release ethic remains very strong fifty years after its launch. It is promoted and taught actively through Vermont Fish and Wildlife publications and learn-to-fish programs for all species of game fish. With creel limits set for most fish species and size limits for many, everyone releases fish today. Catch and release is especially important where fishing pressure is greatest. Today and for the foreseeable future, learning to release a fish properly is as important as learning to properly catch one.

As a group, what do Vermont trout fishers value? It's mixed. Data from a comprehensive 2010 Vermont Angler Survey Report produced for Vermont Fish and Wildlife by researchers at Cornell show that about 40 percent of us favor more management for wild trout in Vermont—that this is "very important." On the other hand, 54 percent of us feel it is "very important" that stocking with catchable-sized trout continue. Vermont Fish and Wildlife management strategies for trout take into consideration both sets of values, and there is a lot of overlap; it's not one fishing preference versus the other here. Fly fishers and bait anglers fish the same rivers, ponds and lakes. At the end of an evening at a place like Miller Pond, it's about how each person measures his or her success differently. And it's about the common need for clean water.

There is strong support for certain types of special regulations in Vermont—length limits (60 percent in favor) and lower creel limits (39.9 percent), for example—but less strong support for other types of regulations, like required catch and release (21 percent) and requirements for artificial flies and lures (27 percent). These data are a window into Vermont's fishing cultures today. Angler attitudes evolve over time. So do anglers' values, scientific knowledge and rules.

However it all goes down, we can hope that the *Hexagenia* hatch at Miller Pond, despite all that changes, keeps showing up around the Fourth of July.

Chapter 20

MILL RIVER

Thursday, July 5, 2018

Mill River is in the Otter Creek drainage. While I wish I could report on extensive explorations of Otter Creek and its tributaries, I cannot. It's a glaring omission that's waiting for someone else to write it. Otter Creek is western Vermont's Connecticut River, smaller in size but every bit as interesting to an angler. My original plans to float sections of Otter Creek in hopes of catching large pike north of Brandon—where the Otter, with a few exceptions, is a warm-water fishery—were foiled by drought and distance. I had also hoped to fish all the important tributaries, beginning with Big Branch and Mill Brook in Danby and working north to the Clarendon, East, Castleton, Middlebury, Lemon Fair and New Haven Rivers. I caught my first Vermont brown trout in the New Haven, a popular river for Burlington anglers, back in my college days there, and I was looking forward to a reunion. All of these rivers and streams are covered ably by Northern Cartographic's *Vermont Trout Streams*. You can hook up with any of them through the Middlbury Mountaineer as well and someday write the book on Otter Creek yourself.

Instead, I visited just one place in the watershed. A popular swimming hole on the Mill River, where the Long Trail and Appalachian Trail—still one and the same at this point—come out of the woods and cross Route 103. My wife was hobbling down off the Long Trail here, and as her driver and provisioner, I was standing by to meet her. Actually, there were few places I'd rather have been on that blistering hot Fourth of July weekend. And I was not alone. There were a hundred or so others with the same idea.

Vermont has a number of small streams that have managed over thousands of years to carve deep gorges. Swimmers know where they are. Drive along the Huntington River in Richmond or Huntington on a hot day, for example, and go to the river where the line of parked cars is longest and you'll find a popular swimming hole. Huntington Gorge itself is dangerous, but there are many other pools along the road.

The Upper Clarendon Gorge on the Mill River in Clarendon, Vermont, just south of Rutland, is prized in the region as an excellent swimming hole where Vermonters, and the occasional visitor, go to cool off on hot July days like this one. Lower Clarendon Gorge, just a few miles south, is even better known. It has the added cachet of being among the first projects of the Vermont River Conservancy (VRC). VRC took ownership of two properties when private owners needed to sell, and then transferred these to the state. Lower Clarendon Gorge is now part of a seventy-two-acre state forest that protects not only the forest and various rare plants and ecotypes but also the public's right to swim.

What's been obvious for a long time to those working in the natural resources management, conservation and stewardship fields—and I hope obvious to anyone reading this far into this book—is that almost everything that gets done in the name of natural resource protection these days is done in partnership. What I particularly love about the VRC is that the role it has had for years, protecting public access to rivers and their swimming holes, was somewhat overlooked, possibly because it was viewed as of lesser importance or because what the organization does is complicated, difficult work involving issues of landowner liability, management and long-term oversight (including rules and the enforcement of them). It's also true that since its founding in 1995 by founding directors Stephan Syz, Tom Willard and Mike Kline, and under its first director Jeff Meyers's able leadership, its mission has evolved. It has completed some ninety-five projects over the years. Each includes some type of legal obligation. But while in the early years it was holding easements or fee simple deeds to swimming holes like Lower Clarendon Gorge, today, with the emphasis in Vermont on water quality and floodplain management, seventy-three of its holdings are river corridor easements.

AFTER TROPICAL STORM IRENE left rivers across the state in ruins, Mike Kline, head of the state's river management program, coordinated a deep look into how rivers work. As Steve Libby, current executive director of the VRC, told me, you can't control rivers: trying to makes them less stable. Most floodplain corridor projects, Libby said, are about the stabilization of sediment transport systems. Paradoxically, that means letting rivers move and meander so they can find their balance point. Lowering the river's energy reduces erosion—working with farmers to plant forested buffers builds stability without trying to permanently fix channels. Sediments still move, but sands, silts and gravels mined by moving water against one bank settle downstream where the water velocity, thanks to a meander, slows. Of course, when a river runs through a town, you don't want that river meandering. Unless the town's given the river wide berth, a bit of containment is in order. The historic closeness of towns to their rivers had everything to do with water power. Gorges like this one are excellent examples of a river's power. Swimming pools carved out of stone—the same power drove this country's Industrial Revolution, version 1.0. What role will water play in version 2.0?

Chapter 21

LITTLE RIVER, MAD RIVER, DOG RIVER

Tuesday, July 10, 2018

In this central Vermont region, there are villages and rivers, mountains and brook trout streams, and though I've lived near them for more than thirty years, I have not lived on them. Middlesex, Moretown, Montpelier, Waitsfield, Warren, Waterbury, Waterbury Center, Stowe; west to Richmond; east over Roxbury Mountain on Warren Road; Northfield and Northfield Falls and the Dog River; and then south from there to Roxbury, site of the first hatchery in Vermont—sitting on the divide. This is the region of the Ben & Jerry's ice cream factory, Green Mountain Coffee, Alchemist Beer (of Heady Topper Double IPA fame) and the Sip of Sunshine IPA by Lawson's Finest Liquids, now brewed at a brand-spanking-new brewery in Waitsfield. This is ski country, with Mad River Glen ("Ski It if You Can"), Stowe, Smugglers' Notch and Sugarbush, all within a forty-minute drive of one another. Long mountain ridges here split the watersheds between the Connecticut River and Lake Champlain.

The Mad River Valley is well known, too, for the pride locals have in the landscape. You could stage a fishing trip here in any one of several lovely places (or all of them): Waitsfield, a ski town that grows sleepy in summer; Montpelier, the state capital, with river walks and biking trails along the Winooski; and Waterbury, the cool craft brewing center with its pubs and restaurants. One could drive through these places, these villages—each a world of its own—stop and fish and never get bored in summer.

But without local knowledge, you cannot reasonably assume that you will catch fish. I, at least, needed a local guide. That would be Clark Amadon, member and on-and-off chair of the Mad Dog Chapter of Trout Unlimited (TU). He has lived in this region for years and been involved in river protection initiatives throughout these three watersheds. He seems to know everyone on a first-name basis and has been active in the TU National Leadership Council and national affairs. I couldn't do better than Clark.

We met at noon at the brilliant Red Hen Baking Company in Middlesex, just a minute or two off I-89. This is the one establishment I know well in Middlesex and make a habit of visiting (I have a sister- and brother-in-law just up the road). Red Hen is the perfect pit stop: clean bathrooms, great bread, coffee, newspapers, bright, neat sitting places, excellent local beer selection. Red Hen, I think, is simply the best bread in Vermont. The bakery shares space with a few local arts businesses too, including the Hive, a collective pottery studio.

Clark Amadon, TU volunteer and head of the Mad Dog Chapter on the Mad River. Clark and the Mad Dog Chapter of Trout Unlimited have devoted thousands of hours to buffer strip development, habitat restoration and fish passage improvements in central Vermont. *Photo by author.*

Our first stop was the Little River, an unexpected bottom-release tailwater fishery in Waterbury. The reach (about three miles long, between the Waterbury Reservoir and the Winooski River) has new mandated minimum-flow and graduated higher-flow regimes, thanks to relicensing agreements with Green Mountain Power. And temperatures from the bottom of the reservoir run at fifty degrees—wear your waders, anglers, even in July! We've got about the best we could hope for, Clark noted, walking me through the long and sometimes contentious Federal Energy Regulatory Commission (FERC) relicensing process.

The Little River is a must-stop for serious fly anglers. There is a two-fish-limit special regulation and some terminal-tackle restrictions. While there is private property along its length, access is good, with a dirt road running from near the mouth to the state park and dam. There is an opportunity, said Clark, for a small destination fishery here, and the word is getting out. A good thing, he added in a charitable fashion. Typically, a local angler might demand a promise in blood that a fishing writer keep quiet about a place like this, that's small and contained and mostly frequented by locals. But there are other opportunities, Clark noted, and we need a body of anglers that gets it, that sees the opportunities coming down the pike in upcoming FERC relicensing processes. He named a few, including Wrightsville Reservoir on the North Branch of the Winooski, where there may have been structures built originally for a bottom release, though never used. The North Branch below Wrightsville has beautiful stretches and plenty of public land; the thought of cold-water additions there would have any angler—fly, spin or bait—drooling. Clark mentioned Marshfield Dam (now a state park called Molly's Falls Pond) and Molly's Brook, far up on the Winooski's main stem. The organization Friends of the Winooski River wants to put much more cold water into Molly's Brook. Now most of that water goes into the penstock—the pipe a few miles long running along Route 2 in Marshfield to the turbines on the side of the hill in Marshfield and then, warmed, back into the river. Bolton Falls dam, a run of the river flow, is also up for renewal. And there is the Green River reservoir dam too, soon entering the relicensing process. Green River is one of the state's wildest canoe camping spots, a consistent common loon producer and a hot bass fishery. You can camp on your own island, swim naked and catch fifteen bass in the evening.

Clark doesn't think that the public understands the significant opportunities that dam-relicensing projects represent today. When these dams came into being many decades ago, they weren't designed or managed with the environmental services in mind that we recognize in rivers today. It's not just the fishing. It's many forms of recreation; it's clean water, flood control, the health of entire natural ecosystems; and it's human health shaped by flow regimes. It's green energy, I added. Well, Clark said, dams represent renewable energy sources, but they aren't by definition "green" energy sources necessarily. We have to make them green, he added. Vermont's waters don't belong to the utilities. They belong to the people of the state.

The Little River is a bright spot, Clark said. He sees lots of woody debris there, not swept out of the system by massive and erratic flows. Tree trunks have time to get established on banks. These, in time, capture more wood. Today we saw five anglers. Over the past weekend, Clark said, there were fifteen. Yes, all types of fishing are welcome here. But Clark added in the same breath that some places in Vermont should be reserved for the catch-and-release fly angler and that the Little River is one such place. He described a visit east by a western Montana friend who found it inconceivable that Vermont has no such water (except the fly fishing–only, catch-and-release Seyon Lodge, owned by the state but managed much like a public fishing club). A trip to the Upper Connecticut, said Clark, will convince anyone that fly anglers respond to such places and the promise of good fishing they hold. (The fly fishing–only section on the Upper Connecticut River is in New Hampshire—well worth buying a three-day license to fish in the state. And there is a New Hampshire catch-and-release section you can fish with a Vermont license in North Stratford at Lyman Falls.) Sure, Clark said, you're going to be fishing in view of other anglers, but that's an acceptable tradeoff. On the other hand, he added, fighting over regulations is a nonstarter in Vermont; fishing regulations are not our focus, he said. He described efforts to lower the current brook trout bag limit of twelve. It's FERC relicensing, winning buffer strips, securing easements and revegetating banks—that's where the action needs to be. TU's job, he told me, with partners like Friends of the Winooski River, is to rally around the work of those partners and to help those partners make local connections with the landowners and businesses that TU often knows well. To plant seeds.

After the side trip to the Little River, we were back in Montpelier, turning up the Dog River valley. I was surprised to learn that the Dog is carrying far fewer fish per mile than it did through the high-flying 1980s into the mid-'90s. From 3,000 or so fish per mile to 300 to 400, is what Clark thought. It's possible that sewage treatment led to fewer trout per mile. There is tertiary sewage treatment here now—much cleaner water throughout the watershed than in the 1980s. Yes, there are some large trout in the system, said Clark.

But overall densities of trout are lower. That hasn't stopped TU from its work to improve streamside habitat and chase cold water.

Clark pointed out various farms, one in particular where there is no wooded buffer and the farmer is planting close to the edge of the river. That farmer is losing ten to twelve feet of land per year, Clark said. You can find that land now in the form of large silt and gravel bars downstream. Farmers can see it too. There are farms throughout the lower portion of the river and for several long stretches elsewhere that have provided fifty-foot buffers, and volunteers over the past fifteen years or so have planted them. And there are many more that Clark thinks will do the same down the road.

We rolled through the farmstead of owners Nate and Jen—hardworking land stewards, according to Clark, although they don't want to be the public face of any campaign, as they don't have a lot of spare time. They grow organic grain and run a dairy that manufactures and bottles whole organic Jersey milk. They make and sell yogurt. The bridge at their place is a convenient access point to the Dog River, and there's a state access point a mile or so upriver. Amtrak runs through the Dog River Valley, and it's never far from view. Passenger and freight trains connect Vermont (and Quebec) to New York and metropolises to the south.

All along the lower river, Clark pointed out tree plantings. He mentioned George's place, Dog River Farm, which maintains a twenty-five-foot buffer. These are relationships with farmers that the TU chapter has cultivated across decades. That's how long it takes to establish trust. While the Natural Resources Conservation Service has plenty of money for high-cost manure storage, some farmers shun it, seeing a round-hole, square-peg problem. But over time, as the chapter built relationships and got some work done, neighbors saw what was going on and changed their view. It's long-term work.

If you asked a farmer around here, Clark said, they'd likely give you permission to access the river across their land. That's a return on a long-term investment (the same is true in the Mettawee Valley). Clark pointed to trees now twenty-five feet high that he helped plant years ago. The bane of revegetating these riverbanks (and those throughout Vermont), he said, is the invasive bamboo-like Japanese knotweed that suppresses tree growth. If you can get trees up above the knotweed canopy, they thrive. Clark referred to knotweed as "like the Great Wall of China." It's on most riverbanks.

The goal is chasing cold water, bringing cold water farther downstream. Clark pointed out important tributaries where rainbow and brook trout are known to spawn. I asked him why the Dog supports so many more fish in its main stem and tributaries, and much more natural reproduction, than the Mad River. It's a smaller watershed, Clark said, but there's much more recharge going on from seeps, springs and cold brooks coming off the mountains than in the broader and flatter croplands of the Mad River.

We visited a dam-removal project in Northfield Falls. The dam's construction suffered from unfortunate timing, built by an engineering professor from Norwich University as a demonstration project for his students, just months before the great flood of 1927. The dam was nearly washed away. Eighty years later, armed with funding from the U.S. Forest Service, U.S. Fish and Wildlife Service, private individuals and foundations, TU finished the job.

To see the post-dam site, we crossed through three identical covered bridges. What's there now is an attractive series of bare ledges that go stepwise down the steep gradient to a large pool and, beside it, an antique farmhouse surrounded by trellises and gardens. Rainbows come in the spring now to spawn, and the brook trout population, long isolated, can move up- and downstream. Water no longer pools and warms in the middle of what is a cold-water source for the Dog. The natural community evolves.

After a quick stop at the Falls General Store in Northfield for a cold drink (Nate and Jen's chocolate milk), we headed up and over Roxbury Mountain by Warren Road and into the Mad River Valley.

A visit to the Mad River, after a tour of the Dog River, is in some ways a study in contrasts. We're out of the constricted valley of the Dog and into a broader valley with the spine of the Green Mountains to the west. It's a study in contrasting local cultures, too, though not in any pejorative sense. People are just people everywhere, shaped by the natural landscape and by the somewhat chaotic twists and turns of human settlement, industry, agriculture and community development. The Mad River Valley is Clark's home.

We came down the mountain and were initially high up in the watershed. Side note, for those of you making the same trek: check out Rootswork, a community nonprofit market in the old East Warren Schoolhouse building high up on Roxbury Road, with a view of the mountains to the west and the traces of their ski runs. It's a lovely building with a great local foods and local goods mission.

Our first stop was the Warren Village Dam in the heart of Warren, about a minute off Route 100, a village that Clark described as tony—kind of the perfect word for my town of Woodstock, too, I pointed out. Both places are big on parades. If you ever get the chance, Clark said, check out Warren's Fourth of July parade. Crazy floats, half-naked people, farm animals and who knows what else. What I got was a picture of eccentric, inventive post-aristocrats living in a secluded colony that might as well be on Mars. This was further reinforced by the story of the dam, an old log structure just waiting to bust apart with the straw that broke the camel's back. It's ugly, said Clark, but some see it as historic. Gone, it would be missed by no one. But the people who own it see the site differently. Perhaps as future value in the war against climate change? A hydroelectric hedge? Visionaries or contrarians, or both? The owners, it turns out, are part of a trust appropriately named Prickly Mountain. Originally, Clark told me, this was a group of unconventional architects who built homes in Warren… perhaps on the side of Prickly Mountain? Clark, I need to add, did no Warren-bashing, other than his "tony" remark. Although he lives downriver, he loves Warren—a stunning place. The bunting and American flags were flying ten days after the Fourth. All in all, one of the best put-together—and highest—historic enclaves in the Green Mountains. It felt like Lincoln, Vermont's (on the west side of nearby Lincoln Gap) doppelganger.

We traveled farther up the watershed into brook trout land to visit a culvert that the partners rebuilt with state and federal funds. The new culvert is designed to avoid the too-common condition of blocking fish passage. It's a large concrete arch with no poured floor, just a natural streambed. Clark told me that within a day or two of construction, brook trout were moving both up and down the tributary.

Shortly thereafter, we turned a 180 for the run downstream. We stopped at a place where didymo algae (*Didymosphenia geminata*, or "rock snot") was first observed in Vermont. Clark pointed out easements gained, buffer strips planted. We drove through the town of Waitsfield and into the broadening valley through which the Mad River flows. This is now officially listed on America's Scenic Byways (the Mad River Byway), a designation that volunteers worked for years to win. Clark and his neighbors Virginia Farley and Jack Byrne worked on it. Don Wexler led the charge.

The Mad is known for its deep pools, famed swimming holes and clear water, but it can't sustain low temperatures in its lower reaches; a gorge/dam separates it from the Winooski. About four thousand trout are put in annually. We aren't going to create a Montana of the East, Clark said. The main stem can't support spawning habitat (presently). Creating a lot of fly fishing–only zones for catch-and-release anglers…it's just not going to happen here. What we can do, he added, is continue to push cold water downstream; the farther down it goes, the healthier we are going to be.

The tributaries are all dynamic, Clark said. He'd recently found a dead wild brown trout on the banks of the river near his home, a trout as bright and fat as any healthy wild brown he'd seen. He thinks there is brown and rainbow trout reproduction going on in some of the tributaries. And brook trout populations in the tributaries are healthy. That's a big plus. Clay Brook, he noted, is a wonderful brook trout fishery. There are many others. And there's promise in that, he said. I agree. Anyone who has not spent a summer day poking up a Vermont mountain tributary with a fly rod and a dry fly has not lived.

On that sublime note, we left the magical charms of the Dog and Mad River landscapes, the gifts and maddening challenges besetting the fishery there and the very real gains the partners have made over the years that, taken as a body of work, are deeply imaginative and impressive. Right on cue, we were passing the Red Hen Baking Company and heading to the park-and-ride.

Never pass up a bathroom or a good cup of coffee.

Chapter 22

THE WHITE RIVER, THIRD BRANCH

Wednesday, July 11, 2018

Have you ever been spooked at night on the Third Branch of the White River? I have. Found knives, strange sounds, sharp smells, encounters with unusual people—or a coyote, or a bemused beaver—and sometimes just a pile of women's clothes (a case, my rational mind tells me, of a tubing expedition and a forgotten starting point). Being spooked on a river is a form of happiness sometimes.

I had stopped by a bridge south of the Roxbury Fish Culture Station at midmorning, high up in the watershed, and rigged my rod for a walk downriver. It was quiet except for a distant chainsaw buzzing up in the hills. I walked down the riprap next to the bridge abutment and downstream. The spooky thing: someone in a tricked-out, tinted-window Hummer racing up and down the dirt road and then stopping on the bridge as if to case me out. "Who does that?" my imaginative wife would have asked. "A meth dealer?" Half in jest, of course. But really, who knows? Vermont is rural, and rural America has its severe social afflictions, drug addiction and selling drugs among them. We're not immune. A $75,000 Hummer in a place smaller than Lost Nation? Go figure.

The good news: Despite the Hummer, the heat and the radically shrunken river, the tributaries were running cold water like tub spigots into the warmer river. You could feel the cold as you moved up into these small tributaries and sometimes even see a cool mist—the sources of that magic cold water being high up in the Roxbury mountains.

Summer drought, 2018, White River Third Branch. Fishing for wild brook trout somewhere north of Randolph. *Photo by author.*

Each pool had its brook trout too. And they were peppy little trout. If you got a hit once and you missed once, then you might as well move downstream. I did. Half a mile more and I found the swimming hole I'd been looking for. In the shade of large maples above the ledge of the river, I stopped harassing fish and took a swim, listening to that distant whine of the chainsaw biting into wood.

The White River illustrates a principal interplay between stocked and wild trout that, I think, is common to many of Vermont's rivers. While stocked trout—hatchery-grown fish—are often the foundation of a fly angler's experience, many river systems support ample populations of wild fish too. These fish rarely get very large, but there are large wild fish here and there, both browns and rainbow trout. Some tributaries can hold upward of two thousand young-of-the-year brook trout per mile, as well as plenty that get to year two and beyond. These fish move seasonally—if not hindered by barriers like perched culverts, warm-water "barriers," old dams or a lack of habitat—back and forth from tributaries to main stems. Chasing them is good sport. That's true especially with rainbow populations, which have been naturalizing here since at least the 1940s.

Earlier that morning, I'd stopped at the Roxbury Fish Culture Station at the tip-top of the Third Branch. Built in 1891, Roxbury was the first state hatchery to come online (there are five now). Damaged by Tropical Storm Irene, Roxbury has been used as an archive and library for Vermont Fish and Wildlife for the past few years. Fisheries biologist Bret Ladago gave me a brief tour, and we talked about his recent assessment of spawning wild trout populations in the White River watershed. They are significant. We talked about the Roxbury Fish Culture Station, too, slated to be rebuilt beginning in September 2018 (at this writing). That's a significant development as well.

While Roxbury was the first official, state-run fish culture station built in Vermont, fish culture and "stocking" goes back farther in time here. Liz Pritchett and Ann Cousins's research traced early stocking efforts to restore depleted fisheries back to 1819, when several Orange County residents planted Lake Champlain fish into Otter Creek in an attempt to restore fish populations there.

Early fish culture efforts in America—based on the European practices of stripping eggs, fertilizing them and raising fry in glass jars—were made in the 1850s by Theodatus Garlick and H.A. Ackerly from Ohio. Garlick published a treatise on fish culture in 1858, and Ackerly opened the first hatchery near Cleveland in the late 1850s. Other private hatcheries followed suit in the early 1860s. Private hatcheries raised fish for the marketplace, and it could be lucrative business.

Of course, when it comes to conservation in Vermont, many roads lead back to George Perkins Marsh. In Vermont in 1856, concern over fish declines prompted the legislature to commission Marsh to study the problem, for the sum of $100. Marsh was fifty-five years old at the time. He'd already served three terms in the U.S. Congress (his Whig Party supported wool tariffs that propped up Vermont sheep farmers) and completed his stint as U.S. minister to Turkey. He was well known in Vermont, with a bit of a reputation as an elitist and intellectual snob. When the opportunity to study fish declines came up, he happened to be back in Vermont trying to recover from near bankruptcy, with a failed railroad project and a failing woolen mill. (His biographer, David Lowenthal, described Marsh as "an indifferent entrepreneur" with "an inability to devote himself wholeheartedly to money-making.")

Marsh issued his fish report to the legislature in 1857, noting that, while the "improvidence" of fishermen was often to blame for fish declines, "in

The Roxbury Fish Hatchery, circa 1896. The Roxbury hatchery was the first in Vermont. Constructed in 1891, it was damaged by Tropical Storm Irene. The hatchery is being rebuilt in 2018. *Courtesy of the Vermont Fish and Wildlife Department.*

taking them at the spawning season, or in greater numbers at other times than the natural increase can supply," there were other environmental degradations at fault: "Sawmills [dams and sawdust pollution], factories and other industrial establishments on all our considerable streams have tended to destroy and drive away fish." Marsh cited "more obscure" causes, too, such as "general physical changes produced by the clearing of land and cultivation of the soil....It is certain that while the spring and autumnal freshets are more violent, the volume of water in the dry season is less in all our watercourses than it formerly was, and there is no doubt that the summer temperatures of the brooks has been elevated." Marsh's report to the legislature on fish declines contained an argument for fish culture as a strategy for restoring native fish stocks. He added—always the visionary—that he anticipated a federal approach would be needed, given that migratory fish cross multiple state boundaries and that no citizen would likely want to invest state tax dollars that benefit landowners living in another state. Much of what he found in his 1856–57 study shows up in *Man and Nature* seven years later: "The artificial breeding of domestic fish has already produced very valuable results, and is apparently destined to occupy an extremely conspicuous place in the history of man's efforts to compensate for his prodigal waste of the gifts of nature."

Formal state fish commissions in the New England states and beyond began forming in the later half of the 1850s, with Massachusetts being the first in 1856. In 1865, New Hampshire, concerned about the loss of Atlantic salmon in the Merrimack and Connecticut Rivers, urged Vermont, Massachusetts and Connecticut to form a four-state commission to study the problem. In 1868, thirty-two thousand Atlantic salmon—raised to the smolt stage from Canadian salmon eggs incubated in the Livingston Stone National Fish Hatchery in Charlestown, New Hampshire—were introduced in the Connecticut River. Vermont obtained another fifty thousand salmon from private hatcheries.

By 1870, the American Fish Culturists' Association had formed, and in 1871, Congress authorized the creation of the U.S. Fish Commission, with Spencer Baird at its helm. Baird was given a $5,000 appropriation to produce a report on the decline of fishes along the Atlantic seaboard. Senator George F. Edmunds of Vermont was the chief sponsor of the legislation that formed the commission (which morphed over time into the National Marine Fisheries Services under the National Oceanic and Atmospheric Administration).

Baird completed his study of fish declines and attached to it a five-hundred-page report by renowned Yale zoologist Addison Verrill. Verrill accompanied Baird and his assistant on many expeditions. His report gives accounts of new species encountered, mostly around the waters off Woods Hole, Massachusetts, situated between the southerly and northerly influenced waters of Vineyard Sound, Buzzards Bay, Cape Cod Bay, Georges Bank and the Gulf of Maine. Baird was a consummate collector of birds, fish, insects, you name it, for the Smithsonian Institution in Washington, D.C., and like his friend Marsh, he became an enthusiastic proponent of fish culture. Congress responded to Baird's call for a federal program of fish culture, giving him the authority to propagate fish in 1872, along with the federal directive to establish a hatchery to collect salmon and rainbow trout eggs on the McCloud River in Northern California. That's where our rainbow trout came from originally. He hired the fish culturalist Livingston Stone from Charlestown, New Hampshire, to develop the hatchery on the McCloud. While the original directive was to focus on commercial food fishes, Baird interpreted his mandate to grow and spread fish (including carp) broadly, jumping right into sport fish aquaculture.

Between 1872 and 1880, the U.S. Fish Commission stocked 6 million Atlantic salmon fry and 8 million shad fry in the Connecticut River. State and federally constructed hatcheries located in Vermont were soon to follow.

Roxbury raised 553,500 trout and salmon in its first year of operation. After Roxbury, new hatcheries were added. Bennington opened in 1916, Salisbury in 1931, Newark in 1940 and Grand Isle in 1991 (a state hatchery in Canaan was sold to a private concern). Two federal hatcheries came online as well. The White River National Fish Hatchery in Bethel (flooded out by Tropical Storm Irene in 2013 and reopened in 2018) raised Atlantic salmon smolts and fry for introduction into the White River as part of the Connecticut River Atlantic salmon recovery effort, and the Pittsford National Fish Hatchery (now called the Dwight D. Eisenhower National Fish Hatchery) raised lake trout and salmon for Lake Champlain (a federal hatchery in Swanton was transferred to the state and then closed).

The early days of fish culture involved the massive harvest and storage of ice. The hatcheries had their meat-storage buildings for trout food too. Stocking was by horse and buggy, and fish eggs and fry were moved across the country in ten specially made railcars. While technologies at every stage of fish culture have dramatically evolved to become environmentally safer, more efficient and more focused on disease prevention and preserving wild genetic stock, the fundamentals of fish culture haven't changed that much over the past 150 years.

Along with changes in fish culture technologies, stocking policies have evolved radically. Stocking is practiced much more strategically now—less random than it was as recently as the 1960s. In a recent study comparing wild brook trout populations in 2016 to population estimates from the 1950s, the author, Richard Kirn (past director of cold-water fisheries at Vermont Fish and Wildlife), noted that the stocking of brook trout, according to "The Vermont Management Plan for Brook, Rainbow and Brown Trout," discourages stocking in wild brook trout waters today. While state stocking of yearling brook trout averaged 1,701,499 fish annually in the 1950s, the averages were down to 243,435 fish annually during the 2000s. In addition, fry and fingerling stocking (one to five inches) was widespread in the 1950s, "with very little consistency, direction or evaluation." The current plan directs that larger trout be stocked at targeted locations (such as trophy waters and larger, accessible waters that have habitat limitations). Today, fry and fingerling stocking of brook trout is generally reserved for remote ponds, "where transport of yearling trout isn't feasible." (In the Northeast Kingdom, volunteer groups help stock remote beaver ponds.)

Kirn's comparison study shows wild brook trout populations holding up well at levels comparable to what similar studies found in the 1950s (although overall densities are higher in the 2000s, mainly due to more young-of-the-year).

The true enemies to wild brook trout are warm water (sixty-eight-plus degrees), the destruction of in-stream and riparian habitat, an increase in severe flood events and dams and culverts that block fish passage. Obviously, stocking can increase our enjoyment of trout fishing, but stocking cannot reproduce the conditions needed to grow native fish.

It will be interesting to see how fish culture evolves in Vermont over the next century, with climate change and other human-wrought changes to the biosphere pressuring us to adopt new social approaches to community development, housing, food production, energy production and transportation—new approaches to how we manage, treat and revere the non-human world.

Much has changed since the early days of fish culture in Vermont. Our dam-building days are shifting from new and recommissioned dams (though not so in the rest of the world) into a dam-deconstruction phase. Will this evolve as climate change necessities press in? Will we see more truly green, environmentally sensitive hydro? How will that be balanced against the chase for more cold water, for improved fish habitat and fish passage? We've given up on one approach to restoring Atlantic salmon to the Connecticut River that did not work, and we are shifting the focus to shad and other river herring that may work and that critically need our attention today. At Lake Champlain, we have the dual goals of supporting an economically valuable sport fishery that requires chemical suppression of another fish (sea lamprey), while increasing funding for clean water (now mandated by the EPA) and restoring healthy native fish populations and their ecosystems, particularly sentinel species such as lake sturgeon.

In the matter of managing recreational trout fishing, the needle is turning toward habitat improvements, restoration of damaged ecosystems and the more selective and strategic placements of sport fish. One way to think of all this is that the focus of fisheries management is more and more on restoring nature's capacity to sustainably produce native abundance. George Perkins Marsh, the nineteenth-century's E.O. Wilson, used the archaic word *usufruct* (from the Latin *usus* and *fructus*, meaning "use and enjoyment") to describe using a resource that is not "yours" without destroying the essence or substance of that resource—restoring the land's capacity year after year to produce abundance. When we had to read *Man and Nature* (nearly unreadable) in college in the 1970s, we were taught that Marsh was first and foremost a utilitarian, to be distinguished from the romantic idealism of the likes of Henry David Thoreau, Ralph Waldo Emerson, Margaret Fuller and the other American transcendentalists. But these days, I think of George Perkins Marsh as an early whistleblower and a restorationist, not only for utility, but for survival, beauty, for upright mind and moral thinking. He took what he remembered from Vermont and honed it against what he learned in Europe and reframed it for America. Fish culture to him was one dimension of the restoration of balance and the assurance of native plenty. A moral imperative.

This all bodes well for the future of fly fishing and other freshwater sport angling in Vermont. It's a matter of sustaining progress, of not moving backward. We can't let global warming overtake us (although perhaps it already has).

In the introduction to *Man and Nature* (1864), Marsh wrote, "But with stationary life, or rather with the pastoral state, man at once commences an almost indiscriminate warfare upon all the forms of animal and vegetable [and other humans'] existence around him, and as he advances civilization, he gradually eradicates or transforms every spontaneous product of the soil he occupies."

How to recharacterize our relationship with nature to one of restoring the capacity of natural systems—"every spontaneous product of the soil"? How to produce and sustain diversity, abundance and resilience?

Chapter 23

JON CONNER

I never tell people where I go fishing, and when I do, I lie.
—*Jon Conner*

Monday, July 23, 2018

I have been an admirer of Jon Conner's for some time, even if he lies to me (I don't think he does that much). Jon is truly one of the unheralded fly fishing gurus around here, with a singular focus on fly fishing that is rare. It's how he stays sane, he told me, in the upside-down politics of the country today. It's how he solves problems. He's also a quiet, humble conservationist, and I admire that.

Jon's pedigree in fishing goes far back. As you may recall, his grandfather on his mother's side, John Wheelock Titcomb (1860–1932), was an early fish culturalist. He served as chair of the Vermont Fish and Game Commission from 1891 to 1902, was chief of the Division of Fish Culture (U.S. Bureau of Fisheries) from 1902 to 1909 and then came back to Vermont to head the Vermont Fish and Game Commission from 1910 to 1916. Titcomb is best known as the first person to successfully bring North American salmonids to Argentina (brook trout). Hired by the Argentine government in 1903 to survey potential locations, he settled on the enormous Nahuel Huapi Lake near Bariloche and the Chilean border as the best bet for a successful introduction. Some 100,000

Fly Fishing & Conservation in Vermont

Jon Conner, great-grandson of John Wheelock Titcomb, one of Vermont's first fish and game commissioners, holding up his catch in Woodstock, Vermont, circa 1954. *Courtesy of Jon Conner.*

fertilized eggs of brook trout made the six-month steamer trip. The fish eggs traveled in refrigerated containers normally used to ship beef from Argentina to Britain. After making the Port of Buenos Aires, the eggs traveled several days south by train and then by horseback across the Pampas to the mountains and lakes on the border. Titcomb's hatchery on Nahuel Huapi was the first in South America.

Jon has upheld the fishing tradition in many ways. He's used a small foundation set up by his parents in honor of his grandfather to improve fishing on the Ottauquechee River, and he's distributed stream tables to area schools and museums. Jon is also a very fine fly tyer who's come up with a few distinctive patterns that everyone who fishes these rivers should have in their fly box.

Jon and his wife Pic's home is a veritable Shangri-La, hidden behind the Sharon hills. There is a small pond by the drive and sheep, chickens and turkeys on a slope just behind the house. Two friendly dogs occupy the space between the drive and the stone walk up to the veranda. The veranda—covered in grapevines and hidden behind low, twisted trunks of walking stick and cedar and other green profusions—connects house and barn, where Jon's shop is. Jon's a builder—of houses, furniture, boats and fishing rods. His wife is a garden designer, so the house has as much green inside as out.

On his fly designs, Jon said, "We don't really care what the trout thinks they are—they work." He ties his sinking flies using a strip of rabbit skin. They look very...something. He ties his floating flies with a paraloop hackle using a "gallows." The body of these flies sits in the water while the hackles—which only extend above and to the sides in a kind of 3D fan—float, with a little grease applied, like a cork. They stay upright. The paraloop method is advanced fly tying, he assured me (graduate seminar stuff and above my paygrade).

This brief interview took place when the rivers were low. Not a good time to go out fishing, so we stayed and chatted in Jon and Pic's Shangri-La.

Tim: What got you fishing in the first place, Jon?

Jon: I started fishing as a little kid—I was born in 1945. It wasn't something conscious. I grew up in Woodstock and was on my bike all over the place along the Ottauquechee River. I had a fishing buddy, Tommy Brownell. He lived in the village; I lived on the edge of the village. In

John Wheelock Titcomb, circa 1900, Vermont fish culturalist. *Courtesy Jon Conner.*

summer, beginning in about fourth grade, that's what we did. At eighteen, I went out to Eastern Washington, near a little town called Twisp, to work for the summer [on my uncle's ranch], *and they had a fly fishing–only pond. Very rural. That was 1963. That's what forced me into fishing with a fly. I just learned the rudiments. Ten years later, I started really going after fly fishing.*

Tim: *Did you settle in Woodstock?*

Jon: *I did. My dad owned the Volkswagen garage in Woodstock* [between where the liquor store and hardware store are today]. *I worked there for quite a time. My dad ran a dealership there* and then a garage with a lift where the old train station is. He owned a Jeep and Rambler dealership too, in a building behind the Woodstock Inn. Late '50s, early '60s.

Tim: What's your fishing range around here today?

Jon: Well, I get about fifty miles or so up the Connecticut River [one of Jon's favorite places is the difficult-to-access Comerford Dam tailwater; big fish there], *and I go around here—you know, the Connecticut, the Ottauquechee and the White River. I tend to fish not too far from home. I'd rather fish for two hours and drive for ten minutes than drive for two hours and fish for ten minutes. And, of course, I go to the ocean. I started doing that around 1996, when I got hooked on stripers. That was with Don Delay. Don and I started fishing together in 1984.*

Tim: What is your advice for the new fly angler coming to Vermont?

Jon: The best thing you can do right off is to go out with a guide for a day or two. It puts you onto fish, as opposed to thrashing about thinking, "Here's fishy water." But 90 percent of the time, you're wrong. You can learn more in a day with a guide than you can learn in a year on your own.

Tim: What about the White River? Do you do much exploring with a fly rod there?

Jon: You know, this stretch right here in Sharon down to West Hartford is great. I fish above the old dam. Rarely below. It can be quite good.

Tim: Are you lying?

Jon: No, not this time. It's a little difficult to really get to this section now. You have to know where you can cross and where you can't. It has always been inaccessible to the hordes. After Irene, it became much more difficult. The floodplain got bombed, and all the trees are down, so it makes it more difficult to access the river. Impenetrable. You need a machete and a chainsaw to get through the tangle of junk.

Tim: Lying now? No, just joking. I have floated that and lost a set of car keys in that section. I, too, had some good fishing but did not catch back my car keys.

Jon: You need at least 450 cfs [cubic feet per second] *to paddle it. It was about 150 cfs yesterday* [when] *I was looking at all the flows.*

Tim: Do have general advice on tackle? Rod weight?

Jon: A 5-weight line, eight to nine feet of length, works in almost all situations. And 4X up to a 6X leader. But no one starting out wants less than 4X, I think.

Tim: Fly patterns? You've developed your own, haven't you?

Jon: I use for most of my sinking flies a little dubbed-fur body with a rabbit fur strip behind it. It's kind of like what I use most all the time. I call it a Rabbit Tail. A little nothing fly. And I make them big too. They have good action and I sort of imagine that they are Isonychia nymphs or a small baitfish, or whatever you want to think it is. They move well in the water, and if you drift them through a pool, there's a pretty good chance a fish will eat that. Rather than trying to get technical meeting the hatch. I never use sinking line, and I don't use strike indicators. Indicators make it so that anybody can catch fish.

Tim: How do you tie these?

Jon: I tie most all of my flies on short-shanked, bent-scud hooks. Daiichi 1120s. The 1130, I use for most of my dry flies. I have a style of dry fly I use that's a little different from the standard. This is what I do [goes out to the car to get his vest and comes back with boxes of flies]. *It's sort of a parachute but a little different. It's called a paraloop. What I do, I put the thread over my little gallows here, and I wind the hackle around the thread. After it's all wound and you put the body on the back, you pull the whole thing over the top of the body so all the hackle stays up on top of the fly.* [You don't wind it around the front hook on the front third of the body.] *They float like corks. The idea is for the hackle to hold the thorax on the surface instead of propped up above the water the way a standard wound hackle would.*

Tim: So, the body sits in the surface film rather than on or above it?

Jon: Exactly. The hackle lets the fly sink a bit. You can throw the fly up into rough water and it stays upright. The body is a bit of peacock herl and the tail a bit of Antron. Often, I use woodchuck for the body. I make dark ones and light ones. Nothing very specific. I do make ones that are supposed to be Hendricksons. But I tie those on Orvis hooks with longer shanks.

My conversation with Jon developed through the afternoon into a full-blown advanced fly tying demonstration using a gallows. I wish I had kept good notes or filmed. With fly tying, words alone often fail, and it's truth in video that rules the day.

Chapter 24

THE LAMOILLE RIVER AND STERLING POND

Wednesday, July 25, 2018

On the way up to meet my wife at Smugglers Notch and fish Sterling Pond—the highest trout pond in the state—and then Lamoille River just west of Jeffersonville, I stopped by to say hello to Bob Shannon, the owner of the Fly Rod Shop. If you need flies, advice, directions or an experienced guide, I highly recommend you check in with Bob. Located on Route 100 in Stowe, his shop is perfectly situated halfway between two of Vermont's great rivers, the Lamoille to the north and the Winooski to the south, with plenty of very good brook trout water in between. What makes the Fly Rod Shop noteworthy, besides that it's been in business for fifty years, is that while Bob's dedicated to fly fishing, his shop covers the gambit. You can buy worms in blue containers, inexpensive spinning gear, graphite fly rods, top-quality tying vices and custom-made nets. There's an entire side room dedicated to tying supplies. He's got a posse of seasoned guides, all excellent, and they're busy all year. I especially admire that Bob's reputation as a fly-angling guide doesn't put him off the job of working with families to introduce the next generation to fishing. That's important.

Bob and I went on to have an interesting conversation about his many years as a local fishing expert in this region.

Tim: What got you into fly fishing, Bob?

Bob: I went to Paul Smith's college [a private forestry college in the Adirondacks of upstate New York], *so that was an important factor. I fell in with a bunch of fly anglers. One of the standing jokes was that we majored in fishing and minored in education. There's water everywhere in the Adirondacks. I graduated in 1981 and moved to Stowe in 1982. There were few, if any, fishing guides around then, and lots of water. I was working as a bartender at a local restaurant/hotel and printed up some business cards and started running a guide service. In 1993 or '94, I began guiding year round by offering trips outside of the country.*

Tim: So you were guiding anglers during the day and bartending at night. Sounds like a nice life. How did you get involved in retail?

Bob: My affiliation with the Fly Rod Shop goes back to when it was originally owned by the Diamondback Fly Rod company. A few years after moving to Stowe, I spent my winters working for the ski patrol and my summers guiding. I connected to the shop back in the 1980s. It was owned by Bill Alley, a real innovator in the story of fly-rod building in Vermont and a great source of information. I approached Bill about working in the shop while also offering fly-fishing tours. His initial reaction was, "This isn't Montana." I said, "Yeah, but while Vermont may not have the numbers of fish or the size, it does offer a pretty special experience." We kind of butted heads over that a little bit, but in the end, I went to work for Bill while continuing to grow my own business, called Fly Fish Vermont. Eventually I had my own small retail location in Stowe. Back then, it was primarily the outfitter part of the business that sustained me.

Tim: Is that typical to most fly shops?

Bob: Most shops are looking to develop the retail service aspect of the business. I kind of started out backwards with the guide service and instructional classes and evolved into the retail end. In 2002, I bought the Fly Rod Shop. But we're still very much a fishing travel company. We get to the Caribbean and South America. We run a lot of trips to Canada. There are seven guides working with me now.

Tim: What about your range in New England? Do you get to the Upper Connecticut River or to coastal Maine, for example?

Bob: My range now is limited to Vermont and New York because I'm not licensed in Maine or New Hampshire to guide. I do offer trips to the eastern side of the Adirondacks and over to Lake Ontario. And then primarily from the central part of Vermont to the northern part of the state. I don't do a lot of trips down south.

Tim: I've found most Vermonters to be focused on their own region. Can you describe this destination with Stowe in the middle?

Bob: I couldn't have picked a better place in Vermont to set up shop. When I first came here in the 1980s, the reason I moved here from the Adirondacks is that off-season survival in the Adirondacks was a lot tougher. What worked well here was that the ski season would end in April, and by the middle of May, I'd be rolling back into my guiding business. Stowe was already a well-developed tourist destination, in spite of its small size; it attracts people looking for things to do. The hiking and the mountain biking—fly fishing was kind of a natural fit. Working in cooperation with the local lodging and hotels, within two years, the guiding business just kind of blossomed.

Tim: What about this location as a destination fishery?

Bob: The huge advantage to Stowe is that we're higher in elevation, with the Green Mountains to the west and the Worcester Range to the east. We have the high peak region, and coming off of that is cold water, every trout fisher's dream. And it's unimpacted by pollution or sediment. We can drive within fifteen minutes from the store and give anglers five to seven different fishing options.

Tim: Can you say a little bit about your client base?

Bob: We get all of the above. But what has evolved is a kind of seasonality where in the early part of the season, and then again in the fall, we tend to get the more experienced anglers. They're here for the cold water, the hatches and specific destinations. During the summer months, early July through August, we're doing much more instruction with families and children new to fishing, and young adults and adults new to fly fishing.

Tim: How do you introduce families to fishing?

Bob: We do a lot with the next generation. I have a program going on now called "Family Gone Fishing." It's not fly fishing. Not yet. It's really just about breaking the ice. We use bait and everyone catches fish. I just returned from a trip this morning before meeting with you. We had three families and a bunch of kids, and we caught seventy fish between us. When kids first get out there, they're very squeamish about touching a fish. By the end, they are literally kissing that perch or sunfish. It's a total transformation. The other thing we see more of is the father or mother that comes into the shop with their thirteen-year-old kid wanting to learn to fly fish. So getting out when they're young to fish with bait is part of this continuum that maybe has learning to fly fish in the future. We bring our program to summer camps and schools, and all summer get families together out on the water.

Tim: The fact that you sell worms must be shocking to some of your diehard fly anglers.

Bob: What do you mean you're selling nightcrawlers!? But I think everyone gets it. If you can remember back far enough in your own life, you remember digging up nightcrawlers and going to a local trout pond on opening day.

Tim: Women are a growing demographic, aren't they?

Bob: Until it was made a thing—women's groups for and led by women—it was a challenge getting women out there. It can be very intimidating. The state's program, Becoming an Outdoors Woman, has been effective. Women are beginning to come into their own in fly fishing. When I go to international fishing shows these days, I'm seeing "women's aisles" with gear designed for women. While I used to run women's angling groups, women are running women's groups now, and that's better, more appropriate. Now women are seeing women modeling comfort in the outdoors. The same is true for the cancer survivor program for women called Casting for Recovery.

Tim: Bob, if you were marooned on a desert isle with a cold-water trout stream and could only have a handful of trout flies, what would they be?

Bob: You have to remember when you come to fish in Vermont that, by and large, these are infertile waters. We just don't have a lot of nutrient-

rich, high-alkaline cold waters here. Fish here tend to be opportunistic feeders. So I steer people away from an intense focus on matching the hatch. I like dark flies—nymph and wet fly patterns—in the early season and light flies in the warmer months. Here are a few suggestions: Light and dark Hendricksons. Tan and olive caddis in the summer. It's always a good idea to bring along a few Parachute Adams. Of course, Woolly Buggers are the go-to, nationally. In a variety of colors, they are a great prospecting fly. And don't forget to put a few terrestrials in your kit.

Tim: Bob, I know you served for eleven years on the Fish and Wildlife board. How has fishing changed over the years here in Vermont for the better? From a policy and program standpoint, what's working well?

Bob: A recent study of our brook trout populations that looked again at plots that were surveyed back in the 1950s showed that brook trout are actually doing very well statewide. I think that will come as a surprise to some people. Here in the valley, every one of those squiggly blue lines coming off the ranges has wild brook trout. Our forests came back in this century, and all those tributaries are shaded and cool. That cool water helps cool down the main stems. We also have an increasing beaver population. Beaver ponds are our hidden gems. While they may only hold trout for four to six years, finding new healthy ponds often means finding a healthy wild trout population. The trophy trout program—eight rivers statewide and numerous trout ponds stocked with two-year-old trout—is a real achievement that was years in the making. It gives anglers in Vermont a chance to catch the fish of a lifetime, and it's good for business. While it's expensive raising two-year-old fish, these fisheries attract anglers from afar. They hire guides; spend money on food, lodging, gear and fishing licenses. It has been measurably good for my guides and our business. If I could change the program—I've suggested a delayed harvest. We have a two-fish-per-day creel limit; of course, many anglers are returning the fish they catch. If we could delay the harvest, say to June 1 or June 15, those fish would have a chance to disperse more widely, and that improves the quality of the fishing experience for many. We're not there yet.

Tim: Do you see any threats to cold-water fisheries that you'd like to mention here?

Bob: I think our main stems are taking it hard. A recent study shows that average water temperatures are up 1 percent over something like the past ten years. Chasing cold water is going to be a century-long endeavor and a challenge to generations. Private landownership along rivers is going to make habitat improvement difficult. Groups like TU chapters and Friends of the Winooski, with their relationships and partnerships with state agencies, are going to become more and more important as educators and connection points to landowners and the general public.

Chapter 25

LAMOILLE RIVER HEADWATERS

Sunday, August 5, 2018

Still in the grips of the heat wave, although the last week of July brought torrential rains. Welcome to climate change. We've had the warmest July on record. (We will have one of the coldest, wettest falls.) The rivers are up again, dirty, and the stream that flows fifty yards from our front door is rollicking and loud. Flash floods have been predicted for Windsor County, fuel to the old saw and new reality that if you don't like the weather in New England, wait a minute. In the age of climate change, that bromide takes on new meaning.

August has been, in general, a good time to avoid fishing Vermont's rivers, at least for as long as I've been fishing them. A good time to visit a lake, go for a swim or find a shaded mountain brook and dabble your way up for brook trout. Today, I was hoping to do the latter. My brother-in-law, Wayne, met me at the Waterbury Park and Ride, where we checked maps and cell reception before heading north on Route 100. Although our politics—like raw kale and quinoa to a Texas T-bone steak—may be hard to mesh, that matters less and less, I think, even as the strains on our democracy caused by the red and blue division matter more and more. I can't really explain the cause of that inverse relationship when it comes to Wayne, but it has to do with blood being thicker than water and older age being wiser than younger age. And it has to do with trout fishing.

We were looking for a brook, brook trout and beaver ponds today in a remote valley—one of hundreds in Vermont, where the farms are tucked up under green mountain ridges and every turn of the dirt road holds a new angle of view. Beyond the farms, there are higher valleys, woods, brooks and eastern brook trout. And, above the valleys, those beautiful green mountains.

Wayne remembered similar brook trout outings with his brothers in upstate New York—and the failed attempts by his father to stock their farm pond with brook trout. Smallmouth bass, he told me, proved the winning choice. I don't think I saw a brook trout until I turned seventeen and spent my first summer working in the White Mountains of New Hampshire, where, gratefully, to this day, brook trout populate backcountry streams.

Eastern brook trout—*Salvelinus fontinalis*, a char—has disappeared from large parts of its ancestral range due to urbanization, pollution and warming water. We've lost habitat in Vermont too, but brook trout populations in Vermont appear to be holding their own in large swaths of the state. A 2017 Vermont Fish and Wildlife study comparing brook trout population estimates from the 1950s to brook trout population estimates in the 2000s, looking at the same 150 sites on 138 streams, shows brook trout holding up well, with comparable numbers of yearling trout between the decades. A 300 percent increase in the numbers of young-of-the-year fish between the 2000s and the 1950s is likely due to improvements in water quality and habitat, made beginning in the 1970s. The changes may also reflect changes in stocking practices. That's reassuring for anglers looking to catch wild brook trout. Vermont's general regulation allows the harvest of up to twelve brook trout daily. That's a contentiously high number, if you ask a Trout Unlimited member what they want. But robust wild populations, low fishing pressure and the large stock of streams argues against reducing bag limits. Other factors come into play, such as the high number of trout anglers now releasing all the fish they catch and the mandate to manage for a wide band of values and attitudes among fishers in Vermont. We weren't planning on bringing any fish home. We just wanted a look at these little jewels. It goes without saying, though, that pan-fried wild trout taste good too.

There is a bowl-like cirque valley under Sterling Mountain in Morrisville, north of Stowe on Route 100. I remember lots of water in those ponds twenty years ago, with thirteen-inch brook. Back then, the beaver had plenty of water to play with and lots of terrain waiting to be dammed. But times change and the typical run of a good beaver pond is four to five years, not twenty, so I wasn't sure what we'd find.

At the end of Beaver Meadow Road in Morrisville, there is an access point—a small dirt parking lot—to the Morrisville Town Forest, which has trails for hiking. These connect to a web of informal single-track

Wild brook trout, typical of those living throughout Vermont's upland watersheds, caught and released at a small stream and beaver flowage in Morrisville. *Photo by author.*

biking trails. Beaver Meadow Trail and the Whiteface Mountain Trail leave from that place. Just over the embankment of the parking area is Mud Brook—not muddy—with plenty of brook trout.

We caught and released a dozen bright brook trout in the six-inch range. With absolutely no casting room, catching these fish was by dangling. Swinging a size-16 Adams over a pool and dabbing it about where the water was deepest, moving the fastest—or sinking a fly close to banks that provided cover. A quick swirl at the fly and for a few moments the fish was on—and then usually off again. This was a stream that during the drought, absent the beaver ponds above, would likely have been bone dry. These fish owed their existence to beaver. A seven-foot single-weight bamboo rod would be perfect here.

So much of natural life in North America depended on the industry of beaver. As master dam builders, they shaped the North American landscape, making what would without them be withered and arid in the West and Midwest verdant and wet. Beavers are master plumbers whose ponds capture sediments, charge and recharge groundwater, prevent flooding and provide habitat. They move through eastern forests like miners, leaving their old ponds eventually to the grassland meadows that followed. These gave indigenous people of the Woodland period their meadows for corn, and later they fed colonists' animals and grew their grain. All along the continuum of the life and death of a beaver pond, beavers supported entire natural communities, birds, mammals, insects, amphibians and native plants. Beavers are landscape shapeshifters.

During this fishing summer, beavers have been a constant companion of mine. There have been few days on the water when beavers were not present, to wake up with a tail slap, to bemuse with an underwater roll or to entertain while they went about their business cutting down trees, stripping and eating the cambium and building their beaver empires.

For an entirely enjoyable and recent treatise on the beaver and the role beavers have played in molding this continent, see Ben Goldfarb's book *Eager: The Surprising, Secret Life of Beavers and Why They Matter* (Chelsea Green, 2018). For context, the beaver was extirpated from Vermont by the early 1800s. They are back—and back with a vengeance.

Here are a few remarkable facts that Ben recounts, to whet your beaver reading and exploring appetite:

- Beaver numbers have been estimated at between 60 million and 400 million before European colonists arrived and trapping began.
- There were some 250 million beaver dams before beavers were trapped to "within a whisker of extinction."
- By the end of the eighteenth century, Massachusetts, Connecticut and Vermont were free of beavers.
- Landscapes were so dramatically unraveled with the beaver's demise that that period can be measured in deposits of organic matter (nutrients) in ocean sediments.
- Studies in Quebec show that small streams, on average, had 10.6 beaver dams per kilometer.
- In Wyoming, that number's been estimated at 52 dams per kilometer.
- In Quebec alone, estimates of 3.2 million cubic meters of sediment storage are thanks to beaver dams.

And the list of beaver delights goes on. When we imagine the streams of pre-European settlement—northern streams prior to the 1600s, before the arrival of the Puritans at Plymouth, when the beaver still ruled—we may have to adjust our thinking from free-flowing water to streams as terraced terrain, made up of rice paddy–like beaver ponds, boggy wetlands, grassy meadows and everything in between. In Goldfarb's words, "Every tertiary and secondary stream had its beaver dams." It must have been a sight, and a puzzle to navigate.

By midafternoon, after a few hours of stream tramping, we hoofed up into the beaver meadows in the cirque valley above, about a three-mile walk. We made it to the first of them, but these were absent much water (entirely predictable, given the dry summer and the old age of these wetlands). After six miles of up and down, we were ready for a cold beer back in Waterbury, the craft brew mecca of central Vermont, and some food to recharge our batteries. So, we never did catch a beaver-pond trout, technically speaking, but we did catch up on the news, on the prospects of retirement, on the gains of grandchildren and on the benefits of being in better shape. In spite of our personal divided politics, we do share the hope of getting back up to beaver pond country someday, using Google Maps and satellite view to find our way.

Chapter 26

GROWING FISH

Thursday, August 9, 2018

If you live in Vermont and fish, or are a fly fisher on vacation, and you get a chance to visit a state fish culture station, take a look. I did. Tom Chairvolotti, fish production supervisor at Vermont Fish and Wildlife, offered to take me through the Ed Weed Fish Culture Station on the west shore of Grand Isle in Lake Champlain, less than a mile from the ferry docks to New York. I wanted to see how salmon, walleye and lake trout are grown in Vermont. We didn't talk about managing fish in the lake—Tom was clear up front that managing Lake Champlain fisheries is the job of fisheries biologists in the field. He's in the business of growing fish and stocking them.

Water quality is really the key to success. Tom began with a description of Ed Weed's water sources. They collect it from two lines running out into the lake. A 3,400-foot-long, 180-foot-deep line collects forty-degree water, and a second, much shorter line in 20 feet of water collects warmer water. This is blended and heated if necessary to bring it up to the temperature required to hatch eggs—generally around fifty degrees. The water is treated to remove nitrogen gas, hit with UV light to kill off bacteria and viruses and then oxygenated. Controlling water temperature has a lot to do with how fast or how slow they want things to go.

We started on walleye. They're early spring breeders. Shortly after ice-out, with water temperatures between thirty-eight and forty-four degrees, biologists capture about twenty-five females from one of three rivers—the

Winooski, the Poultney or the Missisquoi. The Lamoille has a strong enough natural spawning population that it doesn't need inputs of hatchery-raised fish. The females, or hens, are brought to the hatchery and stripped of about 3 million eggs. Walleye eggs stick like chewing gum to everything. So they mix them with a clay compound called fuller's earth, which makes them slippery enough to move into jars for seventeen days of incubation. Once the eggs hatch into sac fry, biologists use two different methods to raise them. Half are fed for about thirty-five days with a dry feed system (fish meal). That's the newer, more intensive approach (walleye are tricky). These stay in the hatchery until release back into the river of origin. The other half are fed for five days on microscopic brine shrimp, about forty to fifty shrimp per drop of water, and then placed in rearing ponds operated by the all-volunteer Lake Champlain Walleye Association, a nonprofit group that partners with Vermont Fish and Wildlife to rebuild and maintain the stocks of walleye in Lake Champlain. The association's fish grow in ponds on various members' properties for about thirty-five to forty days before release. At the time of release back into the mouths of the river they came from, they measure two inches in length.

Landlocked salmon, on the other hand, deliver their own eggs to the hatchery. Salmon imprint on the waters of their birthplace, Tom said—Ed Weed Fish Culture Station in this case. They begin showing up around mid-August, entering a creek and a fish trap close to shore. Staff start stripping salmon eggs in mid-October and can modify water temperatures for the early birds and late arrivals to get them onto the same growth track. By early November, they'll have all the salmon eggs they need. Salmon eggs, about seven thousand per incubation tray, will spend fifty days incubating in fifty-degree water (there are sixteen trays per stack and nine stacks, so the hatchery can raise 1 million salmon if it needs to). At hatching, the yolk-sac fry salmon are transferred into circular tanks in a room next to the incubation area. The round tanks are self-cleaning, each with a biofilter that converts ammonia to nitrite and then nitrate. Once again, oxygen is added, and the water passes through UV light to kill bacteria and viruses. The circular rearing tanks are fitted out with bio-mats that mimic gravel redds. Within a day or two, almost all of the sac fry are hiding under them.

Water temperatures drop through winter, and feeding slows down. There's little growth in winter, Tom said, with water temperatures down around forty degrees. In fact, they have to heat the water in winter to keep it there. By early May, the salmon smolts are 3.5 inches in length; that's about one hundred fish to the pound.

Before leaving the hatchery, all the fish they raise, except brown trout, are fin clipped with a pattern that can identify the year class. Tom told me that a typical salmon won't live in the lake more than five years. They grow fast.

I, too, had to leave the hatchery with my virtual fin clipped. I realized about ten miles down the road that what I had really wanted to learn was the process they use to raise lake trout for Lake Champlain. One of the great unsolved fisheries mysteries in Champlain is why lake trout are not reproducing viably in the lake itself. Is it a problem of fish culture? Of genetics? Of predation? Of habitat? Of available food? Of water chemistry? To date, no one really knows.

Chapter 27

THE WHITE RIVER, WEST BRANCH

Tuesday, August 14, 2018

Most conversations today about river conservation in Vermont come back to Hurricane Irene in one way or another. You'll recall that by the time Irene hit Vermont in August 2011, it had been downgraded to a tropical storm, a very slow-moving one that carried a massive load of moisture from the subtropical Atlantic to the northern New England highlands. An average of six inches of rain fell on the Green Mountains, and some places got as much as eleven inches. The rain was steady and lasted for hours. By about two o'clock in the afternoon, thin mountain soils had become saturated, and surface flows up and down the Green Mountain chain had grown into flash floods, overwhelming hundreds of culverts and taking out miles of roadway, bridges and other infrastructure statewide. Village centers were submerged from Brattleboro and Wilmington to Waterbury and Hardwick. In the central Vermont town of Rochester, hemmed in by the spine of the Green Mountains to the west and the Northfield Range to the east, roadways gouged out by the rivers cut townspeople off from the outside world. Images of National Guard helicopters landing potable water and food on the Rochester Green made national news and are an enduring piece of Irene history.

But it's what happened after the flood that most affected in-stream and riverside habitat around the state. In Rochester, extensive gravel mining to rebuild Route 73, wood excavation, riprapping, grading and straightening modified (de-natured) miles of river. Vermont Fish and Wildlife conducted a post-Irene assessment study. Statewide, some eighty miles of major waterways were lobotomized in a similar fashion—straightened and made neat to the edge of death.

Governor Shumlin didn't waste any time fixing blown-out roads and washed-out culverts, but he didn't pay much attention to the rivers, at least at first. It's understandable, given the devastation to roads, homes and downtowns—the millions of dollars in property damage and the loss of lives—to want to flush water fast through villages and repair critical roadways. We're wedded to the automobile and thoroughly dependent on our road system. Still, a pause, a careful consideration of river ecosystems and human economics together—a conversation between the road builders and the river managers—was long overdue and could have yielded a much better outcome for both. An opportunity to make right by rivers was lost. Vermont Fish and Wildlife estimated that the recovery of the most heavily damaged seventy-five miles, their native fisheries and natural ecosystems, if left to their own devices, would be measured in decades, not years. On the positive side, river repair began almost immediately, and it's yielding some new, needed partnerships.

A few weeks back, I visited the West Branch of the White River in Rochester with Greg Russ, project manager for the White River Partnership, and its engineer intern, Christian Pelletier. We were there to see the new riffles, pools and logjams at a part of the West Fork of the White that had been riprapped, stripped of wood, flattened, gravel-mined and bulldozed post-Irene. (This section is best accessed from the U.S. Forest Service's CC camp parking area, about five miles up from the junction of Route 100 and Route 73.)

Standing together in that piece of repaired river was tranquil. August crickets blended with the soft rush of water moving over gravel. Looking upstream, we could see a hint of past violence in the tumble and jumble of the massive logjams. Water hadn't moved them there—it could have, but not in this case. In fact, the logjams were the central piece of a long-term restoration plan.

The hills that feed the West Branch are steep-sided, including the peaks, high cirque valleys and cliff faces around Brandon Gap. (Side notes: There's a peregrine nesting site on the cliff face of Mount Horrid, and the Long Trail crosses there.) Runoff from the brooks that feed the West Branch was torrential during Irene. Water quickly overwhelmed culverts and bridge abutments. Large swaths of Route 73 were washed away. Irene

White River Partnership project manager Greg Russ, *left*, and engineer/Americorps worker Christian Pelletier monitor habitat improvement work on the West Branch of the White River in Rochester, Vermont. *Photo by author.*

brought down thousands of trees and moved tonnages in rock. That was seven years ago. Roads and bridges are back now, and the entire event is fading from public memory. But these logjams are a reminder of something else entirely. In 2015, 450 sixty-foot-long Norway spruce trunks with root balls attached were cut on forest service land and brought here by truck. Excavators anchored them to the banks along the river according to a plan. Six private landowners and the Green Mountain National Forest worked with the White River Partnership, the State of Vermont and private groups like Trout Unlimited to remake this section of river. The aim was to deepen the river's channels, scour new pools and create cover and shade for fish and other aquatic animals—to mess things up in a good way. In 2016, another five private landowners got involved downstream, and another section of river was remade.

Fundamentally, Greg said, we had to learn to do this work ourselves. The U.S. Forest Service is just such an expert. Forest service specialist Bob Gubernick's experience was large wood restoration projects in the Pacific Northwest and Alaska, where he'd worked for years repairing damaged salmon streams. The West Branch work was more nuanced. The channel of the straightened and graded river had to be reconstructed. Bob designed and oversaw the first phase of the project, spending several weeks in Rochester, mapping out the new river, its twists and pools, installing the jams, overseeing the excavation work and then teaching logjam planning and installation to the local team. Phase II, with consulting help from Gubernick, was managed by the local team entirely, incorporating another 150 logs. In all, several miles of damaged river got a much-needed makeover.

A more recent Phase III did something novel but obviously beneficial when you consider the natural history of rivers and adjacent riparian zones. By linking a new pond—dug at groundwater level in the riparian zone—to a rerouted Brandon Brook (Brandon Brook has presented a challenge, adding warm, sediment-laden water into the system), and then linking the pond to the river, Phase III added hydraulic complexity, opening the door to the possibilities of expanding resilience and diversity. Excavators also built a type of speed bump in the river channel so that floodwaters would back up, pool and overflow into wetlands that had been cut off by channelization and artificial berms along the boundaries. Up and down this section of river, the project created alternative channels to existing wetland habitats on both sides. The river can move now, rediscover itself, roam and overflow into the neighboring floodplain forests. It can calm down.

Considering the violence of rivers, increasing due to climate change, how should managers respond to an increased frequency of major storms in the future? Working with nature is emerging as the preferred route. John Teal, a pioneer in salt marsh restoration, described the work of restoration ecologists as providing the minimal and essential foundations for restoration and leaving the rest to Mother Nature. The logjams I came to see, the placement of stones in a channel, the reshaping of the channel—these are foundational. They provide for future natural processes to do their work—by the movement of water; the colonization by beavers, fish and bugs; the freeze and thaw of ice; the holding power of roots; and the cooling effects of shade. It doesn't take long for new life to take hold given the opportunity. Within a few days of building the log structures, Greg told me, fish were occupying the pools behind them.

From a fisheries standpoint, what was most surprising to Greg Russ was that after the logjams went in, it was brook trout's turn to show up at the party—surprisingly large brook trout. This had been wild rainbow trout water, exclusively, since monitoring began by the forest service in the 1980s. The jams seemed to provide an entrée for brook trout, surely common in the tributaries.

Why brook trout suddenly appeared here is subject to speculation, but the jump in trout density is not. Monitoring has shown numbers "through the roof," according to Greg. A virtual desert is now blooming with fish, to use a mixed metaphor. Greg's gone down with mask and snorkel to see for himself, an exercise that the White River Partnership is repeating in September with groups of schoolchildren from the area, snorkeling the river in search of macroinvertebrates, including the invasive rusty crayfish, as well as fish and other vertebrates.

Just downstream from the tree trunk junkyard and its developing trout pools, we took a look at another project the White River Partnership is managing. It's a bridge replacement on Wing Brook (an excellent cold-water tributary of the West Branch), the last of three culverts blocking fish passage to be removed and reengineered on the brook. This one involves replacing a sixty-foot culvert "tunnel," which had an eleven-foot peak width, with a twenty-two-foot-wide bottomless arch with a reengineered natural stream channel design. The eight-foot-tall bridge abutments are well out of the bank-full channel, so the cost in concrete is much lower than it might have been. The old culvert was perched several feet above the streambed. Restoration involved building in a 4 percent grade connecting the old drop pool with upstream waters. They built a system of seven stone weirs and large rock footers, Christian explained, each dropping the brook by about seven inches. The results will be quite spectacular for brook trout, brown trout and rainbows looking to spawn or needing an accessible cold-water refuge to survive the increasing frequency of drought and high-intensity storms. The bridge's price tag, at a mere $260,000, seems like a very good deal, all things considered.

Culverts are surprisingly complex engineering challenges, and most, from a wildlife-passage standpoint, are failing in Vermont. Christian, who will soon graduate with a master's degree in environmental policy from the Vermont Law School, assessed nearly 200 culverts in the White River watershed this summer. Almost all, he told me, were perched, too shallow and undersized. The Vermont Fish and Wildlife Department assessed 1,500 culverts statewide and found that more than 40 percent provided no aquatic-organism passage at all, and a mere 5 percent provided full passage to juvenile and adult trout (perched or shallow culverts prevent the passage of spring salamanders, wood turtle, mink, native fish—including suckers—and many other aquatic organisms).

Pouring footings outside of the bank full stage for a new bridge over Wing Brook, a tributary of the West Branch of the White River, to improve fish passage up and downstream. The project replaced a perched culvert with a natural streambed. *Photo by author.*

Mary Russ, executive director of the White River Partnership, explained that before Irene, the public normally only associated culverts with functional roadways. Irene provided an opportunity to associate functional roadways with culvert designs, in certain places, that can handle increased storm flows and benefit fish and wildlife too. That gives culverts a kind of connecting status between ecosystem health and the health, safety and welfare of human communities. Partly thanks to Irene—and due to an increasing understanding of the potential effects of climate change on community safety (storm frequency and intensity; average temperature increases; drought and growing forest-fire threats; water supply and quality; dramatic drops in insect population diversity and density due to warmer temperatures; changes to forest species composition; threats to the maple syrup industry, cold-water fisheries, moose populations and the health of the skiing industry; growth of winter tick populations, resultant Lyme disease and other diseases associated with warmer winters; and the list goes on and on and on)—inroads are being made and new partnerships forged.

There's greater public buy-in and an understanding that healthy rivers—rivers well connected to floodplains and tributaries and road systems that are designed with both community safety and river health in mind—can make our region more resilient in the face of future natural disasters. Working in partnership is the way to go. For example, Mary said, the White River Partnership is cooperating with the Vermont Agency of Transportation's road criticality pilot program by doing stream culvert assessments. They're also designing in partnership with other groups, including the Vermont Fish and Wildlife Department, a two-day Rivers and Roads Training Program for road agents and other transportation professional contractors. The workshop incorporates electrofishing, flume-table river modeling and field trips.

Vermonters have a keen appreciation for the environment. Here, it's not hard to see that the roads and rivers go together, that they have from the time of the first humans—small bands of hunters ten thousand years ago. Old indigenous hunting and migratory pathways became the traces that connected colonial outposts and trading centers. These were widened, hardened and paved over time. In mountainous Vermont, our paths followed the valleys and mirrored the rivers; even when they go up over gaps, they follow the tributaries beyond their sources. Cross-disciplinary, cross-bureaucratic, multiagency approaches to river corridor management are becoming the rule, not the exception.

Chapter 28

LAKE WILLOUGHBY

Saturday, August 16, 2018

A few days ago, I traveled north in search of lake trout. I had cajoled an expert to help. Lenny Gerardi—a wiry, fit guy who still hikes twenty-two-mile days at the age of sixty-five—was the state's district fisheries biologist in the Northeast Kingdom (NEK) for much of his career. He also served as division chief and, in various role reversals, as a fish tech (after serving as chief). Now retired, he still knows lake trout as well as any. And he has a motorboat.

I met Lenny at 8:00 a.m. just off I-91 Exit 23, left a car at the White Market in Lyndonville and soon we were heading north. I always feel when I go north of Route 2 that I've entered another country, that I'm traveling through the home of a reticent person who might not want me there, or might. That's part of the NEK's appeal—the extension of an arm's length invitation. Novelist Howard Frank Mosher (*Where the Rivers Flow North*, *Disappearances* and many other novels about life in the NEK) spent much of his career trying to capture the joy and despair of rural life here—the closeness to nature, to hunting and fishing, to whiskey running, to poverty and isolation, to going to war—and capturing the ironies of being extolled, mythologized and ignored all at the same time. He wrote about locals' love of solitude, rural racism and the need for government help that was rarely extended. Writer Annie Proulx (*The Shipping News*, *Heart Songs* and many others) made the people of the Northeast Kingdom subjects of her early tragicomic short stories—the urban escapees with money, up close and personal with the rural people trapped and dreaming of escape with none. Poet and playwright David Budbill (*Judevine*) never got tired of listening to the cadences of an isolated and disappearing Vermont dialect, like a threatened subspecies of Old English, spoken by longtime residents, and he wove them into his poems and plays. Nor did the filmmaker Jay Craven, who made Mosher's stories his movies. I've always thought each was trying to pierce through a cultural barrier as an act of love. I think they came as close as any.

We were headed to Lake Willoughby. At more than three hundred feet deep, Willoughby is one of the deepest and most beautiful lakes in the NEK. Locals around here affectionately refer to it as the Lake Lucerne of America. The steep sides of sentinel mountains Pisgah and Hor mark the narrow southern end. As much as the profile of Camel's Hump, far to the south, has come to symbolize the heart of the Green Mountains, I think of the dramatic gap between Pisgah and Hor—visible as far south and east as Mount Washington in the White Mountains—as the gateway to the northerly reaches of the NEK.

Soon we were backing down the ramp at the public put-in. There was a state employee there, checking props and hulls for exotic plants. We passed muster. Lenny's got a hefty Starcraft aluminum boat he bought from a retired warden (he then sold his other boat to a different retired warden). The Starcraft has a V hull, a pair of downriggers, an old Evinrude 88 outboard engine and a small trolling motor. In lake trout fishing, you troll very slowly, using perhaps ten-pound tippet and a drag that's set loose but not so loose as to free spool. All in all, we had a good setup for this lake, and that upped our chances. It was midweek, and there were almost no other boating anglers about. We were glad to be there, fully aware that catching fish would be a challenge. But then again, Lenny—with his years of gillnetting, electroshocking, measuring and tagging—had insider knowledge. The only other fishermen, a jolly married couple coming off the water, smiled and gave us their dim prognosis. They had no idea of modest Lenny's fishing pedigree.

Deep northern lakes, Lenny explained, are deep enough to maintain a thermocline through the hot months of summer. At eighty or ninety feet, a lake's water temperatures remain stratified. Shallower lakes by midsummer have thoroughly mixed warm and cold water and have achieved an even— and warmer—temperature throughout. While surface temperatures on Willoughby hover around seventy-two degrees (too warm for lake trout), bottom temperatures stick close to the high forties. Lake trout go deep in summer, Lenny said, and feeding slows. Fishing can be challenging.

Out on the water, Lenny set the downriggers at forty and sixty feet, and we began our slow trawls south with the wind behind us, the sun coming in and out of the clouds. For someone used to wading rivers and casting flies, this kind of fishing can feel dauntingly overly focused on technology. A fish finder and downriggers—one electric and one hand-cranked, in Lenny's case—take some of the guesswork out, but there's still a lot of guesswork. It's a big lake, and the fish are far from evenly distributed. So the wind, the points of land, the underwater reefs—these become essential knowledge. I could do this in my rowing canoe with lead line and a Gray Ghost at the terminal end and call it fly fishing, but without eyes on the bottom and the shadows of fish, I'm disadvantaged, which is amplified by my fear of technology and my general paranoia when it comes to being out in a small canoe on a large lake.

In a motorboat, you can drink coffee, fish, converse, eat a sandwich and adjust a line, all the while sitting on a cushioned seat on a stable platform with a live fish well between you and the water. What's not to love? Throw in a casting platform for a change of pace and actually catching fish becomes a bonus—a giant one. Comfort can be a psychological challenge too, but when in Rome, get comfortable. Peel me a grape.

We watched the fish finder. Schools of rainbow smelt look like dark clouds in a fish finder. We passed through them. They didn't pay attention. And then occasionally, we saw these large fishes at both levels that passed through as sickle-shaped and greenish-orange things on the depth finder. These ignored our lures. Most of the fish marking on the finder were close to the surface. Yellow perch? Rock bass (a recent immigrant)? Something else? There are a few other interesting species on the lake, Lenny said—round whitefish, for example, cousin to the white fish found in rivers. Willoughby is the only lake in Vermont that has them. Lingcod, too—holdovers from the lake's saltwater embayment era—are caught mostly through the ice and are bottom dwellers otherwise in summer. They're supposedly very good to eat, but in earlier days they were thought of as "trash" fish, an expression that we hope will soon fall by the wayside. And, of course, there's landlocked Atlantic salmon. The state stocks 7.5-inch smolts, clipping an adipose fin on each fish it stocks. I think the lake trout and salmon may come from the nearby Bald Hill Fish Culture Station, but I'm not sure. Rock bass showed up in the lake in the 1980s, likely through a clandestine introduction—"an enthusiast having his day," Lenny said.

At first, Lenny said, beginning with the work of the U.S. Fish Commission in the 1870s, it was biologists moving fish around. During those early years, the federal government built an enormous infrastructure for fish and fish-egg distribution, including those special railcars designed to move live eggs and fish thousands of miles, complete with ice to cool water, oxygenators and sleeping quarters for the staff who were on hand to keep fish well cared for.

Lake trout introductions in Vermont began sometime around the end of the nineteenth century or the turn of the twentieth, close to the time the original stocks began to disappear in places like the Averill Lakes. But going much farther back in time, how did lake trout find their way back into the upland lakes and ponds of landlocked northern Vermont after the glaciers receded? That's a question that interested Lenny.

Lake trout could have returned via one of up to four possible refugia, each connected to the waterways of the NEK in some way, Lenny said. From an Atlantic refuge, the brackish estuaries of the Atlantic coast, they could have come up through enormous glacial lakes—Lakes Hitchcock and Hancock in the Connecticut Valley. The Mississippian refugium connected the Gulf of Mexico to the Great Lakes. For a time, the Great Lakes were merged into one enormous lake. At some point, the moraine separating Lake Champlain would have given way, a cataclysmic release, and lake trout could have moved into a Lake Champlain that at various times probably extended up the Missisquoi River and possibly into current-day Lake Memphremagog. Or lake trout could have come down from the St. Lawrence River. Salmon came down the St. Francis into Memphremagog and into the Clyde River, before dams on the St. Francis at Sherbrooke, Quebec, cut them off. A northern refuge, the Beringia (Bering Sea today), would have provided possible passage from the west and north, and the Nahanian refugium—roughly the Fraser River drainage—could have linked northern Vermont to a western population.

You can't answer the question of how fish got here by looking at the landscape we have today, Lenny said. It helps to reimagine the landscape of northern Vermont as a water world covered by watery connections that no longer exist today, a vast network of lakes joined by rivers joined to salt bays and ocean.

Lake trout were here when people got here, Lenny said. The Abenakis fished for trout and salmon with weirs on rivers like the St. Francis. They show up in Zadock Thompson's *History of Vermont, Natural, Civil and Statistical* in 1853, although the naming conventions were different. Back in the early days of the Vermont Fish and Game Commission, around 1865, every town had a fish warden whose duty was to report on the status of fishes. Lake trout were in the common mix.

Maidstone Lake, only a few miles from the Upper Connecticut River, had a population of lake trout in the 1970s that were darker than ordinary lakers and lacking in spots. Locals called them lunge. Could these be a remnant population of golden trout, *Salvelinus alpinus oquassa*, a landlocked subspecies of Arctic char thought to have been extirpated from Vermont around the turn of the twentieth century? For a while, Lenny tried to untangle the tantalizing question at Maidstone Lake: Were these lakers, Arctic char or some genetic combination of both?

Initially, Lenny relied on morphological clues. Lake trout, *Salvelinus namaycush*, and Arctic char, *Salvelinus alpinus*, differ in the number of projections they have in the pyloric caeca, an organ situated between a fish's stomach and intestine that increases the surface area of the gut and aids in digestion. Arctic char projections are measurably fewer. So Lenny looked at stomachs. When that was inconclusive, he moved on to genetics, sampling them in a nonlethal way using gillnets to capture them. The department back then had already started fin clipping all the fish. From the start, Lenny could tell a wild fish from a hatchery-raised fish. Lake trout can live thirty-five to fifty years (the state record in Vermont is a thirty-one-year-old, 34.5-pound lake trout, taken from Willoughby near Crescent Beach), so the potential for many age classes occurring together was very high—wild reproducing and stocked lake trout both.

Maidstone's mystery fish turned out to be a normal lake trout with some morphological variation. As Lenny's sampling moved east to west, he did find some genetic variation between lakes that correlated to the influences of the various refugia on these lake trout populations. That was an interesting finding. While lake trout introductions tended to mask those ancestral connections, they could still be detected.

We caught a lake trout and released a lake trout. If you have to measure a lake trout to see if it's legal size—eighteen inches at Willoughby—you might as well save the fish the trouble of measuring, Lenny said, on the quick release. Was this trout wild or a hatchery fish? Lake trout do spawn at Willoughby, Lenny replied, but no one has really nailed down a spawning location yet. Lake trout like a cobble bottom. They don't build redds like brown trout, brook trout or rainbow trout. Instead, the eggs, not sticky, fall down into the loose cobbles. They have identified spawning sites at Lake Seymour; Lenny used scuba equipment to find them. And they do have a spawning location marked at Crystal Lake. Seymour has managed good lake trout spawning even with the arrival of smallmouth bass there. Smallmouth bass tend to cluster around inshore areas when lake trout fry emerge, feasting on them. The vibrant population of lake trout at Caspian Lake spawn on top of rocky stacks found here and there. Finding those spawning sites was a mystery until, diving to sixty feet one day, Lenny found eggs on the stacks. Lake trout typically spawn at night. Halloween in fifty-degree water is a reliable spawning date there. Rocky, windswept shoals; stacks sixty feet down; nighttime…spooky.

Late in the afternoon, turning, we caught a stocker salmon with its telltale missing adipose fin. A handsome fellow that we did not keep.

On our way back to shore, I asked Lenny what he thought had changed the most in fisheries management in Vermont during his near forty-year tenure. He thought about it and then said something surprising, noting that the sensitivity to angler interests and the amount of public involvement has gone through a sea change. There is always the tension between science-based policy, politics and public attitudes. But today, he said, we make it a matter of policy to involve the public. There's way more cross-discipline collaboration going on to problem-solve. He gave the example of a long, simmering debate going back to the mid-'60s between summer camp owners on Willoughby and ice fishermen. Camp owners felt that ice fishing would deplete lake trout. Ice fishermen were adamant about preserving their rights to fish through the ice. The divide seemed unresolvable. Vermont Fish and Wildlife broke the impasse by creating a diverse working group, eight to ten people who represented all views. The group was provided with all the information the department had accumulated, including public surveys and scientific studies. It instructed the group to come up with a regulations package that they all could agree on. And the group did.

The group brought its plan to the Fish and Wildlife Board, and with minor changes, it got its approval, Lenny said. Every three years, Vermont Fish and Wildlife assessed the plan and, based on data, has occasionally made changes. Plans need to be flexible. Not everything works the way you hope it will. You evaluate and adjust. There was interest in creating trophy trout options, for example. We felt these might work at Little Averill Lake and Seymour, Lenny said, and we tried that (with limited success). In the angling community, there is always tension between the keep-the-regulations-simple group and the manage-each-waterbody-individually group. Learning to listen to people has been a big thread for the department, he said.

What else? I asked. Looking at systems more holistically, he replied. One dimension of that is learning to balance what is good for ecosystems with what anglers want. Too often, they want every fish everywhere. The 1980s, for example, saw a huge uptick in public interest in bass fishing. We've had to adapt our plans to that strong and growing interest, he said. Another dimension of taking a holistic view is finding that they can be on the same page with traditional adversaries—for example, when it comes to managing floodplains and fish passage. Richard Kirn and Cosmo Bates developed together guidelines for fish passage. They brought together the people from all sides who deal daily with the issues of floodplain management but from different angles of view. Transportation was involved from the get-go. Instead of years of wrangling, ultimately—thanks to a multidisciplinary approach—they found common ground and common ownership of both the problems and the solutions.

Of course, many improvements have been made to research technology over the years, Lenny added. Microelectronics for fish tracking, for instance. Crowdsourcing. Use of the Internet. The generation of huge data sets. That's been big.

Listening to Lenny, it seems they've learned more in the past ten years than in the previous fifty, thanks to technology. But that collaboration, working in partnership, is one of the oldest, lowest-tech, most powerful tools of all. The challenges to fisheries mount, yet collaborative tools for managing an unknown future are rising to the occasion. People are changing. But managing fish and wildlife, with all this new technology wiring brains together, is still a labor of love.

Chapter 29

THE LEICESTER RIVER

Tuesday, September 11, 2018

Making tentative gestures toward fishing more on the western side of the state—particularly within the Otter Creek watershed, which I have, without intention, neglected—I asked a friend, Catlin Fox, what he knew about the Neshobe River. He and his wife, Annie Claghorn, own and run a small organic dairy in Leicester called Taconic End Farm. (Leicester is pronounced "Lester"; leister, incidentally, is also the name for an eight- to twelve-foot-long fishing spear, *nodamawogan* in the Abenaki language.) The Taconic Mountains appear to actually end in their meadows, with the rock ledges, like whales sounding, diving into the earth. The Neshobe River is nearby and is said to have some decent cold-water fishing above the town of Brandon. I got interested. But Catlin told me I should paddle down the Leicester River instead.

The Leicester River is less a river and more a creek. It begins at Lake Dunmore in the Green Mountains to the east and flows west into Otter Creek. Catlin and Annie's farm lies at the confluence of Otter Creek and the Leicester River. Their lower meadows flood almost annually, to the extent that you can't drive a car to the river. There are large pike and sometimes big browns in the shallows of their cornfields.

The Leicester, Catlin told me, has an incredibly productive fishery, with shoals of various warm-water fishes by late summer. (My mind went to northern pike and pickerel, possibly small- and largemouth bass, bluegills, sunfish, perch, black crappie, brown bullhead—who knows? He wasn't sure.) We could float the Leicester in a canoe from Route 7 to Otter Creek. His canoe. So, we made a date for early August. Then life got in the way, and we didn't get out until September 11.

Otter Creek is said to be the longest river in Vermont. I have had a problem accepting that since on the eastern side of the state there is the Connecticut River, which flows from the Atlantic to the Canadian border. Otter Creek, whose headwaters are in the vicinity of Danby in the Valley of Vermont, flows north to the southern reaches of Lake Champlain. How could Otter Creek be longer than the Connecticut River? For the simple reason that the Connecticut isn't, technically speaking, part of Vermont… but come on! New Hampshire may "own" the Connecticut River on paper, but the river's in all other ways a resource that belongs to Vermonters too. Really it "belongs" to no one. The Otter, however, is longer than you might think it is, if measured by its meandering banks. Otter Creek is *Bikogtegw* in the Abenaki language, meaning "crooked river." It squiggles north through wet bottomland farms, floodplain forests and some of the state's largest swamps. Thanks to Otter Creek, with its enormous capacity to absorb floodwaters, many towns west of the mountains were hit less hard in 2011 when Tropical Storm Irene came through (although Brandon on the Neshobe was hit pretty hard) than those of us on the east side.

The Leicester is part of the largest interior wetlands complex in Vermont, which is also, according to the Vermont chapter of the Nature Conservancy, the biggest and most biologically diverse wetland in New England (the Missisquoi wetlands and river delta in the northeastern corner of Vermont rival these in size). Cornwall Swamp Wildlife Management Area is to the north, and Brandon Swamp Wildlife Management Area is to the south. In between lies the Leicester River and its complex of open marshes, flooded forests and low hammocks.

Farmers, more than the rest of us, have to knoweth where they dwell. Reading the seasons and weather and knowing the lives and cultivations of plants and animal husbandry, soil science, compost management and nutrient chemistry—these are their stock in trade. And they also need floodplain and river knowledge since their pastures adjoin them in some cases. Like pen and paper to a writer, these are fundamental parts of the farmer's toolbox. Catlin and Annie have gotten to know their place, including their animals—a remarkably well-managed herd of Jersey cows. But Catlin's curiosity seems to expand ever outward beyond the farm, just about more than anyone I know. He reads vociferously with a deep interest in family history. He has a better-than-working knowledge of the local birds, amphibians, freshwater invertebrates, fish and mammals. He has a geologist's interest in bedrock geology, a botanist's in wild edibles and herbs and an anthropologist's in early peoples, their tools, their language, their food and their nomadic ways. Otter Creek was an important byway, home and summer fishing camp to the Abenakis and their early ancestors. Native American use of Otter Creek dates back to 1000 BC. When we put in that afternoon—down a steep bank off Route 7, through poison ivy and onto a river strewn with deadfalls and beaver dams—I knew we were in for an exciting ride.

Actually, the deadfalls disappear about a quarter mile south of Route 7, and the river corridor broadens into a wide-open emergent wetland. The river meanders through it slowly, covered by a green sheen of duckweed. Out on the edges of the open marsh, low uplands support forests with clusters here and there of standing dead trees. There are no homes other than wood duck homes and no roads but the river road. Great blue herons, common egrets, green herons and a wave of molting female wood ducks accompanied us downstream. We seemed to be driving schools of fish too. While I made halfhearted attempts to cast flies to the fleeing fish, Catlin gave a running commentary on the place, including the birds—an osprey, bald eagle and marsh hawk flew overhead. We passed close enough to a great horned owl, wings spread over a kill, that I believe we could have reached it with a paddle. But what prey? Wood duck, muskrat? An unusual time of day to see an owl. The schools of small fish rippling the surface of the water generally beelined to cover near shore. Instead of catching them, we only disturbed them. Year-one northern pike? Otter Creek is said to be a good northern pike fishery, and pike, along with the uncommon brassy minnow, is listed for lowland rivers like these in the southern Champlain Basin. Marshes are nurseries for all manner of life, and this place felt like an eminently fine fish nursery (and wood duck nursery; I counted eighteen molting wood ducks in one group).

Soon enough, the wetlands narrowed and the river straightened. We pulled up onto what Catlin described as an island, grabbed something to drink and eat and went exploring. The island had a name and a story. It had been home to Abenaki summer fishers and hunters. Potsherds had been found here, and Catlin picked up pieces of gray knapped stone—the remains of an arrow or spearpoint—showed them to me and then replaced them. These might have been parts of an "Otter Creek" projectile point, predating the bow and arrow. (Catlin tells me this information is available in William

A. Ritchie's "New York Projectile Points: A Typology and Nomenclature" in the 1971 *New York State Museum Bulletin* 384.)

Back down on the river, we pulled a few freshwater clams for closer inspection—one of our most diverse little groupings of invertebrate life, bivalves, with seventeen native species in Vermont. There is another bulletin if I'm interested, Catlin told me. And I was.

The end of the float found us, some dozen beaver dams later, at the confluence of Otter Creek. It had been quite an eye opener, a perfect introduction to the pleasures and wonders of fishing in the Otter Creek watershed. Fishing is so often an apt analogy for learning. If I'd had a few small northern pike in my memory palace as a result of traveling down this river, I wouldn't have objected, but we had to pull the canoe up a steep and slippery bank and onto the back corner of one of Catlin and Annie's meadows. "Oh," said Catlin about the rather badly battered canoe, "I'll just leave it here for now." It was getting close to the evening milking, and he had to get moving.

Chapter 30

THE UPPER CONNECTICUT RIVER

Saturday, September 29, 2018

All summer I had been trying to get to the Upper Connecticut River for an outing with Brian Ganley to fish with some of his split-cane bamboo rods. The Upper Connecticut is a favorite destination of his, and it's my old stomping grounds, having spent most of my late teens and twenties living and working summers up there—the last two at the federal salmon hatchery in Milan, not far from the Connecticut River. I've tipped a canoe in the Thirteen Mile Woods and caught large native brook trout at Lyman Falls, all back in the 1970s.

Much has been written about this part of the fishing world. The Upper Connecticut—from North Stratford, New Hampshire, north to the Connecticut Lakes on the Canadian border—has a long and storied trout and salmon fishing history and is a popular destination fishery. Next to Lake Champlain and the Battenkill, it's the biggest and oldest of destination fisheries in Vermont and New Hampshire.

Fortunately, those holding a Vermont fishing license can fish the river up to Beecher Falls at the New Hampshire and Quebec border. The river turns northeast there and enters New Hampshire toward Pittsburg. If you've got a few days, consider purchasing a New Hampshire license. The New Hampshire reaches of the Upper Connecticut and environs—from Fourth Connecticut Lake down to West Stewartstown—offer spring and fall salmon fishing in the lakes and the river sections that connect them, as well as stillwater, fly fishing–only opportunities on remote ponds and miles of wild brook trout waters. Big rainbows, brook trout and browns are caught regularly in the special-regulations waters of the main stem. The most popular reaches for fly anglers are between Second Connecticut Lake and the inlet to First Connecticut Lake, including a three-mile fly fishing–only, catch-and-release section; what's deemed the trophy section between the First Connecticut Lake dam to the inlet to Lake Francis; and the ten miles below Murphy Dam, a tailwater sending cold water into the river all summer. See Christophe Perez's *Eastern Fly Fishing* article "Fly-Fishing Frontier" on the Upper Connecticut for a good overview of the fishing between lakes, with maps and hatch and fly information (streamer imitations of smelt).

There's another reason to purchase a New Hampshire license. At the Upper Connecticut, you're within striking distance of the Upper Ammonoosuc, the Ammonoosuc, the Androscoggin, the Magalloway, Umbagog Lake and the Rapid River, all in all some of the best fishing for large wild brook trout in the Northeast.

But our focus here is the forty-mile stretch between West Stewartstown and North Stratford. At Stewartstown, New Hampshire, and Canaan, Vermont, the Connecticut disgorges out of the woolly Great North Woods and enters into a wider, quieter plain, much like the broad floodplains of the piedmont region farther south. Above Stewartstown, it's rocky, wooded lakes and ponds; dams; large, deep pools and freestone stretches; and boggy beaver streams. Below, it's agricultural land, corn and hay, and a river that meanders. The water is cold and clear. Although farming often leaves banks unstable and eroding, and there are long gravel bars in places out in the middle of the river, floating and wade fishing are excellent throughout. Some farmers have used novel approaches to stabilizing banks here. You might see a row of upright junk cars. During a float on one of the northern sections of this reach, you'll be looking at a big mountain (3,140-foot Monadnock) with a fire tower from about every conceivable angle as the river loops southward.

While these reaches are best floated, and there are on the order of thirty professional drift boat guides willing to take you, there's plenty of good wade fishing throughout. You can float them on your own, although public put-in and take-out options are limited. On prime weekends, you'll be sharing the water with catch-and-keep bait anglers, anglers casting lures and others fly fishing, but fishing pressure is spotty enough that you can usually find some water to yourself. And find the fish, too, especially early and late in the season.

Before leaving for the upper river, I called an old friend for intel. Kenny Hastings has been running a drift boat guide service (Osprey Fishing Adventures) longer than anyone else on the reaches south of Canaan, Vermont. He trailered his boat across the country after eight years of living and working as a guide on Wyoming's big rivers and set up shop on his old homeground, the Upper Connecticut, in 1982. Kenny's told me often that he believes the Upper Connecticut has great potential that has yet to be realized. With a catch-and-release rule, wardens to enforce the regulation and limits on the number of outfitters, the forty miles below Stewartstown and Canaan could grow lots of very large fish again.

As for the fishery this year, he told me that the high water temperatures this summer had been tough but that the fishery survived the summer, thanks in part to bottom releases at Murphy Dam. As for the fishing in the catch-and-release water below Lyman Falls, he said that New Hampshire Fish and Game had put more browns farther downstream (the warmer water end), and that was good. But my assessment of fishing pressure was too optimistic, he told me. All the attention that the Upper Connecticut River gets attracts more than fly anglers. Plenty of bait anglers show up, too, and they are harvesting more fish, often in the catch-and-release water, so the fish don't get much of a chance to grow. And the number of registered guides is getting out of control. New Hampshire Fish and Game needs to do a better job of managing them, he said. And biologists should set limits on the number of permits issued; permits, once granted, should be in perpetuity. Guides can then buy and sell them like mortgages. I hate to say it, he told me, but it's coming to that.

His main point was that the central problem is a lack of money. New Hampshire's "no income tax" policies don't work for the stewardship of fish and game. There just isn't enough money generated by the sale of equipment and licenses, and furthermore, Vermonters, "who are three out of five of the anglers on the river," aren't contributing to the management of the resource. (Ouch! I don't know the particulars, but if true, then we need to find a way to support the improved management of this fishery. It may have more potential than most to become truly world-class. However, the Vermont Fish and Wildlife Department suffers the same fiscal woes and limits that New Hampshire Fish and Game's does. We need to find new ways to finance the restoration and management of nature.) Could this be and should this be, I wonder, a twin-state cooperatively managed fishery? What if both states had a trout stamp program? What if all recreational equipment was taxed, and some of that went to building a truly outstanding destination fishery on the Connecticut? Kenny described arriving back here with no money in 1982. In his first year of guiding, he had two clients. He worked three other jobs to get by, eventually becoming a high school teacher in Colebrook. But in those early years, he told me, he and his wife—coming east from Idaho—would do a two- or three-day float, using a rough camp they'd put together downstream, and they'd have one hundred trout days between them, with several fish in the three-pound range. With different management, he said, we could see that again.

The day Brian Ganley and I fished in late September, we got a reprieve from the cool, wet weather we'd had for weeks. The river was high but clear and cold, and the sun came out. We fished around Lemington and Bloomfield, never making it to the catch-and-release section at Lyman Falls dam in North Stratford. The fish we caught, all rainbows, took small dark nymphs fished above and into pocket water, and small streamers fished into logjam pools.

We parked in farmers' fields that Ganley had used before; at road pull-offs just above the river; and, late in the day, at the little red schoolhouse in Lemington—no longer a school, but Lemington's miniature town hall. The river there takes a few turns, and the pools are large and enticing on those corners. There is a new state access spot on the recently protected 1,100-acre Johnson Farm upstream, with more than six miles of river frontage. The Nature Conservancy, the Vermont Land Trust and Vermont Fish and Wildlife worked together for more than four years to protect that farm and forestland.

Fishing with a bamboo rod, I learned quickly, cleared up a chronic casting problem I'd ignored for years. Used to much stiffer graphite, I was putting a wider loop on the back cast, thanks to more generous and softer bamboo, and that immediately cured hooking up on my own leader knot. I also got to like the feel of bamboo in my hands—the light weight and the aesthetics. The rod performed well with a fish on, a nice working companion.

Ganley ignored his own creations and fished with an old H.L. Leonard he owned though had never used. It had an unusual locking reel seat, and he was having trouble aging the rod because of it. As if it were a requirement to balance out the rod's antique technology, Ganley also brought a drone and camera to take photos for his developing website. He's gearing up to make rods full time. It's strange having a drone floating thirty feet above you, and then fifteen feet behind you and then gone. Disconcerting—but then you focus on casting to a seam where the water flows around the trunk of a half-submerged tree and you forget the drone. Besides, the sun was breaking through, and it felt nice to be out on the river in the North Country again, just before fall really sets in. The climate change experts predict heavier precipitation for our region in fall, winter and spring. I feel that in my heart and bones, so it's nice to feel the sun instead.

Where are you when you're fishing the Upper Connecticut right here, south of Canaan, north of North Stratford? You're close to the headwaters of a river that flows four hundred miles to the Atlantic. If you're on the bank, you're standing on the eastern edge of Vermont; if in the water, then you're in New Hampshire. To the west the hills rise up, and the forest takes over from farmland. That's a cultural boundary, the edge of the Northeast Kingdom (NEK). This eastern side of the NEK is in Essex County, and it's the part of the NEK I know best. My wife was born in St. Johnsbury, and her family on her father's side comes from Glover, in Orleans County, not far from here.

For a regional perspective, if you could sit on that drone and get up one hundred feet, to the west you'd be looking at the hills and valleys of the Nulhegan Basin—brook trout kingdom. The Yellow, Black and East Branches of the Nulhegan come together southwest of us and enter the Connecticut River at North Stratford. One of the most significant invisible boundaries is the one encompassing the twenty-six-thousand-acre Silvio O. Conte National Fish and Wildlife Refuge's Nulhegan Basin Division. Silvio O. Conte was a congressman from Massachusetts with an avid interest in the environment and a particular love for the Connecticut River. He introduced legislation creating the refuge in the 1990s. Conte is a refuge with an unorthodox boundary: the entire eleven-thousand-square-mile watershed of the Connecticut River, which takes in landscape features as diverse as cities, several million people, remote northern hills, bogs and orchards and urban woodlands. The traditional refuge, maybe a waterfowl unit, probably had a fence around it—but not here. While the old refuge was staffed with experts, the new refuge has a few experts and a throng of amateur volunteers. Most of the stewardship work in the coming years will be done by state, nonprofit and federal agencies partnering with those volunteers—citizen conservationists.

For years, the focus in the Nulhegan Basin, and across state lines at Nash Stream, has been repairing fragmented brook trout fisheries. Streams were cut by roads and blocked by dams (including a blighted response to a dam washout on Nash Stream). Poor culvert design, clearcutting, in-stream channel straightening and sedimentation—all the usual surly suspects come into play. This fall, TU had crews in the Nulhegan Basin enhancing habitat on the Yellow Branch. It's epic work that sets in motion ecological changes that can help blunt the impacts of climate change and improve the fishing. Eastern brook trout are a sentinel species because they connect to rare orchids and everything else, including thin-soiled and steep headwaters, particularly susceptible to poor logging practices and torrential rains.

You're still up on the drone. Bordering Conte at the south end is the 22,000-acre West Mountain Wildlife Management Area, owned by the State of Vermont and managed by Vermont Fish and Wildlife. Both refuges were part of a land deal in 1998 whereby 132,000 acres of Champion International paper company lands were sold to the State of Vermont. The state established the West Mountain Wildlife Management Area; the U.S. Fish and Wildlife Service created the Conte refuge's Nulhegan unit; and 84,000 acres were sold to Essex Timber Company with conservation easements, management plan oversight and public access granted (later sold to the Plum Creek Timber Company). The state investment of $4.5 million was a big win for the region, although not everyone living in the NEK thought so at the time. For groups afraid of losing their rights to hunt and fish—to travel by ATV or snowmobile, to trap and to continue to lease a camp on what used to be industrial timber lands (Champion, Diamond International, Weyerhaeuser and so on)—fear of loss is scary, particularly an expansion of state lands, perhaps with purposes sounding alien to hunting and fishing. (And occasionally they are, because some places should not be open to either.)

What worked for decades up here was a vibrant forest-based manufacturing economy where jobs in a pulp mill or sawmill, or as a logger or log truck driver or a furniture maker, were all but guaranteed. Much of that economy has been lost. The paper mills are gone; the number of working loggers (four to five hundred in the state today) and large-scale harvests are down; and furniture plants—Ethan Allen, for example—have all but gone away. (Ethan Allen plants at Island Pond and Beecher Falls are shuttered, although the plant in Orleans is still operating.) The perception that hunting and fishing are threatened is a powerful fear (hunting and fishing are still a means to getting food when money and jobs are scarce), although these public lands do the opposite, by securing and holding public rights for both and creating the possibility of a future economy that can grow in new directions. Still, as industrial large-scale ownerships continue to wane, and non-industrial large-scale ownerships are on the rise, predicting the future gets harder. TIMOs, or Timberland Investment Management Organizations, are on the rise—and what they are, how they will behave and what will happen to the Northern Forest economy from an ecological and economic standpoint are not known. (TIMOs have the ring of tax shelters for rich people, but combined with the sale or donation of development rights that restrict subdivision and require management plans, they could have significant public benefits.)

Up here, the reservation and protection of wild lands and working forestlands is good news for brook trout fly anglers. In the Nulhegan Basin, groups like TU are improving fish passage, adding woody habitat, repairing stream channels, taking out dams, making straightened rivers crooked, changing out perched culverts, reconnecting floodplains and generally restoring and enhancing the places that brook trout and other aquatic life live. These big forest tracts are climate change research labs too.

Whatever your social perspective, newly minted large blocks of protected, publicly owned working forestlands are a rare and special thing in Vermont and New Hampshire—good for the future of fishing and for the future of rural communities.

Chapter 31

LITTLE AVERILL LAKE

Tuesday, October 2, 2018

Big Averill and Little Averill Lakes sit like a pair of blue gumdrops on the Canadian border in Essex County on the eastern side and northern edge of Vermont's Northeast Kingdom (NEK). Little Averill, at 483 acres, is just over half the size of Big Averill. Each is big enough and deep enough (more than one hundred feet) to support robust populations of wild lake trout and other salmonids. Back in the day, the catch included Atlantic salmon, but native landlocked salmon were extirpated around the 1900s. Sport fishing since then has relied on stocked salmon fry and smolts. If you're lucky, you could catch a trophy lake trout. This year, I wanted to see Little Averill again, catch a trophy lake trout and spend a night at Quimby Country, in that order. Quimby's is the oldest continuously operating North Country sport (and family) camp in Vermont, and it's under new ownership.

You can access Little Averill by a small public boat landing on the west side of the lake. There is a smattering of camps there, most concentrated along the entrance road off Route 114. The cottage owners are protective of their fiefdom. They've changed the name of the entry road from Little Averill Road to Jackson Road. There are no signs announcing a public access, only a "Smile, You're on Camera" sign and a "County Sheriff Patrols, Takes Note of Suspicious Vehicles" sign. I suppose that's needed because of suspicious vehicles like mine. The lake is not hard to find; nonetheless, it seems this part of the world is still not sure it wants or even likes "outsiders." (Although, the access is likely by permission of a landowners' association, so we are grateful to the neighbors of the fiefdom.) There is a junction (no signage, but go right) before the access and then the landing itself with its posters alerting you to special rules. (Little Averill has special regulations that limit the taking of lake trout over twenty inches to one a day. Lake Seymour has the same trophy fish regulation.) We are also alerted to the presence of loons on the lake, as well as the rules concerning fishing around loons. Ingested fishing line and sinkers kill more loons than any other cause.

Bundled up in plenty of wool, tech clothing and commercial fishing gear, I launched out into the gray world. Me, the loons and imagined schools of trophy lakers. Absent skill or much lake trout experience, hope and patience are the twin engines of my occasional lake trout fishing ventures. Still, without fishing luck or skill, I was glad to be here—Little Averill's about as pretty as the world gets, even with a cloud covering most of it. When I pushed out to the middle of the lake, let out all the lead line on a drift and began my long trawl to the south, the clouds lifted and rose, like curtains at

Lilly and Gene Devlin in the fall of 2018 at the end of their first year as majority owners of Quimby Country, the oldest "sport fishing" camp in Vermont (now a family resort). *Photo by author.*

the beginning of an opera, to reveal the stage's leafy backdrop—a trio of steep-sided mountains covered by the scarlets, oranges, browns, greens and blues of a foliage going wild at the end of its run. The opera's story line is right out of Queen Scheherazade: the life and death (and three wishes) of a magical golden fish.

For thousands of years, Little and Big Averill Lakes provided a charmed home for the mythical golden trout, *Salvelinus alpinus oquassa*, now extirpated from all of its range in New Hampshire and Vermont but still found in a few lakes in Maine, as well as surviving in lakes in Idaho and other far-flung regions where introductions occurred in the late nineteenth century. Golden trout are landlocked Arctic char. They also go by the common names blueback trout in Maine and Sunapee trout or white trout at Lake Sunapee, New Hampshire. Oquassa is the town in Maine's Rangeley Lakes district where the species (or subspecies—there has been a lot of speculation and disagreement among taxonomists over the years) was first described. (It was a Dr. T.H. Bean in 1887 who lumped them all—blueback, Sunapee and golden trout—into *Salvelinus alpinus oquassa*.)

For a time, an alternate nomenclature recognized the golden/Sunapee trout and blueback trout as two separate subspecies. The celebrated trout taxonomist Robert J. Behnke, in his 2002 book *Trout and Salmon of North America*, agreed with Bean's final nomenclature and listed the golden/Sunapee/blueback trout together as *S. alpinus oquassa*. But earlier in his thinking, Bean had called the golden trout by a golden name: *Salvelinus aureolus oquassa* (as *aurum* in Latin for gold).

In the Quimby scrapbooks that go back to their earliest years in the 1890s, golden trout are referred to as *aureolus*, and much is made of their presence in the lakes. In fact, Quimby's fishing brand image was wrapped up in gold. Lake Sunapee folks took pride in their Sunapee trout cache too. There is a particularly amusing and energetic newspaper exchange between a Lake Sunapee native and George Quimby over who discovered golden trout first. In a letter to the *White River Herald Tribune* in 1926, Ralph Davis wrote in response to claims by Mr. George Quimby (on the provenance of golden trout), "The fish of which Mr. Quimby speaks is described in Jordan and Evermann's 'American Food and Game Fishes' as Sunapee Trout or American Saibling (*Salvelinus aureolus*). It was first discovered, described, and named at Sunapee Lake NH in 1888." George Quimby fired back a letter to the *Tribune*, claiming much earlier knowledge of the so-called golden trout at the Averill Lakes, including a letter from John Wheelock Titcomb (Sharon resident Jon Conner's fish culturist grandfather), who recounted a visit to the Averill Lakes around 1883: "He requested that Mart Noyes send him a specimen and he received one not long after his visit." According to other writers, there were much earlier observations of these fish, going back to the early 1870s at Sunapee and linked to the first introductions of rainbow smelt there. The more pressing question at the time for New Hampshire fish commissioner Colonel Elliot B. Hodge was whether or not these fish were native or planted there. He visited the lake with T.H. Bean in 1890 and laid out his argument that they're indigenous (and not planted European char).

As for the disappearances of Artic Char in the early 1900s, Robert Behnke thought that hybridization with introduced lake trout (also a char) was the culprit. Others say the introductions of Atlantic salmon and rainbow smelt, a forage fish often stocked with salmon and lake trout, took out the remnant char. There are fourteen sites in Maine where *S. oquassa* can be found and caught (the four ponds in the Deboullie Public Reserved Land are your best bet). Behnke noted that there is an established population of *S. alpinus oquassa* in Idaho at Sawtooth Lake. Introductions were also tried in lakes at the headwaters of the Salmon River and in the Snake River below Shoshone Falls.

I hoped to catch a Little Averill Lake trophy lake trout but did not prevail (not for lack of trying). What I was sure was a strike turned out to be a black stick that I did manage to bring to net. Four passes later and ready for a wood fire at Quimby's, I rowed back to the put-in, the wind and rain so strong at that point that on the last swing, I had to row backward to slow the boat down. Instead of a fish, I caught some version of the past.

LILLY AND DEAN, a young couple from the Middlebury area with two young children, are the new majority-interest owners of Quimby Country. They've injected a huge amount of enthusiasm and good ideas up here in this historic and hallowed fishing place. Charles Quimby, the original owner, liked to call Quimby's (originally named the Cold Spring House, then Cold Spring Camp) "the only Maine sporting camp in Vermont," a pretty accurate description in the 1890s but not so accurate today. Quimby Country is a family camp now, with boating and swimming, hiking and great meals in the nineteenth-century lodge setting on Forest Lake—and, yes, fishing. These are changes that actually began back in the 1920s under Charles's daughter, Hortense Quimby.

In the early years, advertising for the Cold Spring Camp was all about the fishing and good health. Fishing meant catching with live bait, eating and perhaps salting and boxing large and aged fish to take home. By 1919, the camp was advertising landlocked salmon, square-tailed trout, the "famous golden aureolus," lake trout, black bass and pickerel. The Canaan hatchery at the time was putting out 1 million fish per year. Claims to the health benefits of the spring began to grow in inverse proportion to the quality of the fishing. "The Cold Spring House," wrote Hortense, "is rapidly gaining a reputation of a health resort....Malaria is unknown in this region." The Cold Spring claimed to cure a long list of ailments, including, "Lithaemia, Dyspepsia, Constipation, Nephritis, Biliousness, renal and hepatic calculi, and all diseases attended by or caused by deficient elimination of waste in the human body."

Early fishing clients came up along the Connecticut River by train to Canaan and then switched tracks and trained on a trunk line to Norton. From there, it was a brief horse-drawn stagecoach ride to Big Averill Lake and then a wood-fired steamboat ride down the lake. Finally, a short wagon ride got them to the lodge on Forest Lake.

The fishing in the early years was incredible. And it stayed good well beyond the turn of the century. Catches during the early 1900s were brook trout up to five pounds, lake trout and Atlantic salmon in the six- to ten-pound range and *S. aureolus*. Vermont Fish and Game commissioner John Wheelock Titcomb began introducing lake trout and salmon to the lakes around 1900. But stocking couldn't make up for overharvesting. Photos from the 1890s and early decades of the twentieth century show men with big catches laid out in the grass before them. Trying to sustain those catches took a lot of Charles Quimby's attention, and it was a losing battle. When Charles died in 1919, Hortense, who'd been trained as a teacher at a normal school (a historical term for teacher-training colleges), was teaching in New Jersey. She rushed home to care for him and, after his death, took over the camp. In many ways, Quimby Country's success into the twenty-first century, and the evolution of modern trout fishing in Vermont, is Hortense's story.

When I got to my cabin, there was a fire going in the woodstove, and my wet clothes were soon hanging on hooks on the back wall. The cottages here form two lines, a front rank and a staggered back rank, all with views to the west of Forest Lake. Quimby lodge is original—with improvements—a turn-of-the-century, well-lit place with a covered porch, windows along the lake side, a sitting room, a fireplace and a dining room with new shiny wood-like vinyl floors and straight-backed chairs. There's a mounted lake trout on the wall. And a moose head.

Cold Spring Camp, Averill Lakes. Lake trout, salmon and brook trout catch, circa 1920. *Courtesy of Quimby Country.*

The cottages at Quimby's are painted yellow—not too bright, not too dull, golden or a variety of mustard yellow, a bit brighter than German mustard but in that vein. If you've ever thought about painting your house yellow, you know the choices are too numerous—that you're much more likely to get yellow wrong than right and have to paint your house over again, or paint it white. Here, the cottages are painted a good yellow and named after famous trout flies (Hortense's idea). My cottage is named Hare's Ear, a popular nymph in these parts, but there's also Parmechene Belle, Jock Scott and others. The trout flies themselves are mounted and framed under glass just inside each cottage door.

As the fishing came to rely more and more on stocking, Hortense saw an opportunity in fly fishing, which was gaining in popularity among her clients. She helped push that transition along by retraining her guides in the art of casting the fly. She recognized fly fishers as having less interest in limiting out and thus a lighter impact on the fish populations—which, at the time, required a lot of expense to maintain. She also began promoting lower bag limits and catch-and-release fishing, not only on the Averills but statewide. She saw fly fishing, catch-and-release practices and low bag limits translating to more fish, bigger fish and fish less costly to grow. Hortense also saw a continuing prime role for fish culture, and she invested in salmon rearing

Hortense Quimby, owner of Cold Spring Camp, was one of Vermont's most active fisheries conservationists in the early twentieth century. *Courtesy of Quimby Country.*

pools and other hatchery infrastructure at the south end of Big Averill, along the brook that flows in from Little Averill.

It was Hortense who shrewdly repositioned Quimby's as a family-oriented resort, adding lawn games, tennis, horseback riding, hiking, swimming and sailing. Hortense fished, hunted and smoked the occasional pipe. She posed with a spaniel at her side. Sometimes she posed in a canoe. While I can imagine an unmarried sport fisher visiting Cold Spring in 1923 being starstruck by Hortense, anecdotal evidence suggests that she could be hard-edged, a bit imperious. Guests were, apparently, scared of Hortense.

Still, even with a tough, no-nonsense exterior and a steely inner resolve, she was a woman, particularly a single adult woman, in the rural wilds of northern Vermont. Life can't have been easy. Red-haired Hortense was brave, courageous, independent, selfless and also self-interested in the way a responsible business owner must be. After the devastating flood of 1927, she volunteered for six weeks with the Red Cross in Montpelier. In her life, she exhibited some of the most admirable human traits and few of the lesser strain. She worked well with others, formed partnerships and gave back to the community. She wrote well, explaining her positions. She was dedicated to the camp but also to fisheries conservation statewide. She was an innovator, having devised salmon-rearing pools to keep up salmon populations in the Averills. As owner of the camp, she adapted to changing times and kept the business—an important employer in this region—going. She urged her neighbors to get with the times. She was cultivated, a savvy countrywoman and an outdoorswoman who routinely showed up in front of legislative committees but not so rough cut that she couldn't wear pearls. She once served as host on an African cruise. She was not afraid of using her God-given skills to promote what she believed was right.

On the subject of spiritual thought, in her first journal—dedicated to news clips as opposed to photos—she sprinkles in writings and sermons from preachers she admired, professing indirectly an interest in philosophical religious thought that bent to the unity of all things, Universalism, which was popular in Vermont at the time. She saw a huge role for conservation in the state of Vermont at a time when public awareness of the need to conserve fish and wildlife was just emerging, but still likely before most people knew what the word "conservation" meant. She wasn't afraid to speak out.

Hortense was once quoted as saying, "If I must have a hobby, as many contend we all should, then fish are mine and I will fight for their cause." How clear is that declaration! She could have given Lee Wulff a run for his money. Hortense Quimby lived an interesting life. She could be the titular character in Howard Frank Mosher's book *Mary Blythe*. The book closes with Mary and her new husband starting up a sport fishing camp somewhere in the Kingdom. At the start of that venture, fishing from a bridge, Mary foul hooks what turns out to be an enormous snapping turtle. Hours later, she manages to bring it in.

You just know things are going to go well for Mary (and Hortense).

Chapter 32

JOBS POND

Thursday, October 4, 2018

Rain, rain, everywhere I go. But rain or shine, a trip to Jobs Pond—another gumdrop, a drop-dead beauty of a small wild brook trout pond in the Northeast Kingdom—is advisable. I stopped here on Lenny Gerardi's advice, and I was glad I did. Jobs Pond in Newark, Vermont, is special-regulations water designed by state biologists to grow and maintain a population of large wild brook trout (Lenny also suggested Martin's Pond, with the same protected slot). There is a twelve- to fifteen-inch protected slot limit and a two-trout daily limit, only one of which can be greater than fifteen inches. Bait is somewhat restricted. No minnows, live or dead, are allowed (although worms are, which is a bit baffling given the higher hooking mortality, but I understand the social value of worms). Motors are allowed, under five miles per hour. It's a tight put-in and a small pond at thirty-nine acres, much more amenable to small rooftop boats. And there are loons.

When I visited, there was one other fisherman—a guy named Keith who was about my age (with a camp on Little Averill and a ton of local knowledge), paddling around in a fishing kayak. Keith was casting plugs that imitated crayfish, and he'd had great luck the week before, with evidence on his mobile phone of two fifteen-inch-plus fish he'd released. I went to my sinking line and a dark streamer, size 12. The rain came in sudden sheets. Then it would stop and the clouds would clear halfway up the cliff, and then the clouds would drop and the rain would come again.

The first fish I "caught" was stolen by a loon. A nice brook trout, easily fifteen-plus inches. Net out, I had him close to the canoe, then he ducked under the boat and began stripping line, which I thought was strange. Then a loon that had been bird-dogging me a bit surfaced with the fish sideways in its bill. This was a fisherman's no-no; concerned that I'd hook the loon, I gave my line a firm tug, the fish popped out and I began retrieving again. The loon went under. Damn little U-boats! So the story ended. The loon got his fish and I…well, I got my fly back anyway.

The conventional wisdom is that if a loon is hanging around your boat, give it good leeway. Leave it be. It's taken conservation strategists and a large corps of dedicated volunteer loon watchers nearly fifty years to bring loons back from the edge of extinction in Vermont. The direction to anglers around loons is to paddle away and find another corner to fish, one without loons. But what if that loon has had a taste or two of trout brought to table here by an angler and is hanging close (I think the incidence of this is rare), hoping for a hit? One suggestion is to use a tippet ring several feet back from your fly with lighter tippet that will break off more easily at the ring. That way, if a loon does come calling and ingests the fish, you can break the line off without leaving a tangle of monofilament for the loon to get bolloxed up in. By all means, never use lead sinkers—they're illegal and they're killers. Also, flatten that barb and avoid big treble hooks—anything to minimize the chances of foul-hooking a loon.

The second fish I caught was within the protected slot limit—probably thirteen to fourteen inches. I brought it quickly to the net, but as I gazed down at the fish in the net in the water, the loon passed under the boat within a foot or two of my hand, swimming by like a shark with wings. What a lovely sight, and I did feel graced by that loon, who had arguably more rights to that pond and that fish than me.

Chapter 33

SAVING THE MISSISQUOI

Sunday, October 28, 2018

> *Following the European discovery of Lake Champlain in 1609 by its namesake, Samuel de Champlain, the ensuing 400 years brought substantial physical changes to the watershed, lake sediments, and hydrological connections within the lake. Two fish species, Lake Trout and Atlantic Salmon, were extirpated, 15 fish species were added, and 16 species have been listed as endangered, threatened, or of special concern/susceptible. Chemical inputs from land use and industries have caused algal blooms and have contaminated fish tissue. These changes in the biological, physical, and chemical characteristics of the lake present practical and philosophical challenges to management: to what extent have ecosystem services been compromised, is restoration possible, and should restoration, rather than acceptance of an altered system, be the goal?*
> —*J. Ellen Marsden and Richard W. Langdon,*
> "*The History and Future of Lake Champlain's Fishes and Fisheries,*"
> Journal of Great Lakes Research

In Vermont's northwestern corner, New York, Vermont and Quebec come together at a spot in Lake Champlain just north of Rouses Point. A bit east is the Alburgh Tongue, a peninsula jutting down from Quebec that contains the modest but festive town of Alburgh, with its small villages of Alburgh, Alburgh Center and South Alburgh. East from Alburgh and across the northeastern arm of Lake Champlain is Hog Island, most of which is either farmland or U.S. Fish and Wildlife Service refuge (the wet parts). My sister and brother-in-law have a small camp at the south end of Hog Island. I've spent many a summer day there with my family enjoying the beauty of the lake and fishing some. Now, sitting on their deck on this warm afternoon near the end of the fishing season, I can see across Maquam Bay, down the northeast arm of Lake Champlain and south toward Burton Island and St. Albans Bay; Burlington is far out of view. Today, there isn't a single boat out, and the surface is serene, still as a looking glass. It's a good place to consider the end of the fishing season—this being such a fishy corner of the world.

There are so many rivers, streams, lakes and corners of the state I haven't gotten to, as well as many I've visited that I haven't included in this record of a fishing summer: Lake Memphremagog's north-flowing rivers, like the Clyde with its fall salmon run; the Willoughby and its famed spring rainbow run; the Black and the Barton; Saxtons River; the Waits River; and nearby Seyon Pond, with its creaky rowboats and the state's fly fishing–only, catch-and-release lake—the closest we have to a public trout club. There's also Cow Mountain Pond in Granby, a small pond we walked into one late afternoon—a place out of time, with hefty wild brook trout. There are dam removals I haven't reported on, including the work of Connecticut River steward Ron Rhodes's project removing the old Norwich Reservoir dam (owned by the Norwich Fire & Water District) on Charles Brown Brook. Ron's our Johnny Appleseed of dam removals. He's removed at least five dams and has many more in his sights. About 750 truckloads of sediment later, and there's forty-five new miles of connected brook trout water to explore.

This deck is a nice spot to look back at a fishing season and an equally good spot to consider a vision for the future of the lake stretched out before me—Vermont's most pressing environmental challenge today. What we're hearing from scientists, from Lake Champlain itself, is that all is not well with this ecosystem, in spite of tranquil lake vistas and the backdrop of New York's Adirondacks. These northern arms of the lake, in particular, are troubled—shallow and impaired with an overabundance of phosphorus. Beautiful Missisquoi and Maquam Bays are eutrophying. Nutrient loading has led to blue-green algae blooms and a loss of native fishes. Dams in Swanton village have blocked migratory fish passage, since not long after the American Revolution. Invasive aquatic plants have colonized bottom sediments in these bays. Some invasive fish are common now, while other native fish—mostly of the small and humble variety but including the likes of lake trout, Atlantic salmon, walleye, muskie and lake sturgeon—are

Ron Rhodes, Connecticut River steward, Connecticut River Conservancy, surveys a recent dam removal site in Norwich, Vermont. *Photo by author.*

much reduced or depending on fish culture and sea lamprey supression for renewal. Paradoxically, the fishing here in the bays and throughout the delta of the Missisquoi Delta is still considered good by many, and the area gets a lot of fishing attention. But it's also true that anglers suffer from shifting baselines today—we've simply lost our collective memory of how good the fishing used to be.

So, what's the vision for restoring this place? What does the future hold for anglers, swimmers, cottage owners, visitors, Vermonters and all who come up for a brief stay? For the fish, plants and aquatic systems that depend on clean water and ample intact habitat? If we consider fish as the virtual canary in the mineshaft, what would it take to restore fish populations here to historic proportions? Are the odds against restoration to any reasonably close standard—considering past losses, current conditions and climate change—so high that we shouldn't try?

Chris Smith, state coordinator of the Partners for Fish and Wildlife Program, U.S. Fish and Wildlife Service, who sees himself as a glass-half-full guy, doesn't think so. He grew up in Franklin County and has twenty-three years of service with U.S. Fish and Wildlife and many more than that paying attention to aquatic conservation in Vermont. He sees a lot of signs of hope and progress. The rapid development of the Vermont Rivers Program over the past twenty years, with its foundation in river science, for example, and the establishment of new partnering organizations, including the Missisquoi River Basin Association. While phosphorus reduction is a very daunting task, NRCS is bringing a whole suite of new tools to the job of clean water. Farmland trusts, like the Vermont Land Trust, are now fully engaged in the work of intercepting farmland runoff with newly developed policies on buffer strip requirements, vital to clean water efforts. There is no one single big fix, Smith said. We got to where we are today by one thousand small cuts across 150 years: development strategies, the intensification of agriculture, overfishing, diking and damming. We need to recognize that no silver bullet is going to heal it. We also have here the most extensive wetland resources in Vermont and possibly in New England. Missisquoi is internationally recognized as a Ramsar site (named after the international convention on wetlands in Ramsar, Iran). This is a great foundation for restoration. Yes, the bays are impaired, but the biomass in the system is amazing. We still have a tremendous resource. It's bound up but ready to take off.

How important, historically, were the fisheries of the Missisquoi? James Ehlers, executive director of Lake Champlain International—an environmental advocacy group that puts on the annual Lake Champlain International Fishing Derby and has been working for swimmable, drinkable and fishable water for nearly forty years—says the evidence of remarkably abundant fish populations is irrefutable, found in records kept by town clerks and in logbooks by commercial anglers. Fish were sustenance and currency both. Even Benedict Arnold kept logs documenting trade in barrels of salmon.

Bernie Pientka, a biologist for the Vermont Fish and Wildlife Department who's overseeing the fisheries of the Missisquoi River Basin, points to the Missisquoi as a primary fishing ground. You can't separate the river and bay from the greater lake ecosystem, he added—neither the biota, nor the sediments, nutrients or other pollutant inputs. Many lake-dwelling fishes use the river for part of their life cycle, for spawning and early growth—notably walleye and the endangered lake sturgeon—and then return to the lake, ranging widely there. Other fish never leave the river. The Missisquoi is critical, he added, historically contributing importantly to the overall diversity of the Lake Champlain ecosystem. The state-listed endangered stonecat, *Noturus flavus*, is found in the river, as are three species of native redhorse sucker: shorthead, greater and silver. Little is known of these populations or their distribution status. All three are considered species of special concern.

Some of the earliest descriptions of fishing the Missisquoi come down through stories from the Western Abenakis. John Moody, an ethnohistorian who has been working with the Abenakis and other indigenous peoples since the 1970s, recounted records of enormous catfish, carp (introduced in Vermont in the 1870s), sturgeon, salmon, muskellunge, pike and walleye. The Abenakis are a fishing people who trace their ancestry to Paleo-Indians—bands of hunter-gatherers who crossed from Asia into North America across the Bering land bridge ten thousand years ago. The Abenakis used a type of stone plummet called *senigan*, bone hooks and rawhide line in times before European contact. They employed stone weirs and ash-strip woven fish traps called *adelahigan* at the base of the weirs. Long, three-pronged spears called *nodamagwojik alnobaiwi* were used to spear large sturgeon, lake trout, pike and salmon along the shorelines and from bark canoes. Fishing has always been a huge part of the story for the Abenakis and still is, Moody said. Going back to the year without a summer, 1816, it was fishing that kept people from starving when crops failed. Fish were legal tender. There are Abenakis today who still live subsistence lifestyles, growing, putting by and catching their own food. The Missisquoi River, Moody said, remains a fundamental part of Abenaki culture. So does dancing.

What degraded fish populations and natural aquatic communities in the Missisquoi in the first place? There were potentially many factors, including introductions of nonnative fish, sedimentation, predation by sea lamprey, perhaps overfishing and certainly the loss of spawning runs due to dams and dikes. The loss of the Missisquoi River spawning run with the construction of the Lower Swanton Dam in 1791 was an early major blow. The dam built at Taquahunga Falls, about five miles from the lake, is nonfunctioning today, but it once powered Swanton's golden age of industry. The first dam in Swanton Village was developed by none other than Ira Allen, who by then had contrived to claim much of the land of colonial Swanton belonging to the Abenakis, whose oldest villages were there. Water ran sawmills, gristmills, textile mills, tanneries, a marble cutting and polishing industry and a World War I munitions factory. Swanton's story is partly the story of Vermont's eighteenth- and nineteenth-century rivers and streams. Waterpower all across the state and region fueled the early years of the Industrial Revolution. Vermont was an important player as a food producer and a supplier of lumber, quarried stone and forged tools.

Lower Swanton Dam. *Photo by author.*

The dam's impact on Missisquoi fisheries was significant. It cut off about the seven miles of fish spawning habitat between Swanton Village and Highgate Falls. Migratory fish including walleye and the endangered lake sturgeon, both of which make spawning runs up Lake Champlain rivers in the spring, were among the losers. While commercial harvest of lake sturgeon were probably never very great, walleye were harvested using seine nets in Missisquoi Bay during spawning runs at an average of 38,584 fish between 1893 and 1904. That number had fallen to about 30,000 fish by the 1950s. Numbers dropped precipitously, and the commercial harvest of walleye was ended in 1971. There is little question in the restoration community that the dam should be removed. But there's a rub.

The village sees costs and benefits differently. In spite of the improvement to fisheries the removal of the dam would bring, the village would like to build a hydroelectric plant at the Lower Swanton Dam. As Swanton Village manager Reggie Beliveau Jr. put it, Swanton Village has been in the hydroelectric business for a long time. The village fathers bought the site at Highgate Falls, seven miles upstream from the Lower Swanton Dam site, in 1894, eventually building a hydroelectric site there. Swanton Village was the first municipality in Vermont to own its own hydroelectric plant. Electric rates in Swanton are among the lowest in Vermont at 11.9 cents per kilowatt hour. Hydroelectric generation remains an important part of the town's economy, identity, history and character.

Many locals seem supportive of a hydroelectric project in the village, according to the village manager. Resident Ron Kilburn told me, for example, that even losing half the Lower Swanton Dam to a fishway would be, to him, an unacceptable loss. Kilburn is a historian of early industrial structures. He's chair of the Swanton Historical Society, which has overseen the renovation and construction of a museum in the old train station in town. He's been a longtime opponent of dam removal.

"Swanton does take great pride in its historic and current relationship to the lake and river," Beliveau told me. There are big challenges. Recent floods, for example, foretell future and accelerating climate change effects. He's aware of pollution problems that the town must fix. In 1995, the state helped Swanton fund a stormwater/wastewater separation to keep stormwaters out of the sewage treatment plant to prevent sewage overflows during large storm events; the separation solved one problem but created another. Untreated urban runoff and sediment laden with hydrocarbons, fecal coliform bacteria and fertilizer runoff now went directly into the lake, adding to mounting eutrophication problems in Maquam and Missisquoi Bays. Today, a "swirl basin" takes care of about one-third of that urban runoff, and there is a "stone garden" at Academy Road that captures another, smaller percentage. In hindsight, storm separation wasn't a great idea, Beliveau said. Now what's needed is a major upgrade to the sewage treatment plant that can improve the treatment of, among other things, phosphorus discharges. Upgrades are expensive. Like many small towns in Vermont, Swanton struggles to bring new businesses into town, and just passing a school budget can be a challenge.

"We've always thought," Beliveau said, "that there is a marriage here. Rather than be dictated to. The fisheries people just want to tear out the dam. It's part of our history. We get a lot of feedback from the community to keep the dam." A hydroelectric dam in lower Swanton isn't only about the potential lease payments that the dam operators would make to the village, he said. Along with the green power generation, Swanton could have a learning center connecting high school students, area tech centers and the community college in St. Albans to energy alternatives and climate change. He mentioned having solar panels and a wind generator on site too.

Just focusing on walleye and sturgeon, how big an improvement to the fisheries might the removal of the dam bring about? According to a habitat suitability study for the Missisquoi conducted by Madeleine Lyttle, fishery biologist for the U.S. Fish and Wildlife Service, suitable spawning habitat would "increase by 65 to 1,210 times what is currently available for lake-run spawning walleye. Additionally, an increase of 303 to 342 times the current level could be realized by lake sturgeon" if fish had access to habitat above Lower Swanton Dam. Walleye, Chris Smith told me, is a famously boom-and-bust species. Spawning in the Missisquoi today is limited to a small area below the Lower Swanton Dam, and the annual walleye season runs only four days or so. The egg sack fry float out into the lake, and once the egg sack is gone, fry need to feed on zooplankton. So it's this fairly precarious situation. The expansion of spawning habitat means we might see a longer season, a spawning run that stretches in time and space. There might be three or four surges of spawning activity, and that could translate to more successful and consistently larger year classes in general.

Bill Scully, for all intents and purposes, is the face of hydro-development at Swanton. His LLC would lease the Lower Swanton Dam site from the village and run the hydroelectric operation. He's no fly-by-night operator. Well informed in environmental history, the Clean Water Act and Vermont law and policy, and aware of the threats of climate change, Bill's got experience in recommissioning defunct hydroelectric sites in Vermont. He recommissioned the Vermont Tissue Mill Dam site on the Walloomsac River in Bennington and the Pownal Tannery hydroelectric plant on the Hoosic River in North Pownal. His position is that not only is more hydro-development necessary if Vermont is to meet its long-term climate change objectives, but that hydroelectric development can also yield large environmental benefits, including fish passage and the removal of toxic sediments. There is such a thing as environmentally sensitive hydro, Bill told me, using the examples of the Walloomsac and the Hoosic, two rivers that were toxic messes before recommissioning. Dams trap sediments that, in industrial and agricultural settings, are often laden with pollutants. In both previous cases, he said, redevelopment resulted in removing and land-filling highly contaminated sediments from the riverbed.

The sediments at the Lower Swanton Dam haven't been tested yet. That's next. But in a Phase II Environmental Site Assessment report, funded by the EPA and conducted for the Northwest Regional Planning Commission, the consultant identified possible sources of contamination. Over the years, the lower dam site has seen a long list of boutique industrial enterprises, from bog iron production to a paper recycling plant more recently. For nearly 150 years, there's been rail traffic, including the transport of asbestos. There could be PCBs furans, dioxins from paper recycling waste, heavy metals, semi-volatile organic compounds, spills of petrochemicals, the atmospheric deposition of partially burned hydrocarbons and PCB-laden dialectic fluids from transformers onboard train engines—and that's not even considering what washes down from farms in the form of pesticide residues, fertilizer nutrients and bacteria. Until there's testing, no one really knows what's there. It should be noted that the dam removers would have to deal with sediment removal as well—this has been the case for years, and dam removal specialists are well versed in the law. The only big difference when it comes to sediment removal is who pays.

As far as fish passage goes, Bill described a theoretical design that would remove about half of the old dam and devote that area to a river-like fish passage system, leaving what he thinks would be adequate flow for a scaled-down hydroelectric plant—say, between 1.5 megawatts and 500 kilowatts, "tending toward the low end." There's ample flow, he said, for both a low-head hydroelectric power plant and a fish passage technology that would get large numbers of lake sturgeon and walleye upstream to spawning habitat.

Finding an upstream fish passage that would work to move a high percentage of migrating fish upstream is only half the challenge. Downstream passage for walleye, lake sturgeon fry and other native fishes would need to be addressed. These are questions for fisheries biologists and engineers who design fish passages. According to Chet MacKenzie, chief fisheries biologist for the Lake Champlain Sturgeon Recovery Plan, designing fishways that work to get large percentages of migrating fish upstream to spawn and downstream to the lake again is extremely difficult. Sturgeon, because they are large and heavy bottom-dwellers, present special challenges to dam and fishway designers. Salmon are stronger swimmers that use bursts of speed and leaping to make it up falls and fishways—less so sturgeon. Walleye and sturgeon drift downstream in their sack fry form, settling into the shelter of rocks and plants on their way to the lake. Finding ways to keep them out of turbines on their way back downstream has proven particularly challenging. From a fisheries-restoration standpoint, it would be better to remove the entire dam. But given all the data available, what is possible?

The Lower Swanton Dam isn't the only challenge to restoring the Missisquoi. Lake-wide agricultural development may have played the longest role as villain. Clearing the forests for agriculture (and industry and village) led to massive sediment flows into the lake. By 1800, 60 percent of the old-growth forest in the Champlain Basin was gone. The Merino sheep boom that began in the 1830s further accelerated land clearing. Beaver, moose and mountain lion were extirpated, and so were salmon and lake trout. Sedimentation increased. Later, dairy farming led to vast increases in nutrient loading. While dairy had been here since early colonization, it took off with the advent of railroads. By 1880, there were thirty-five thousand dairy farms in Vermont, all sending sediments, organic matter, nitrogen and phosphorus into waterways. When refrigerated railcar technology arrived in the 1920s, Vermonters began shipping fluid milk to distant urban markets. Dairy farming continued to expand onto marginal lands, including unstable uplands and sensitive wetlands, increasing soil erosion and nutrient loading. By 1980, 35 percent of the basin's wetlands—important nutrient-enrichment buffers—had been drained.

Few farmers in the nineteenth century were employing soil conservation practices. (Frederick Billings of Woodstock, Vermont, was one exception.) Government programs that promoted soil conservation didn't come about until the late 1920s, early 1930s. By the 1960s, farmers had begun growing their own feed corn, converting pasturage to tilled fields. That led to heavier inputs of fertilizers, pesticides, herbicides, antibiotics and petrochemicals. Recent trends favoring large dairies in the United States, including in Vermont, have pushed many small dairy farmers out and driven runoff up. The most vivid example of the nutrient enrichment problem that Vermont faces may be Lake Carmi, not far from the banks of the Missisquoi. Closed to swimming during the summer of 2018 due to repeated blue-green algae blooms, Lake Carmi—glowing a sickly green and on the receiving end of nutrient inputs from an upstream mega-farm—prompted the Vermont House of Representatives to approve a bill declaring the lake in crisis. Carmi is a microcosm of the Missisquoi basin, not an isolated case. According to James Ehlers, there are streams flowing into the lake around St. Albans that qualify by EPA standards as dead zones.

Yet the agricultural runoff problem, in some ways, seems like the easiest one to solve. We have the data on the size of the problem, since it relates directly to the number of farms and acres in cultivation, and we know where runoff and erosion problems are greatest. A farm's impact on water quality is not equal across the landscape because of the variation of that landscape, the variety of soils, farming practices and the susceptibility of waterbodies. We know that buffer strips work. We know a lot about buffer strips. We know that cover crops work. We understand that pasture management practices—the switch from growing annual grains to growing perennial grass and pasture rotation—can have a huge impact on the chemicals that run off with water and sediment. We know Quebec farmers are doing better than our farmers because of how their provincial government manages milk supply. Much is known. The NRCS has been working in the basin for decades. We have the technical infrastructure, the community connections, voluntary resources, nonprofit partners and governmental agencies—we have the restoration infrastructure needed. If we lack anything, it's the political will and the inner fire to make change. Were a town like Swanton willing to remove a dam, the resources would flood in to help. The benefits in terms of tourism development could be enormous.

We fear loss. Maybe that's why we resist change. Across the country, restored fisheries and water quality has led to expanding economic opportunity and prosperity. No one I met in the river restoration business this summer in Vermont ever framed water quality work or floodplain management as occurring at the expense of a rural community. Solutions that don't work for everyone are nonstarters. Cleaning up Lake Champlain is all-hands-on-deck work. The Missisquoi is a vital piece of that.

The challenge reminds me of the reemergence of the Abenakis over the past six decades in Missisquoi. By their own description, they are the People of the Dawn Land who have endured a long, dark winter—suffering through four centuries of abuse, including warfare and disease, racism, loss of lands, denials of their existence and eugenics targeting. To survive, they assimilated; they melted into the fabric of society; intermarried; adopted western religion; became, at times, invisible, hidden; became transient; and moved across various borders, all the while not forgetting their stories.

Then, in the 1960s, the Abenakis began to reemerge. What marked the beginning were civil protests in Swanton in the form of fish-ins on the Missisquoi. Groups of Abenakis fished flagrantly without fishing licenses to win their ancestral fishing and hunting rights back. Reemergence has slowly led to tribal recognition in Vermont, to new awareness in the broader community, to social and educational programs aimed at improving the current lives and future prospects of area children and to the reemergence of Abenaki language and ways. Abenaki emergence represents a unique view of the river of the future.

When I met with Eugene Rich, chief of the Missisquoi Abenaki Tribal Council, he told me that whether or not the dam is removed is not a big issue for the Abenakis right now. There are other pressing social issues. Supporting families, running a foodshelf, working to improve high school graduation rates and winning federal tribal recognition. He also said that "without clean water, you've got nothing."

When Rich spent time last summer on the University of Vermont's research vessel, the *Melosira*, he was told the story of the geological formation of Lake Champlain by a young student intern onboard. But what came instantly to his mind, he said, was an Abenaki story of the mythic creation of the lake by Odzihozo, "the transformer," or "he who created himself." Odzihozo was not a god but rather a supernatural being that made himself first and then crawled around, still without his legs (these were very slow growing), transforming the world, making the mountains, rivers and valleys of the Abenaki homeland. Lake Champlain, or *Bitawbágw*, was his last great act. You can see Odzihozo in the frozen form of Rock Dunder, the same outcropping that the British mistook for an American frigate during the Revolutionary War.

Maybe "restoration" happens when we reemerge along with the Missisquoi River and the lake. We learn from the patience and perseverance of the Abenakis. We reconsider core values and assumptions. We reframe restoration of a river and lake as part of our own cultural survival and evolution—not disconnected from the lake and the river. The journey begins with the oldest story: combined with all the scientific data and new expertise we have— and, like a mayfly, newly emerged—we get to work restoring new land. Not disconnected from anything.

Appendix A

RECIPES

Hot-Smoked Trout Paté

Note from the chef: Dear reader, trout flesh is so subtle in flavor, one wants to be very careful not to overwhelm it.

4 tablespoons unsalted butter
4 tablespoons cream cheese
4 tablespoons fresh lemon juice
¼ teaspoon salt
pepper and cayenne to taste
½ pound hot-smoked trout flesh, from an approximately ¾ pound fish

In a food processor, cream together the butter, cream cheese, lemon juice, salt, pepper and cayenne until smooth. Add ½ of the trout and process until incorporated. Flake the remaining trout, add to food processor and spin briefly until just barely mixed in. Use on cucumber canapés, as a crêpe filling or in Belgian endive boats. Makes about 1½ cups.

Broiled Trout with Hazelnut Butter

Note from the chef: Hazelnuts are beginning to appear in many of my friends' gardens, so I thought they might make an interesting pairing with trout. This is a locally based, spontaneously created recipe.

Appendix A

fennel fronds
olive oil
a ½-pound cleaned, whole, skin-on trout
coarse sea salt and freshly ground pepper
4 tablespoons hazelnuts
3 tablespoons unsalted butter
2 teaspoons lemon juice
about 8 small, freshly dug yellow- and purple-fleshed potatoes

Arrange the fennel fronds on a baking sheet. Lightly oil the trout on both sides and lay it on the fennel. Sprinkle with coarse sea salt and freshly ground black pepper. Preheat the broiler. Broil the fish about 4 inches from the heat source until the skin is browned and crisp. Carefully flip the trout over and sprinkle with salt and pepper. Return to the broiler and cook until the second side is brown and crisp. At this point, the fish will be cooked through.

Toast the hazelnuts either in the oven or in a skillet until the skins release easily. Grate or finely grind 2 tablespoons of the hazelnuts and coarsely chop the remaining 2 tablespoons. Melt the butter in a skillet and brown it gently. Add the grated hazelnuts and continue to cook for another 2 to 3 minutes. Add the chopped hazelnuts and cook to heat through. Stir in the lemon juice.

Meanwhile, cook the potatoes in gently boiling water until tender. Arrange the fish on a serving platter, surround with the halved potatoes and drizzle fish and potatoes with the hazelnut butter. Resist the temptation to skin the trout. It will be crisp and delicious and provides a lovely contrast to the tender flesh.

Poached Trout with Garden-Fresh Sauces

Note from the chef: Friends Brian and Melissa supplied me with a gift of a 2-pound lake trout that had fennel fronds and lemon slices tucked into its cavity. The fronds came from a planting of perennial fennel in the garden— the non-bulbing variety that furnishes the fragrant seeds used in Italian sausage. We stove-top smoked the fish in a Cameron smoker/cooker over maple chips on medium-high heat for 30 minutes. The flesh was so tender

Appendix A

and delicate it seemed best to take care not to overwhelm its flavor with anything more assertive than a few sauces with subtly contrasting flavors. The winning candidates were a tarragon chive sauce and raïta. I didn't make any, but in Europe the classic accompaniment for poached fish is a Sauce Raifort Chantilly, so I'm including a recipe for that as well. We laid out the fish on a bed of greens and had potato salad as an accompaniment. One thing I love about these sauces is that I was able to source almost all the ingredients either from my own garden or from another very local source.

Tarragon Chive Sauce
⅔ cup mayonnaise (I used homemade)
1 ⅓ cups sour cream
⅓ cup fresh tarragon
3 tablespoons minced chives
1 teaspoon lime juice
salt and pepper to taste

In a food processor, pulse together the mayonnaise, ⅓ cup sour cream and tarragon until smooth. Transfer to a bowl. Mix in the remaining 1 cup sour cream, chives, lime juice and salt and pepper. Chill.

Variations include minced parsley added with the chives or sorrel leaves pureed with the first three ingredients.

Appendix A

Raïta

1 cucumber (about ½ pound)
1 teaspoon salt
1 ½ cups whole milk plain yogurt (I used homemade)
¼ cup diced red onion or shallot
¼ teaspoon ground coriander
⅛ teaspoon cayenne
4 teaspoons lemon juice
3 tablespoons chopped cilantro
¼ teaspoon salt
pepper

Peel the cucumber, slice it in half lengthwise and scrape the seeds from the center. Grate it coarsely into a collander, layering it with the salt. Drain at least 30 minutes. Transfer to a bowl and add the remaining ingredients. Chill.

Sauce Raifort Chantilly

1 cup heavy cream
4 tablespoons prepared horseradish
1 teaspoon lemon juice
1 teaspoon Dijon mustard
pinch cayenne

Whip the cream to stiff peaks and then blend in the remaining ingredients.

Trout Baked in White Wine, with a Saffron Cream Sauce

½ teaspoon unsalted butter
1 ½-pound whole, cleaned, skin-on trout
½ cup crisp white wine
1 tablespoon olive oil
½ cup chopped yellow onion
3 red bell peppers, seeded and cut into long strips
sea salt and pepper

Appendix A

fresh basil leaves to taste, sliced and whole
¼ cup heavy cream
saffron threads

Melt the butter in a baking dish just large enough to hold the trout. Arrange the trout in the dish and pour the wine over it. Preheat the oven to 350 degrees Fahrenheit. Bake the trout for 5 minutes, carefully flip the trout over and then bake for another 5 minutes. Remove the trout to a plate and carefully skin and fillet it. Meanwhile, heat the oil in a skillet. Add the onion and cook until soft. Add the peppers, season with salt and pepper and cook until very lightly browned and tender. Add the sliced basil leaves and heat through.

Pour the juices from the baking dish into a saucepan and boil to reduce by about one half. Add the cream and about ¼ teaspoon of saffron threads and cook rapidly to reduce further. Transfer the peppers to a serving dish and arrange the trout fillets over them. Pour the cream sauce over the fish and garnish with a light sprinkling of saffron threads and fresh basil leaves. Serve with steamed Vermont brown rice.

Appendix A

Pickled Northern Pike

From Ali Thomas's mother. Ali is an environmental educator with Vermont Fish and Wildlife Department's Let's Go Fishing Program. Originally sourced from Pete Finneman, a Minnesota fisherman.

Brine Solution
1 cup canning salt
4 cups water

3 pounds northern pike
sliced lemons
sliced onions

1. Cut the pike into small pieces.
2. Soak the pike in the salt brine mixture for 48 hours in a glass jar/container.
3. Drain the pike and soak in white vinegar for 24 hours. Pour the pickling solution (below) over the pike so it just covers the pike in the jar.
4. Drain the pike and pack it in jars while layering it with sliced lemons and sliced onions.

Pickling Solution
2 cups white vinegar
2 cups sugar
6 teaspoons pickling spice

Boil together and let cool before pouring over the pike.

5. Pour pickling solution over the top of the pike-packed jars just enough to cover.
6. Put the jars in the refrigerator for at least 10 days before eating. It can stay in the refrigerator for months.

Appendix B

THE UPRIGHT CADDIS EMERGER

By *Thomas Ames*

hook: curved sedge or shrimp hook, size 14–20
thread: waxed to match body color, 6/0 or 8/0
body: fur dubbing, ginger or olive
wing: deer hair, natural
legs: ginger cock neck feather, parachute style

I designed the Upright Caddis Emerger fly to mimic the moment of emergence when a caddis fly climbs out of its pupal shuck and shakes its wings preparing to fly....Many caddis flies emerge right on the water's surface. This is the moment when the insect is most vulnerable and a fish is most likely to grab it.

I became interested in the study of aquatic insects for this very reason; it allows me to make use of the connection between an interesting subject and a fun activity. I've designed a lot of flies. Many work some of the time, but it's a great feeling when you create one that works most of the time—when caddis flies are hatching and fish are eating them.

Like anything worth doing, it takes a lot of practice to learn how to tie flies. Look at this fly with a magnifier to see how it is put together. Then store it away in a safe place. If you ever do take up fly fishing, you will have at least one fly that works.

Appendix B

Upright caddis emerger. Original fly design by Thomas Ames Jr. *Photo by Thomas Ames.*

Author's note: Thomas Ames Jr. is a fly angling friend, elementary school teacher and resident of Norwich, Vermont. His books—Hatch Guide for New England Streams; Fishbugs; *and* Caddisflies: A Field Guide to Eastern Species for Anglers and Other Naturalists—*are essential reading for the fly angler, from beginner to expert.*

SELECTED BIBLIOGRAPHY

Bass Management Team. "Statewide Management Plan for Largemouth and Smallmouth Bass." Vermont Fish and Wildlife Department, 2017.

Brink, Jeanne A., and Gordon M. Day. *Alnôbaôdwa: A Western Abenaki Language Guide*. Barre: Vermont Historical Society, 1992.

Evans, Jackson. *The Sound of Falling Water: A History of Water Use and Industry at Swanton Falls*. Burlington, VT: UVM Historic Preservation Program, 2006.

Fisheries Technical Committee. "Strategic Plan for Lake Champlain Fisheries." Lake Champlain Fish and Wildlife Management Cooperative, USFWS, Essex Junction, Vermont, 2010.

Forest and Stream (December 18, 1890).

Forest and Stream 61 (1903).

Friends of the Winooski. "Living in Harmony with Streams: A Citizen's Handbook to How Streams Work." 2016. https://winooskiriver.org/lhsguide.php.

Goldfarb, Ben. *Eager: The Surprising, Secret Life of Beavers and Why They Matter*. White River Junction, VT: Chelsea Green Publishing, 2018.

Greenberg, Paul. "How Vermont Tackled Farm Pollution and Cleaned Up Its Waters." Food and Environment Reporting Network, June 22, 2017. https://thefern.org/2017/06/troubled-waters.

Hager, Albert D., and Charles Barrett. *Report of the Fish Commissioners of the State of Vermont*. Montpelier, VT: Walton's Steam Printing Establishment, 1867.

Hall, Marcus, ed. "The Nature of G.P. Marsh: Tradition and Historical Judgement." *Environment and History* 10, no. 2 (2004).

Haviland, William A., and Marjory W. Power. *The Original Vermonters: Native Inhabitants, Past and Present*. Hanover, NH: University Press of New England, 1994.

Howe, Eric A., J. Ellen Marsden and Wayne Bouffard. "The Movement of Sea Lamprey in Lake Champlain Basin." *Journal of Great Lakes Research* 32, no. 4 (2006).

Huanping, Huang, Jonathan M. Winter and Erich C. Osterberg. "Mechanisms of Abrupt Extreme Precipitation Change Over the Northeastern United States." *Journal of Geophysical Research: Atmospheres* 123, no. 4 (2018).

Jackson, Donald A. "Ecological Effects of Micropterus Introductions: The Dark Side of Black Bass." *Black Bass: Ecology, Conservation and Management, American Fisheries Society Symposium* 31 (2003): 221–32.

Johnson Company. "Phase I Environmental Site Assessment, Swanton Lower Dam, Swanton, Vermont." Prepared for Northwest Regional Planning Commission, St. Albans, Vermont, 2017.

Joint Fisheries Commission (United States and Britain), William Wakeham and Richard Rathbun. *Report of the Joint Commission Relative to the Preservation of the Fisheries in Waters Contiguous to Canada and the United States (Submitted Dec. 31, 1896)*. Ottawa, Ontario, Canada: S.E. Dawson, 1897.

Kendall, W.C. *The Fishes of New England: The Salmon Family*. Part 1, *The Trout or Charrs* [sic]. N.p., 1914.

Klyza, Christopher M., and Stephen C. Trombulak. *The Story of Vermont: A Natural and Cultural History*. 2nd ed. Hanover, NH: University Press of New England, 1999.

Ladago, Bret J., J. Ellen Marsden and Allison N. Evans. "Early Feeding by Lake Trout Fry." *Transactions of the American Fisheries Society* 145, no. 1 (2016): 1–6.

Langdon, Richard W., Mark T. Ferguson and Kenneth M. Cox. *Fishes of Vermont*. Waterbury: Vermont Department of Fish and Wildlife, 2006.

Lowenthal, David. *George Perkins Marsh: Prophet of Conservation*. Seattle: University of Washington Press, 2003.

Lyttle, Madeline. "Spawning Habitat Suitability for Walleye and Lake Sturgeon in the Missisquoi River." Prepared for the Lake Champlain Fisheries Technical Committee of the Lake Champlain Fish and Wildlife Management Cooperative.

Maillett, Edward, and Richard Aiken. "Trout Fishing in 2011: A Demographic Description and Economic Analysis." Report 2011-4. U.S. Fish and Wildlife Service, 2015.

Selected Bibliography

Marsden, J. Ellen, and Richard W. Langdon. "The History and Future of Lake Champlain's Fishes and Fisheries." *Journal of Great Lakes Research* 38 (2012): 19–34.

Marsh, George Perkins. *Man and Nature: or Physical Geography as Modified by Human Action*. New York: Scribner, 1864.

———. *Report, Made Under Authority of the Legislature of Vermont, on the Artificial Propagation of Fish*. Burlington, VT: Free Press Print, 1857.

McPhee, John. *The Founding Fish*. New York: Farrar, Straus and Giroux, 2003.

Merwin, John. *The Battenkill: An Intimate Portrait of a Great Trout River—Its History, People, and Fishing Possibilities*. New York: Lyons & Burford, 1993.

Noon, Jack. *The Bassing of New Hampshire: How Black Bass Came to the Granite State*. Warner, NH: Moose Country Press, 1999.

Pearo, Linda, Fred Wiseman, Madeline Young and Jeff Benay. "New Dawn: The Western Abenaki, a Curriculum Framework for the Middle Level." Franklin Northwest Supervisory Union Title IX Indian Education Program, Swanton, Vermont, 1997.

Pierce, Ken. *A History of the Abenaki People*. Burlington: University of Vermont, Instructional Development Center, 1977.

Power, Marjory W., and James B. Petersen. *Seasons of Prehistory: 4000 Years at the Winooski Site*. Montpelier, VT: Division for Historic Preservation, 1984.

Pritchett, Liz, and Ann Cousins. "Fish Culture Resources of Vermont." National Register of Historic Places Multiple Property Documentation Form. Received by the National Park Service on February 7, 1994. https://npgallery.nps.gov/GetAsset/8d50f4ea-b812-4573-9ea0-3cbf7cf9e7c5.

Responsive Management. "Vermont Department of Fish and Wildlife Media and Communications Survey." Harrisonburg, VA, 2018.

Scully, William F. "Climate Change and The Clean Water Act: Vermont's Energy Terroir and the Questions that Aren't Being Asked." Recurrent Hydro, 2018. www.recurrenthydro.org.

Shea, Peter, and Dick Leyden, ills. *The Atlas of Vermont Trout Ponds*. Burlington, VT: Northern Cartographic, 1987.

Thompson, Zadoc. *The Natural History of Vermont*. Rutland, VT: Charles E. Tuttle Company, 1853.

Titcomb, John W., Henry G. Thomas, Horace W. Bailey and Edward A. Davis. *Sixteenth Biennial Report of the Fish Commissioners of the State of Vermont*. Montpelier, VT: Argus and Patriot Book and Job Printing House, 1902.

Vermont Fish and Wildlife Conservation Group. "Clyde River Salmon Restoration." http://www.vtfwcg.org/clyde-salmon-restoration.

Selected Bibliography

Vermont Fish and Wildlife Department. "Evaluation of Wild Brook Trout Populations in Vermont Streams." Vermont Fish and Wildlife Department Annual Report, project no. F-36-R-19. Study title: "Salmonid Inventory and Management." Period covered: July 1, 2016, to June 30, 2017. Montpelier, Vermont, 2018.

———. "Impacts to Stream Habitat and Wild Trout Populations in Vermont Following Tropical Storm Irene." Vermont Fish and Wildlife Department Annual Report, project no. F-36-R-14. Study title: "Aquatic Habitat Conservation and Restoration." Period covered: July 1, 2011, to June 30, 2012. Montpelier, Vermont.

———. "Lake Champlain Lake Sturgeon Recovery Plan." Prepared by Chet MacKenzie. Vermont Fish and Wildlife Department (Agency of Natural Resources), Montpelier, Vermont, 2016.

———. *Vermont Stream Crossing Handbook*. Burlington, VT: Queen City Printers, 2010.

———. "White River Angler Survey." Vermont Fish and Wildlife Annual Report, project no. F-36-R-20. Study title: "Creel and Angler Surveys." Period covered: July 1, 2016, to June 30, 2017. Montpelier, Vermont, 2018.

———. "White River Wild Trout Evaluations." Vermont Fish and Wildlife Department Annual Report, project no. F-36-R-20. Study title: "Salmonid Inventory and Management." Period covered: July 1, 2016, to June 30, 2017. Montpelier, Vermont, 2018.

Watson, W.C. "The Salmon of Lake Champlain and Its Tributaries." Excerpted from *Report of Commissioner of Fish and Fisheries: The Atlantic Salmon, 1873–1874 and 1874–1875*. Washington, D.C.: Government Printing Office, 1876.

Weber, Lawton, ed. *Vermont Trout Streams*. 2nd ed. Burlington, VT: Northern Cartographic, 2002.

ABOUT THE AUTHOR

Tim Traver grew up fishing the saltwater bays, marshes and rivers of southern New England and has had a passion for fishing and fisheries science ever since. He's worked as a commercial fisherman, at a federal Altlantic salmon hatchery and as director of a coastal wildlife refuge. He has thirty-five years of experience in the land conservation and science education fields in Vermont, including serving as executive director of the Upper Valley Land Trust and the Vermont Institute of Natural Science. He lives with his family in Taftsville, Vermont, near the banks of the celebrated Ottauquechee River. His writing credits include *Sippewissett: Or, Life on a Salt Marsh*; *Lost in the Driftless: Trout Fishing on the Cultural Divide*; and numerous articles for magazines and newspapers.

Visit us at
www.historypress.com